WORLD OF SCIENCE

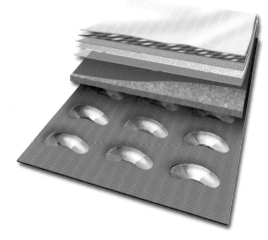

Miles Kelly
PUBLISHING

First published in 2006 by Miles Kelly Publishing Ltd
Bardfield Centre, Great Bardfield, Essex, CM7 4SL

Copyright © Miles Kelly Publishing Ltd 2006

This edition published in 2007

The sections in this book are also available
in hardback, paperback and flexi format.

2 4 6 8 10 9 7 5 3

Editorial Director Belinda Gallagher
Art Director Jo Brewer
Cover Designer Jo Brewer
Editorial Assistant Gemma Simmons
Picture Research Manager Liberty Newton
Reprographics Anthony Cambray, Mike Coupe, Stephan Davis, Ian Paulyn

ISBN: 978-1-84236-803-9

Printed in China

British Library Cataloguing-in-Publication Data
A catalogue record for this book is available from the British Library

All artwork is from the Miles Kelly Archives

www.mileskelly.net
info@mileskelly.net

WORLD OF SCIENCE

Contents

SPACE

PLANET EARTH

WEATHER

OCEANS

INSECTS AND SPIDERS

REPTILES AND AMPHIBIANS

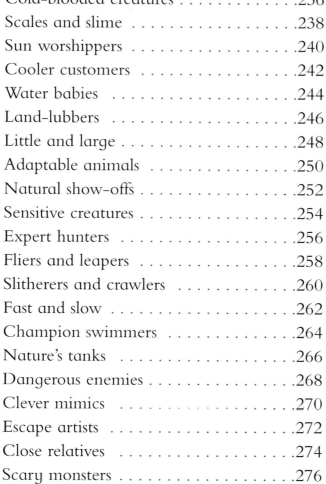

BIRDS

MAMMALS

SCIENCE

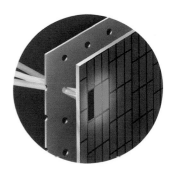

HUMAN BODY

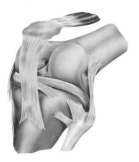

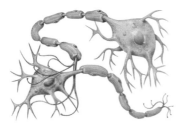

INVENTIONS

SPACE

Take a trip around the Universe and discover
everything you need to know about space.

Planets • Stars • Moons • Comets
Asteroids • Meteors • Galaxies • Rockets
Telescopes • Constellations • Space stations
Astronauts • Satellites • Moon missions

Surrounded by space

Space is all around the Earth, high above
the air. Here on the Earth's surface we are
surrounded by air. If you go upwards, up a
mountain or in an aircraft, the air grows thinner
until there is none at all. This is where space
begins. Space itself is mostly empty but there are
many exciting things out there such as planets,
stars and galaxies. People who travel in space are
called astronauts.

▶ In space, astronauts wear
spacesuits to go outside the
space shuttle as it circles the
Earth. Much farther away are
planets, stars and galaxies.

Our life-giving star

Prominence

Sunspot

The Sun is our nearest star. It does not look like other stars because it is so much closer to us. Most stars are so far away they look like points of light in the sky. The Sun is not solid like the Earth, but is a giant ball of superhot gases, so hot that they glow like the flames of a bonfire.

Nothing could live on Earth without the Sun. Deep in its centre the Sun is constantly making energy which keeps its gases hot and glowing. This energy works its way to the surface where it escapes as heat and light. Without it the Earth would be cold and dark with no life at all.

Solar flare

The Sun is often spotty. Sunspots appear on the surface, some wider than the Earth. They look dark because they are cooler than the rest of the Sun. Solar flares, explosions of energy, suddenly shoot out from the Sun. The Sun also throws huge loops of gas called prominences out into space.

▲ The Sun's hot, glowing gas is always on the move, bubbling up to the surface and sinking back down again.

When the Moon hides the Sun there is an eclipse. Every so often, the Sun, Moon and Earth line up in space so that the Moon comes directly between the Earth and the Sun. This stops the sunlight from reaching a small area on Earth. This area grows dark and cold, as if night has come early.

▼ When the Moon casts a shadow on the Earth, there is an eclipse of the Sun.

▶ When there is an eclipse, we can see the corona (glowing gas) around the Sun.

WARNING:

Never look directly at the Sun especially through a telescope or binoculars. It is so bright it will harm your eyes or even make you blind.

Sun

Moon

Shadow of eclipse

Earth

I DON'T BELIEVE IT!

The surface of the Sun is nearly 60 times hotter than boiling water. It is so hot it would melt a spacecraft flying near it.

A family of planets

The Sun is surrounded by a family of circling planets called the Solar System. This family is held together by an invisible force called gravity, which pulls things towards each other. It is the same force that pulls us down to the ground and stops us from floating away. The Sun's gravity pulls on the planets and keeps them circling around it.

The Earth is one of nine planets in the Sun's family. They all circle the Sun at different distances from it. The four planets nearest to the Sun are all balls of rock. The next four planets are much bigger and are made of gas and liquid. The tiny planet at the edge of the Solar System, Pluto, is a solid, icy ball.

Moons circle the planets, travelling with them round the Sun. Earth has one Moon. It circles the Earth while the Earth circles round the Sun. Pluto also has one moon. Mars has two tiny moons but Mercury and Venus have none at all. There are large families of moons, like miniature solar systems, around all the large gas planets.

Saturn

Uranus

Neptune

Pluto

▲ The nine planets are all different. Mercury, nearest the Sun, is small and hot. Then Venus, Earth and Mars are rocky and cooler. Beyond them Jupiter, Saturn, Uranus and Neptune are large and cold, while Pluto is tiny and icy.

There are millions of smaller members in the Sun's family. Some are tiny specks of dust speeding through space between the planets. Larger chunks of rock, many as large as mountains, are called asteroids. Comets come from the edge of the Solar System, skimming past the Sun before they disappear again.

I DON'T BELIEVE IT !

If the Sun was the size of a large beach ball, the Earth would be as small as a pea, and the Moon would look like a pinhead.

21

Planet of life

The planet we live on is the Earth. It is a round ball of rock. On the outside where we live the rock is hard and solid. But deep below our feet, inside the Earth, the rock is hot enough to melt. You an sometimes see this hot rock showering out of an erupting volcano.

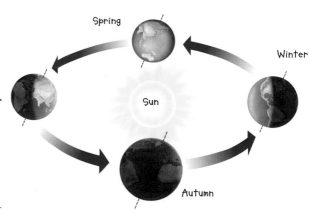

Outer core

Inner core

The Earth is the only planet with living creatures. From space the Earth is a blue and white planet, with huge oceans and wet masses of cloud. People, animals and plants can live on Earth because of all this water.

Spring

Winter

Summer

Sun

Autumn

Sunshine gives us daylight when it is night on the other side of the Earth. When it is daytime, your part of the Earth faces towards the Sun and it is light. At night, your part faces away from the Sun and it is dark. Day follows night because the Earth is always turning.

▲ The Earth tilts, so we have different seasons as the Earth moves around the Sun. These are the seasons for the northern half of the Earth.

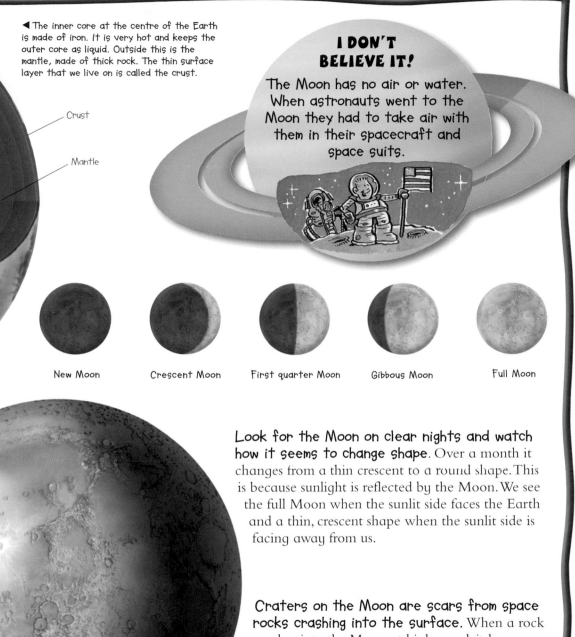

◀ The inner core at the centre of the Earth is made of iron. It is very hot and keeps the outer core as liquid. Outside this is the mantle, made of thick rock. The thin surface layer that we live on is called the crust.

Crust

Mantle

I DON'T BELIEVE IT!

The Moon has no air or water. When astronauts went to the Moon they had to take air with them in their spacecraft and space suits.

New Moon

Crescent Moon

First quarter Moon

Gibbous Moon

Full Moon

Look for the Moon on clear nights and watch how it seems to change shape. Over a month it changes from a thin crescent to a round shape. This is because sunlight is reflected by the Moon. We see the full Moon when the sunlit side faces the Earth and a thin, crescent shape when the sunlit side is facing away from us.

Craters on the Moon are scars from space rocks crashing into the surface. When a rock smashes into the Moon at high speed, it leaves a saucer-shaped dent, pushing some of the rock outwards into a ring of mountains.

The Earth's neighbours

Venus and Mars are the nearest planets to the Earth. Venus is closer to the Sun than the Earth while Mars is farther away. Each takes a different amount of time to circle the Sun and we call this its year. A year on Venus is 225 days, on Earth 365 days and on Mars 687 days.

▲ All we can see of Venus from space are the tops of its clouds. They take just four days to race right around the planet.

Venus is the hottest planet. It is hotter than Mercury, although Mercury is closer to the Sun and gets more of the Sun's heat. Heat builds up on Venus because it is completely covered by clouds which trap the heat, like the glass in a greenhouse.

Venus has poisonous clouds with drops of acid that would burn your skin. They are not like clouds on Earth, which are made of droplets of water. These thick clouds do not let much sunshine reach the surface of Venus.

▼ Under its clouds, Venus has hundreds of volcanoes, large and small, all over its surface. We do not know if any of them are still erupting.

Radio aerial

Solar panel

Camera

Winds on Mars whip up huge dust storms that can cover the whole planet. Mars is very dry, like a desert, and covered in red dust. When a space probe called *Mariner 9* arrived there in 1971, the whole planet was hidden by dust clouds.

◄ *Mariner 9* was the first space probe to circle another planet. It sent back over 7000 pictures of Mars showing giant volcanoes, valleys, ice caps and dried-up river beds.

Mars has the largest volcano in the Solar System. It is called Olympus Mons and is three times as high as Mount Everest, the tallest mountain on Earth. Olympus Mons is an old volcano and it has not erupted for millions of years.

Olympus Mons

PLANET-SPOTTING

See if you can spot Venus in the night sky. It is often the first bright 'star' to appear in the evening, just above where the Sun has set. Because of this we sometimes call it the 'evening star'.

There are plans to send astronauts to Mars but the journey would take six months or more. The astronauts would have to take with them everything they need for the journey there and back and for their stay on Mars.

Valles Marineris

◄ An enormous valley seems to cut Mars in half. It is called Valles Marineris. To the left is a row of three huge volcanoes and beyond them you can see the largest volcano, Olympus Mons.

25

The smallest of all

Pluto is the smallest planet. It is less that half the width of the next smallest planet, Mercury. In fact it is smaller than our Moon. It is so small and far away that it was not discovered until 1930.

▲ Pluto is too far away to see any detail on its surface, but it might look like this.

Pluto is the farthest planet from the Sun. If you were to stand on its surface, the Sun would not look much brighter than the other stars. It gets very little heat from the Sun and its surface is completely covered with solid ice.

Space probes have visited every planet except Pluto. So astronomers will have to wait for close-up pictures and detailed information that a probe could send back. Even if one was sent to Pluto it would take at least eight years to get there.

No one knew Pluto had a moon until 1978. An astronomer noticed what looked like a bulge on the side of the planet. It turned out to be a moon and was named Charon. Charon is about half the width of Pluto.

▼ If you were on Pluto, its moon Charon would look much larger than our Moon does, because Charon is very close to Pluto.

Mercury looks like our Moon.
It is a round, cratered ball of rock.
Although a little larger than the
Moon, like the Moon it has no air.

MAKE CRATERS

You will need:
flour   baking tray
a marble or a stone

Spread some flour about 2 centimetres
deep in a baking tray and smooth over
the surface. Drop a marble or a small
round stone onto the flour and
see the saucer-shaped crater
that it makes.

◀ Mercury's many craters show how often it was
hit by space rocks. One was so large that it
shattered rocks on the other side of the planet.

▼ The Sun looks huge as it rises on Mercury.
A traveller to Mercury would have to keep
out of its heat.

The sunny side of Mercury is boiling
hot but the night side is freezing
cold. Being the nearest planet to the
Sun the sunny side can get twice as hot
as an oven. But Mercury spins round
slowly so the night side has time to cool
down, and there is no air to trap the
heat. The night side becomes more than
twice as cold as the coldest place on
Earth – Antarctica.

The biggest of all

Jupiter is the biggest planet, more massive than all the other planets in the Solar System put together. It is 11 times as wide as the Earth although it is still much smaller than the Sun. Saturn, the next largest planet, is more than nine times as wide as the Earth.

Jupiter

Jupiter and Saturn are gas giants. They have no solid surface for a spacecraft to land on. All that you can see are the tops of their clouds. Beneath the clouds, the planets are made mostly of gas (like air) and liquid (water is a liquid).

The Great Red Spot on Jupiter is a 300-year-old storm. It was first noticed about 300 years ago and is at least twice as wide as the Earth. It rises above the rest of the clouds and swirls around like storm clouds on Earth.

▼ Jupiter's fast winds blow the clouds into coloured bands around the planet.

▼ There are many storms on Jupiter but none as large or long lasting as the Great Red Spot.

▼ Jupiter's Moon Io is always changing because its many volcanoes throw out new material from deep inside it.

▶ Although Saturn's rings are very wide, they stretch out in a very thin layer around the planet.

The shining rings around Saturn are made of millions of chunks of ice. These circle around the planet like tiny moons and shine by reflecting sunlight from their surfaces. Some are as small as ice cubes while others can be as large as a car.

Jupiter and Saturn spin round so fast that they bulge out in the middle. This can happen because they are not made of solid rock. As they spin their clouds are stretched out into light and dark bands around them.

I DON'T BELIEVE IT!
Saturn is the lightest planet in the Solar System. If there was a large enough sea, it would float like a cork.

Jupiter's moon Io looks a bit like a pizza. It has many active volcanoes that throw out huge plumes of material, making red blotches and dark marks on its orange-yellow surface.

So far away

Uranus and Neptune are gas giants like Jupiter and Saturn. They are the next two planets beyond Saturn but much smaller, being less than half as wide. They too have no hard surface. Their cloud tops make Uranus and Neptune both look blue. They are very cold, being so far from the Sun.

▲ There is very little to see on Uranus, just a few wisps of cloud above the greenish haze.

Uranus seems to 'roll' around the Sun. Unlike most of the other planets, which spin upright like a top, Uranus spins on its side. It may have been knocked over when something crashed into it millions of years ago.

Uranus has more moons than any other planet. Twenty-one have been discovered so far, although one is so newly discovered it has not got a name yet. Most of them are very small but there are five larger ones.

◄ Miranda is one of Uranus' moons. It looks as though it has been split apart and put back together again.

Neptune had a storm that disappeared. When the *Voyager 2* space probe flew past Neptune in 1989 it spotted a huge storm like a dark version of the Great Red Spot on Jupiter. When the Hubble Space Telescope looked at Neptune in 1994, the storm had gone.

Neptune has bright blue clouds that make the whole planet look blue. Above these clouds are smaller white streaks. These are icy clouds that race around the planet. One of the white clouds seen by the *Voyager 2* space probe was called 'Scooter' because it scooted around the planet so fast.

Neptune is sometimes farther from the Sun than Pluto. All the planets travel around the Sun along orbits (paths) that look like circles, but Pluto's path is more squashed. This sometimes brings it closer to the Sun than Neptune.

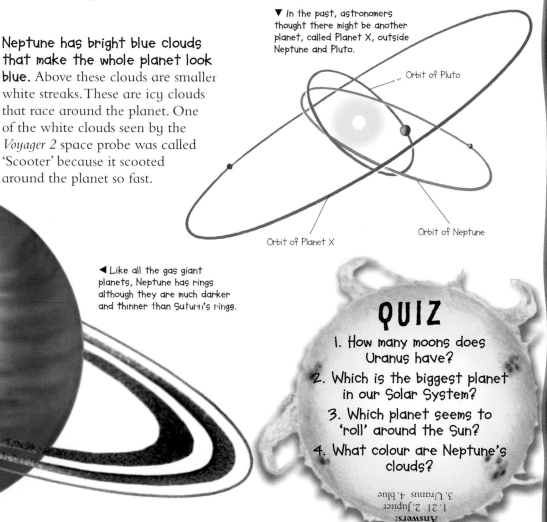

▼ In the past, astronomers thought there might be another planet, called Planet X, outside Neptune and Pluto.

Orbit of Pluto

Orbit of Neptune

Orbit of Planet X

◄ Like all the gas giant planets, Neptune has rings although they are much darker and thinner than Saturn's rings.

QUIZ

1. How many moons does Uranus have?

2. Which is the biggest planet in our Solar System?

3. Which planet seems to 'roll' around the Sun?

4. What colour are Neptune's clouds?

Answers:
1. 21 2. Jupiter
3. Uranus 4. blue

31

Comets, asteroids and meteors

There are probably billions of tiny comets at the edge of the Solar System. They circle the Sun far beyond the farthest planet, Pluto. Sometimes one is disturbed and moves inwards towards the Sun, looping around it before going back to where it came from. Some comets come back to the Sun regularly, such as Halley's comet that returns every 76 years.

▶ The solid part of a comet is hidden inside a huge, glowing cloud that stretches into a long tail.

A comet is often called a dirty snowball because it is made of dust and ice mixed together. Heat from the Sun melts some of the ice. This makes dust and gas stream away from the comet, forming a huge tail that glows in the sunlight.

Comet tails always point away from the Sun. Although it looks bright, a comet's tail is extremely thin so it is blown outwards, away from the Sun. When the comet moves away from the Sun, its tail goes in front of it.

Asteroids are chunks of rock that failed to stick together to make a planet. Most of them circle the Sun between Mars and Jupiter where there would be room for another planet. There are millions of asteroids, some the size of a car, and others as big as mountains.

▶ Asteroids travel in a ring around the Sun. This ring is called the Asteroid belt and can be found between Mars and Jupiter.

Meteors are sometimes called shooting stars. They are not really stars, just streaks of light that flash across the night sky. Meteors are made when pebbles racing through space at high speed hit the top of the air above the Earth. The pebble gets so hot it burns up. We see it as a glowing streak for a few seconds.

QUIZ

1. Which way does a comet tail always point?

2. What is another name for a meteor?

3. Where is the asteroid belt?

Answers:
1. Away from the Sun
2. Shooting star
3. Between Mars and Jupiter

▼ At certain times of year there are meteor showers when you can see more shooting stars than usual.

A star is born

Stars are born in clouds of dust and gas in space called nebulae. Astronomers can see these clouds as shining patches in the night sky, or dark patches against the distant stars. These clouds shrink as gravity pulls the dust and gas together. At the centre, the gas gets hotter and hotter until a new star is born.

▼ 3. Clumps of gas in this nebula start to shrink into the tight round balls that will become stars.

▶ 1. The gas spirals round as it is pulled inwards. Any left over gas and dust may form planets around the new star.

▶ 2. Deep in its centre, the new star starts making energy, but it is still hidden by the cloud of dust and gas.

Stars begin their lives when they start making energy. When the dust and gas pulls tightly together it gets very hot. Finally it gets so hot in the middle that it can start making energy. The energy makes the star shine, giving out heat and light like the Sun.

▲ 4. The dust and gas are blown away and we can see the star shining. Maybe it has a family of planets like the Sun.

Young stars often stay together in clusters. When they start to shine they light up the nebula, making it glow with bright colours. Then the starlight blows away the remains of the cloud and we can see a group of new stars, called a star cluster.

▶ This cluster of young stars, with many stars of different colours and sizes, will gradually drift apart, breaking up the cluster.

QUIZ

1. What is a nebula?

2. How long has the Sun been shining?

3. What colour are large hot stars?

4. What is a group of new young stars called?

Answers:
1. a cloud of dust and gas in space 2. about 4 billion years 3. bluish-white 4. star cluster

Smaller stars live much longer than huge stars. Stars use up their gas to make energy, and the largest stars use up their gas much faster than smaller stars. The Sun is about half way through its life. It has been shining for about 5 billion years and will go on shining for another 5 billion years.

Large stars are very hot and white, smaller stars are cooler and redder. A large star can make energy faster and get much hotter than a smaller star. This gives them a very bright, bluish-white colour. Smaller stars are cooler. This makes them look red and shine less brightly. Ordinary in-between stars like our Sun look yellow.

Large white star

Medium-sized star

Small red star

35

Death of a star

Stars begin to die when they run out of gas to make energy. The middle of the star begins to shrink but the outer parts expand, making the star much larger.

Supernova explosion

Ordinary star

▶ At the end of their lives stars swell up into red giant stars or even larger red supergiants.

Red giant star

Red giant stars are dying stars that have swollen to hundreds of times their normal size. Their expanding outer layers get cooler, making them look red. When the Sun is a red giant it will be large enough to swallow up the nearest planets, Mercury and Venus, and perhaps Earth.

A red giant becomes a white dwarf. The outer layers drift away, making a halo of gas around the star. The starlight makes this gas glow and we call it a planetary nebula. All that is left is a small, hot star called a white dwarf which cannot make energy and gradually cools and dies.

Black hole

◀ After a supernova explosion, a giant star may end up as a very tiny hot star or even a black hole.

Very heavy stars end their lives in a huge explosion called a supernova. This explosion blows away all the outer parts of the star. Gas rushes outwards in all directions, making a glowing shell. All that is left is a tiny hot star in the middle of the shell.

I DON'T BELIEVE IT!

Astronomers only know that black holes exist because they can see flickers of very hot gas near one just before they are sucked in.

Black dwarf star

White dwarf star

▲ When the Sun dies it will become 100 times bigger, then shrink down to 100 times smaller than it is now.

After a supernova explosion the largest stars may end up as black holes. The remains of the star fall in on itself. As it shrinks, its gravity gets stronger. Eventually the pull of its gravity can get so strong that nothing near it can escape. This is called a black hole.

Billions of galaxies

The Sun is part of a huge family of stars called the Milky Way Galaxy. There are billions of other stars in our Galaxy, as many as the grains of sand on a beach. We call it the Milky Way because it looks like a very faint band of light in the night sky, as though someone has spilt some milk across space.

▶ Seen from outside, our Galaxy would look like this. The Sun is towards the edge, in one of the spiral arms.

Curling arms give some galaxies their spiral shape. The Milky Way has arms made of bright stars and glowing clouds of gas that curl round into a spiral shape. Some galaxies, called elliptical galaxies, have a round shape like a squashed ball. Other galaxies have no particular shape.

I DON'T BELIEVE IT!

If you could fit the Milky Way onto these two pages, the Sun would be so tiny, you could not see it.

There are billions of galaxies outside the Milky Way. Some are larger than the Milky Way and many are smaller, but they all have more stars than you can count. The galaxies tend to stay together in groups called clusters.

▲ A cluster of galaxies has many different types, with large elliptical and spiral galaxies and many small irregular ones.

▶ These two galaxies are so close that each has pulled a long tail of bright stars from the other.

▼ From left to right these are spiral, irregular, and elliptical galaxies, and a spiral galaxy with a bar across the middle.

There is no bump when galaxies collide. A galaxy is mostly empty space between the stars. But when galaxies get very close they can pull each other out of shape. Sometimes they look as if they have grown a huge tail stretching out into space, or their shape may change into a ring of glowing stars.

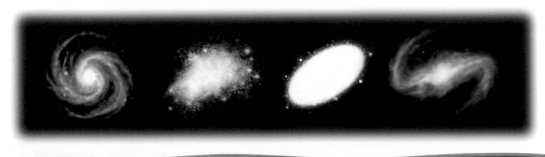

What is the Universe?

The Universe is the name we give to everything we know about. This means everything on Earth, from tiny bits of dust to the highest mountain, and everything that lives here, including you. It also means everything in space, all the billions of stars in the billions of galaxies.

The Universe started with a massive explosion called the Big Bang. Astronomers think that this happened about 15 billion years ago. A huge explosion sent everything racing outwards in all directions. To start with, everything was packed incredibly close together. Over time it has expanded (spread out) into the Universe we can see today, which is mostly empty space.

▼ 1. All the parts that make up the Universe were once packed tightly together. No one knows why the Universe started expanding with a Big Bang.

▼ 2. As everything moved apart in all directions, stars and galaxies started to form.

The galaxies are still racing away from each other. When astronomers look at distant galaxies they can see that other galaxies are moving away from our galaxy, and the more distant galaxies are moving away faster. In fact all the galaxies are moving apart from each other. We say that the Universe is expanding.

The Universe may end with a Big Crunch. This means that the galaxies would all start coming closer together. In the end the galaxies and stars would all be crushed together in a Big Crunch, the opposite of the Big Bang explosion.

We do not know what will happen to the Universe billions of years in the future. It may keep on expanding. If this happens old stars will gradually die and no new ones will be born. Everywhere will become dark and cold.

▼ 3. Today there are galaxies of different shapes and sizes, all moving apart. One day they may start moving towards each other.

DOTTY UNIVERSE
You will need:
a balloon
Blow up a balloon a little, holding the neck to stop air escaping. Mark dots on the balloon with a pen, then blow it up some more. Watch how the dots move apart from each other. This is like the galaxies moving apart as the Universe expands.

▼ 4. The Universe could end as it began, all packed incredibly close together.

41

Looking into space

People have imagined they can see the outlines of people and animals in the star patterns in the sky. These patterns are called constellations. Hundreds of years ago astronomers named the constellations to help them find their way around the skies.

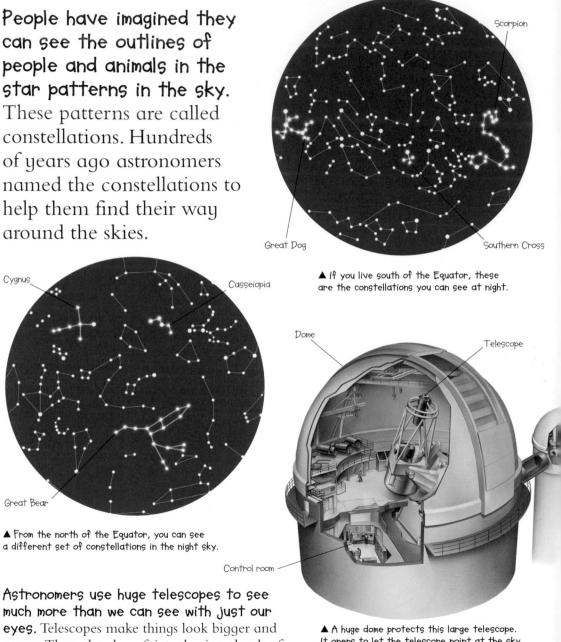

▲ If you live south of the Equator, these are the constellations you can see at night.

▲ From the north of the Equator, you can see a different set of constellations in the night sky.

Astronomers use huge telescopes to see much more than we can see with just our eyes. Telescopes make things look bigger and nearer. They also show faint, glowing clouds of gas, and distant stars and galaxies.

▲ A huge dome protects this large telescope. It opens to let the telescope point at the sky, and both the dome and telescope can turn to look at any part of the sky.

Space telescopes look even further to find exciting things in deep space. On Earth, clouds often hide the stars and the air is always moving, which blurs the pictures made by the telescopes. A telescope in space above the air can make clearer pictures. The Hubble Space Telescope has been circling the Earth for more than 10 years sending back beautiful pictures.

▲ The Hubble Space Telescope takes much more detailed pictures and can see farther than any similar telescope.

Astronomers also look at radio signals from space. They use telescopes that look like huge satellite TV dishes. These make pictures using the radio signals that come from space. The pictures do not always look like those from ordinary telescopes, but they can spot exciting things that most ordinary telescopes cannot see, such as jets of gas from black holes.

MOON-WATCH
You will need:
binoculars
On a clear night look at the Moon through binoculars, holding them very steady. You will be able to see the round shapes of craters. Binoculars are really two telescopes, one for each eye, and they make the Moon look bigger so you can see more detail.

▼ Radio telescopes often have rows of dishes like these to collect radio signals from space. Altogether, they act like one much larger dish to make more detailed pictures. The dishes can move to look in any direction.

Three, two, one... Lift-off!

To blast into space, a rocket has to travel nearly 40 times faster than a jumbo jet. If it goes any slower, gravity pulls it back to Earth. Rockets are powered by burning fuel, which makes hot gases. These gases rush out of the engines, shooting the rocket forwards.

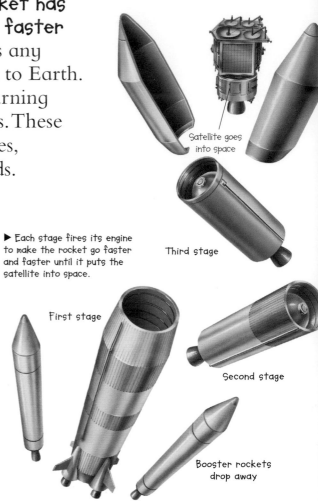

Satellite goes into space

Third stage

▶ Each stage fires its engine to make the rocket go faster and faster until it puts the satellite into space.

First stage

Second stage

Booster rockets drop away

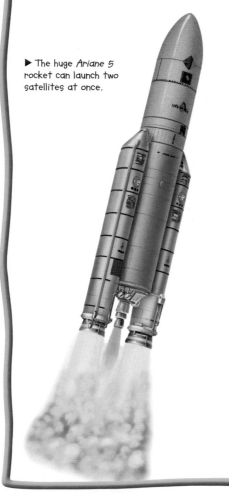

▶ The huge *Ariane 5* rocket can launch two satellites at once.

A single rocket is not powerful enough to launch a satellite or spacecraft into space. So rockets have two or three stages, which are really separate rockets mounted on top of each other, each with its own engines. When the first stage has used up its fuel it drops away, and the second stage starts. Finally the third stage takes over to go into space.

The space shuttle takes off from Earth as a rocket. It has rocket engines that burn fuel from a huge tank. But it also needs two large booster rockets to give it extra speed. The boosters drop away after two minutes, and the main rocket tank after six.

ROCKET POWER

You will need:
a balloon

If you blow up a balloon and let it go, the balloon shoots off across the room. The air inside the balloon has rushed out, pushing the balloon away in the opposite direction. A rocket blasting into space works in a similar way.

The shuttle lands back on Earth on a long runway, just like a giant glider. It does not use any engines for the landing, unlike an aircraft. It touches down so fast, the pilot uses a parachute as well as brakes to stop it on the runway.

▼ The shuttle puts down its wheels and lands on the runway.

▲ The shuttle is blasted into space by three rocket engines and two huge booster rockets.

Living in space

Space is a dangerous place for astronauts. It can be boiling hot in the sunshine or freezing cold in the Earth's shadow. There is also dangerous radiation from the Sun. Dust, rocks and bits from other rockets speed through space at such speed, they could easily make a small hole in a spacecraft, letting the air leak out.

Manned Manoeuvring Unit (jet pack)

Camera

Visor

Joy stick control

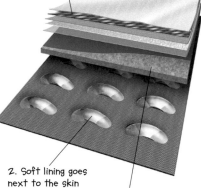

1. Outer layers protect from the fierce heat of the Sun

2. Soft lining goes next to the skin

3. This layer seals the suit from the vacuum of space

▲ In a spacesuit, many layers of different materials are needed to keep the astronaut safe.

Spacesuits protect astronauts when they are out in space. These are very bulky because they are made of many layers to make them strong. They must hold the air for astronauts to breathe and protect them against speeding dust and harmful radiation. To keep the astronauts cool while they work outside the spacecraft, tubes of water under the spacesuit carry away heat.

SPACE MEALS

You will need:
dried noodles

Buy a dried snack such as noodles, that just needs boiling water added. This is the kind of food astronauts eat. Most of their meals are dried so they are not too heavy to launch into space.

Everything floats around in space as if it had no weight. So all objects have to be fixed down or they will float away. Astronauts have footholds to keep them still while they are working. They strap themselves into sleeping bags so they don't bump into things when they are asleep.

Glove

esa

▲ Sleeping bags are fixed to a wall so astronauts look as though they are asleep standing up.

Spacesuit

Astronauts must take everything they need into space with them. Out in space there is no air, water or food so all the things that astronauts need to live must be packed into their spacecraft and taken with them.

Home from home

A space station is a home in space for astronauts and cosmonauts (Russian astronauts). It has a kitchen for making meals, and cabins with sleeping bags. There are toilets, wash basins and sometimes showers. They have places to work and controls where astronauts can check that everything is working properly.

The International Space Station, ISS, is being built in space. This is the latest and largest space station. Sixteen countries are helping to build it including the US, Russia, Japan, Canada, Brazil and 11 European countries. It is built up from separate sections called modules that have been made to fit together like a jigsaw.

I DON'T BELIEVE IT!

The US space station *Skylab*, launched in 1973, fell back to Earth in 1979. Most of it landed in the ocean but some pieces hit Australia.

Key
1. Solar panels for power
2. Docking port
3. Space shuttle
4. Control module
5. Living module
6. Soyuz ferry

Each part is launched from Earth and added to the ISS in space. There they are fitted by astronauts at the ISS using the shuttle's robot arm. Huge panels of solar cells are added. These turn sunlight into electricity to give a power supply for the space station.

◄ When all the pieces have been put into place, the International Space Station will look like this as it circles the Earth.

The crew live on board the ISS for several months at a time. The first crew of three people arrived at the space station in November 2000 and stayed for over four months. When the space station is finished there will be room for seven astronauts and they will have six modules where they can live and work.

The US shuttle carries astronauts, supplies and equipment up to the ISS. It docks for about a week before returning to Earth. Russia has a *Soyuz* spacecraft for ferrying people to and from the space station and a *Progress* ship which brings fresh supplies.

Robot explorers

Robot spacecraft called probes have explored all the planets except Pluto. Probes travel in space to take close-up pictures and measurements. They send the information back to scientists on Earth. Some probes circle planets taking pictures. For a really close-up look, a probe can land on the surface.

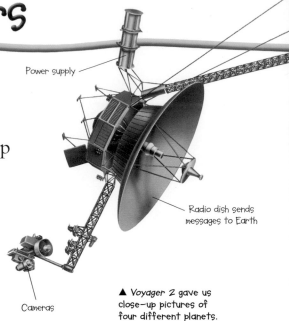

Power supply

Radio dish sends messages to Earth

Cameras

▲ Voyager 2 gave us close-up pictures of four different planets.

In 1976, two *Viking* spacecraft landed on Mars to look for life. They scooped up some dust and tested it to see if any tiny creatures lived on Mars. They did not find any signs of life and their pictures showed only a dry, red, dusty desert.

Two *Voyager* probes left Earth in 1977 to visit the gas giant planets. They reached Jupiter in 1979, flying past and on to Saturn. *Voyager 2* went on to visit Uranus and then Neptune in 1989. It sent back thousands of pictures of each planet as it flew past.

▼ The *Viking* landers took soil samples from Mars, but found no sign of life.

▲ When *Galileo* has finished sending back pictures of Jupiter and its moons, it will plunge into Jupiter's swirling clouds.

Galileo has circled Jupiter for more than six years. It arrived in 1995 and dropped a small probe into Jupiter's clouds. Galileo sent back pictures of the planet and its largest moons. It was discovered that two of them may have water hidden under ice thicker than the Arctic ice on Earth.

◄ *Sojourner* spent three months on Mars. The small rover was about the size of a microwave oven.

QUIZ

1. When did the *Voyager* probes fly past Jupiter?
2. Which probe sent pictures of Jupiter's clouds?
3. Which probes tested the dust on Mars for signs of life?
4. What was the name of the *Mars Pathfinder* rover?

Answers:
1. 1979 2. *Galileo*
3. *Viking* 4. *Sojourner*

Mars Pathfinder carried a small rover called *Sojourner* to Mars in 1997. It landed on the surface and opened up to let *Sojourner* out. This rover was like a remote control car, but with six wheels. It tested the soil and rocks to find out what they were made of as it slowly drove around the landing site.

Watching the Earth

Hundreds of satellites circle the Earth in space. They are launched into space by rockets and may stay there for ten years or more.

▶ Weather satellites look down at the clouds and give warning when a violent storm is approaching.

Communications satellites carry TV programmes and telephone messages around the world. Large aerials on Earth beam radio signals up to a space satellite which then beams them down to another aerial, half way round the world. This lets us talk to people on the other side of the world, and watch events such as the Olympics Games while they are happening in faraway countries.

▼ Communications satellites can beam TV programmes directly to your home through your own aerial dish.

Weather satellites help the forecasters tell us what the weather will be like. These satellites can see where the clouds are forming and which way they are going. They watch the winds and rain and measure how hot the air and the ground are.

▶ The different satellites each have their own job to do, looking at the Earth, or the weather, or out into space.

Earth-watching satellites look out for pollution. Oil slicks in the sea and dirty air over cities show up clearly in pictures from these satellites. They can help farmers by watching how well crops are growing and by looking for pests and diseases. Spotting forest fires and icebergs that may be a danger to ships is also easier from space.

▼ Pictures of the Earth taken by satellites can help make very accurate maps.

▲ Satellite telescopes let astronomers look far out into the Universe and discover what is out there.

Satellite telescopes let astronomers look at exciting things in space. They can see other kinds of radiation, such as x-rays, as well as light. X-ray telescopes can tell astronomers where there may be a black hole.

I DON'T BELIEVE IT!

Spy satellites circling the Earth take pictures of secret sites around the world. They can listen to secret radio messages from military ships or aircraft.

Voyage to the Moon

The first men landed on the Moon in 1969.
They were three astronauts from the US
Apollo 11 mission. Neil Armstrong was the
first person to set foot on the Moon. Only
five other *Apollo* missions have landed on
the Moon since then.

**A giant *Saturn 5* rocket launched
the astronauts on their journey
to the Moon.** It was the largest
rocket that had ever been built.
Its three huge stages lifted the
stronauts into space, and
then the third stage
gave the spacecraft
an extra boost to
send it to
the Moon.

Command Module

Lunar Module

Legs folded for journey

◀ The distance from
the Earth to the
Moon is nearly
400,000 kilometres.
That is about as far
as travelling round
the Earth 10 times.

**The Command Module that
carried the astronauts to the
Moon had no more room than an
estate car.** The astronauts were
squashed inside it for the journey,
which took three days to get there
and another three to get back. On
their return, the Command Module
with the astronauts inside, splashed
down in the sea.

Thrusters

Main engine

Service Module with
fuel and air supplies

▲ The Lunar and Command
Modules travelled to the Moon
fixed together, then separated
for the Moon landing.

The Lunar Rover was a moon car for
the astronauts to ride on. It looked
like a buggy with four wheels and two
seats. It could only travel about as fast
as you can run.

No one has been back to the Moon
since the last *Apollo* mission left in
1972. Astronauts had visited six different
places on the Moon and brought back
enough Moon rock to keep scientists busy
for many years. Maybe one day people
will return to the Moon and build bases
where they can live and work.

The Lunar Module took
two of the astronauts to
the Moon's surface. Once
safely landed they put on
spacesuits and went outside
to collect rocks. Later they
took off in the Lunar Module
to join the third astronaut
who had stayed in the
Command Module, circling
above the Moon on his own.

**I DON'T
BELIEVE IT!**

On the way to the Moon
an explosion damaged the
Apollo 13 spacecraft, leaving
the astronauts with little
heat or light.

PLANET EARTH

Discover all the astonishing natural features of our planet, and how we can help to preserve them.

Mountains • Earthquakes • Caves • Crystals
Volcanoes • Geysers • Rocks • Glaciers • Fossils
Gemstones • Atmosphere • Hurricanes • Tornadoes
Snowstorms • Deserts • Grasslands • Rainforests
Rivers • Lakes • Oceans • Animals • Plants

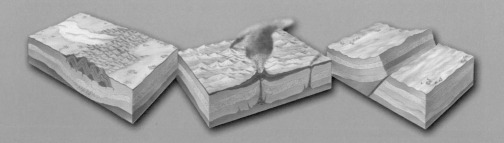

The speedy space ball

The Earth is a huge ball of rock moving through space at nearly 3000 metres per second. It weighs 6000 million, million, million tonnes. Up to two-thirds of the Earth's rocky surface is covered by water – this makes the seas and oceans. Rock that is not covered by water makes the land. Surrounding the Earth is a layer of gases called the atmosphere (air). This reaches about 700 kilometres from the Earth's surface – then space begins.

Where did Earth come from?

The Earth came from a cloud in space.
Scientists think the Earth formed from a huge cloud of gas and dust around 4500 million years ago. A star near the cloud exploded, making the cloud spin. As the cloud spun around, gases gathered at its centre and formed the Sun. Dust whizzed around the Sun and stuck together to form lumps of rock. In time the rocks crashed into each other to make the planets. The Earth is one of these planets.

5. The Earth was made up of one large piece of land, now split into seven chunks known as continents

▶ Clouds of gas and dust are made by the remains of old stars that have exploded or simply stopped shining. It is here that new stars and their planets form.

1. Cloud starts to spin

4. Volcanoes erupt, releasing gases, helping to form the first atmosphere

3. The Earth begins to cool and a hard shell forms

2. Dust gathers into lumps of rock which form a small planet

At first the Earth was very hot.
As the rocks crashed together they warmed each other up. Later, as the Earth formed, the rocks inside it melted. The new Earth was a ball of liquid rock with a thin, solid shell.

Huge numbers of large rocks called meteorites crashed into the Earth. They made round hollows on the surface. These hollows are called craters. The Moon was hit with rocks at the same time. Look at the Moon with binoculars – you can see the craters that were made long ago.

▶ The Moon was also hit by rocks in space, and these made huge craters, and mountain ranges up to 5000 metres high.

▼ Erupting volcanoes and fierce storms helped form the atmosphere and oceans. These provided energy that was needed for life on Earth to begin.

The oceans and seas formed as the Earth cooled down. Volcanoes erupted, letting out steam, gases and rocks from inside the Earth. As the Earth cooled, the steam changed to water droplets and made clouds. As the Earth cooled further, rain fell from the clouds. It rained for millions of years to make the seas and oceans.

I DON'T BELIEVE IT!

Millions of rocks crash into Earth as it speeds through space. Some larger ones may reach the ground as meteorites.

In a spin

The Earth is like a huge spinning top. It continues to spin because it was formed from a spinning cloud of gas and dust. It does not spin straight up like a top but leans a little to one side. The Earth takes 24 hours to spin around once. We call this period of time a day.

Mid–day

Evening

The Earth's spinning makes day and night. Each part of the Earth spins towards the Sun, and then away from it every day. When a part of the Earth is facing the Sun it is day-time there. When that part is facing away from the Sun it is night-time. Is the Earth facing the Sun or facing away from it where you are?

◄ If you were in space and looked at the Earth from the side, it would appear to move from left to right. If you looked down on Earth from the North Pole, it would seem to be moving anticlockwise.

The Earth spins around its Poles. The Earth spins around two points on its surface. They are at opposite ends of the Earth. One is on top of the Earth. It is called the North Pole. The other is at the bottom of the Earth. It is called the South Pole. The North and South Poles are so cold, they are covered by ice and snow.

▲ The Earth moves around the Sun in a path called an orbit. It takes a year to make this journey. In that time it spins round 365 and a quarter times.

Morning

Night

▲ As one part of the Earth turns into sunlight, another part turns into darkness. It is morning when a part turns into sunlight, and evening when it turns into darkness.

MAKE A COMPASS

A compass is used to find the direction of the North and South Poles.

You will need:

a bowl of water   a piece of wood
a bar magnet   a real compass

Place the wood in the water with the magnet on top. Make sure they do not touch the sides. When the wood is still, check the direction the magnet is pointing in with your compass, by placing it on a flat surface. It will tell you the direction of the North and South Poles.

The spinning Earth acts like a magnet. At the centre of the Earth is liquid iron. As the Earth spins, it makes the iron behave like a magnet with a North and South Pole. These act on the magnet in a compass to make the needle point to the North and South Poles.

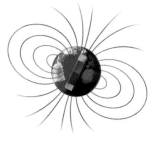

▲ These lines show the pulling power of the magnet inside the Earth.

Inside the Earth

There are different parts to the Earth. There is a thin, rocky crust, a solid middle called the mantle and a centre called the core. The outer part of the core is liquid but the inner core is made of solid metal.

At the centre of the Earth is a huge metal ball called the inner core. It is 2500 kilometres wide and is made mainly from iron, with some nickel. The ball has an incredible temperature of 6000°C – hot enough to make the metals melt. They stay solid because other parts of the Earth push down heavily on them.

Around the centre of the Earth flows a hot, liquid layer of iron and nickel. This layer is the outer core and is about 2200 kilometres thick. As the Earth spins, the metal ball and liquid layer move at different speeds.

▼ If the Earth could be cut open, this is what you would see inside. It has layers inside it like an onion.

Crust

City

Upper mantle

Volcano

Lower mantle

Rising hot rock

Plates moving apart

The largest part of Earth is a layer called the mantle, which is 2900 kilometres thick. It lies between the core and the crust. Near the crust, the mantle is made of slow-moving rock. When you squeeze an open tube of toothpaste, the toothpaste moves a little like the rocks in the upper mantle.

The Earth's surface is covered by crust. Land is made of continental crust between 20 and 70 kilometres thick. Most of this is made from a rock called granite. The ocean bed is made of oceanic crust about eight kilometres thick. It is made mainly from a rock called basalt.

The crust is divided into huge slabs of rock called plates. Most plates have land and seas on top of them but some, like the Pacific Plate, are mostly covered by water. The large areas of land on the plates are called continents. There are seven continents – Africa, Asia, Europe, North America, South America, Oceania and Antarctica.

Very, very slowly, the continents are moving. Slow-flowing mantle under the crust moves the plates across the Earth's surface. As the plates move, so do the continents. In some places, the plates push into each other. In others, they move apart. North America is moving three centimetres away from Europe every year!

Outer core

Inner core

◄ There are gaps in the Earth's crust where hot rocks from inside can reach the surface.

Hot rocks

There are places on Earth where hot, liquid rocks shoot up through its surface. These are volcanoes. Beneath a volcano is a huge space filled with molten (liquid) rock. This is the magma chamber. Inside the chamber, pressure builds like the pressure in a fizzy drink's can if you shake it. Ash, steam and molten rock called lava escape from the top of the volcano – this is an eruption.

▲ These volcanoes are a shield volcano (top), a crater volcano (middle) and a cone-shaped volcano (bottom).

Volcanoes erupt in different ways and have different shapes. Most have a central tube called a pipe, reaching up to the vent opening. Some volcanoes have runny lava, like those in Hawaii. It flows from the vent and makes a domed shape called a shield volcano. Other volcanoes have thick lava. When they erupt, gases in the lava make it explode into pieces of ash. The ash settles on the lava to make a cone-shaped volcano. A caldera, or crater volcano, is made when the top of a cone-shaped volcano explodes and sinks into the magma chamber.

Cloud of ash, steam and smoke

Layers of rocks from previous eruptions

Lava flowing away from vent

Huge chamber of magma (molten rock) beneath the volcano

Molten rock spreading out under the volcano and cooling down

Hot rocks don't always reach the surface. Huge lumps of rock rise into the crust and can become stuck. These are batholiths. The rock cools slowly and large crystals form. When the crystals cool, they form a rock called granite. In time, the surface of the crust may wear away and the top of the batholith appears above ground.

◀ When a volcano erupts, the hot rock from inside the Earth escapes as ash, smoke, flying lumps called volcanic bombs and rivers of lava.

MAKE YOUR OWN VOLCANO

You will need:

bicarbonate of soda   a plastic bottle
food colouring   vinegar   sand

Put a tablespoon of bicarbonate of soda in the plastic bottle. Stand the bottle in a tray and make a cone of sand around it. Put a few drops of red food colouring in half a cup of vinegar. Tip the vinegar into a jug then pour it into the bottle. In a few moments the volcano should erupt with red, frothy lava.

There are volcanoes under the sea. Where plates in the crust move apart, lava flows out from rift volcanoes to fill the gap. The hot lava is cooled quickly by the sea and forms pillow-shaped lumps called pillow lava.

Boil and bubble

A geyser can be found on top of some old volcanoes. If these volcanoes collapse, their rocks settle above hot rocks in the old magma chamber. The gaps between the broken rocks make a group of pipes and chambers. Rainwater seeps in, collecting in the chambers, where it is heated until it boils. Steam builds up, pushing the water through the pipes and out of a cone-shaped opening called a nozzle. Steam and water shoot through the nozzle, making a fountain up to 60 metres high.

▲ Geysers are common in the volcanic regions of New Zealand in Oceania. In some areas they are even used to help make electricity.

In the ocean are hot springs called black smokers. They form near rift volcanoes, where water is heated by the volcanoes' magma chambers. The hot water dissolves chemicals in the rocks, which turn black when they are cooled by the surrounding ocean water. They rise like clouds of smoke from chimneys.

In a hot spring, the water bubbles gently to the surface. As the water is heated in the chamber, it rises up a pipe and into a pool. The pool may be brightly coloured due to tiny plants and animals called algae and bacteria. These live in large numbers in the hot water.

◄ The chimneys of a black smoker are made by chemicals in the hot water. These stick together to form a rocky pipe.

Wallowing in a mud pot can make your skin soft and smooth. A mud pot is made when fumes break down rocks into tiny pieces. These mix with water to make mud. Hot fumes push through the mud, making it bubble. Some mud pots are cool enough to wallow in.

Mud pot

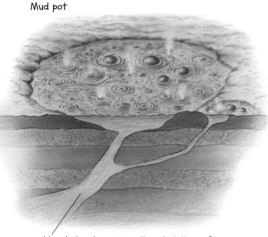

Very hot water mixes with mud at the surface

▲ The bubbles in a mud pot grow as they fill with fumes. Eventually they pop and the fumes escape into the air.

In Iceland, underground steam is used to make lights work. The steam is sent to power stations and is used to work generators to make electricity. The electricity then flows to homes and powers electrical equipment such as lights, televisions and computers.

Steam and smelly fumes can escape from holes in the ground. These holes are called fumaroles. Since Roman times, people have used the steam from fumaroles for steam baths. The steam may keep joints and lungs healthy.

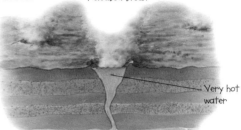

Fumarole   Released steam

Very hot water

▲ Under a fumarole the water gets so hot that it turns to steam, then shoots upwards into the air.

MAKE A GEYSER

You will need:
a bucket   a plastic funnel
plastic tubing

Fill a bucket with water. Turn the plastic funnel upside down and sink most of it in the water. Take a piece of plastic tube and put one end under the funnel. Blow down the other end of the tube. A spray of water and air will shoot out of the funnel. Be prepared for a wet face!

Breaking down rocks

Ice has the power to make rocks crumble. In cold weather, rainwater gets into cracks in rocks and freezes. Water swells as it turns to ice. The ice pushes with such power on the rock that it opens up the cracks. Over a long time, a rock can be broken down into thousands of tiny pieces.

Ice breaking down rock

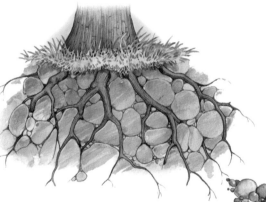

A tree root pushing its way through rock

Living things can break down rocks. Sometimes a tree seed lands in a crack in a rock. In time, a tree grows and its large roots smash open the rock. Tiny living things called lichens dissolve the surface of rocks to reach minerals they need to live. When animals, such as rabbits, make a burrow they may break up some of the rock in the ground.

Warming up and cooling down can break rocks into flakes. When a rock warms up it swells a little. When it cools, the rock shrinks back to its original size. After swelling and shrinking many times some rocks break up into flakes. Sometimes layers of large flakes form on a rock and make it look like onion skin.

▶ The flakes of rock break off unevenly and makes patterns of ridges on the rock surface.

Glaciers break up rocks and carry them away. Glaciers are huge areas of ice which form near mountain tops. They slide slowly down the mountainside and melt. As a glacier moves, some rocks are snapped off and carried along. Others are ground up and carried along as grit and sand.

Region where glacier forms

Moving ice

Where the glacier melts is called the snout

▶ Snow falls on mountain tops and squashes down to make ice. The ice forms the glacier which slowly moves down the mountainside until it melts.

Rocks in rivers and seas are always getting smaller. Water flows over rocks, gradually wearing them down. The water also dissolves minerals from the rock. As well as this, sand and grit in the water slowly grind away the rock surfaces.

I DON'T BELIEVE IT!
In one part of Turkey, people have cut caves in huge cones of rock to make homes.

Wind can blow a rock to pieces, but it takes a long time. Strong winds hurl dust and sand grains at a rock, which slowly blast pieces from its surface. It then blows away any tiny loose chips that have formed on the surface of the rock.

Arch

Settling down

Stones of different sizes can stick together to make rock. Thousands of years ago, boulders, pebbles and gravel settled on the shores of seas and lakes. These have become stuck together to make a rock called conglomerate. At the foot of cliffs, broken, rocky pieces collected and stuck together to make a rock called breccia. The lumps in breccia have sharp edges.

▲ Pieces of rock can become stuck together by a natural cement to make a lump of larger rock, such as breccia

▲ Natural cement binds grains of sand together to make sandstone.

Sandstone can be made in the sea or in the desert. When a thick layer of sand builds up, the grains are pressed together and cement forms. This sticks the grains together to make sandstone. Sea sandstone may be yellow with sharp-edged grains. Desert sandstone may be red with round, smooth grains.

If mud is squashed hard enough, it turns to stone. Mud is made from tiny particles of clay and slightly larger particles called silt. When huge layers of mud formed in ancient rivers, lakes and seas, they were squashed by their own weight to make mudstone.

▶ Mudstone has a very smooth surface. It may be grey, black, brown or yellow.

Limestone is made from sea shells.
Many kinds of sea animal have a hard shell. When the animal dies, the shell remains on the sea floor. In time, large numbers of shells build up and press together to form limestone. Huge numbers of shells become fossils.

▶ Limestone is usually white, cream, grey or yellow. Caves often form in areas of limestone.

SEE ROCK SETTLE

You will need:

sand   clay   gravel
a plastic bottle

Put a tablespoon of sand, clay and gravel into a bowl. Mix up the gravel with two cups of water then pour into a plastic bottle. You should see the bits of gravel settle in layers, with the smallest pieces at the bottom and the largest at the top.

Chalk is made from millions of shells and the remains of tiny sea creatures.
A drop of sea water contains many microscopic organisms (living things). Some of these organisms have shells full of holes. When these organisms die, the shells sink to the sea bed and in time form chalk.

I DON'T BELIEVE IT!

Flint is found in chalk and limestone. Thousands of years ago people used flint to make axes, knives and arrow heads.

▲ Most chalk formed at the time of the dinosaurs, but chalk is forming in some places on the Earth today.

Uncovering fossils

The best fossils formed from animals and plants that were buried quickly. When a plant or animal dies, it is usually eaten by other living things so that nothing remains. If the plant or animal was buried quickly after death, or even buried alive, its body may be preserved.

A fossil is made from minerals. A dead plant or animal can be dissolved by water. An empty space in the shape of the plant or animal is left in the mud and fills with minerals from the surrounding rock. Sometimes, the minerals simply settle in the body, making it harder and heavier.

▶ This is a fossil skull of *Tyrannosaurus rex*, a dinosaur that roamed the Earth around 70–65 million years ago.

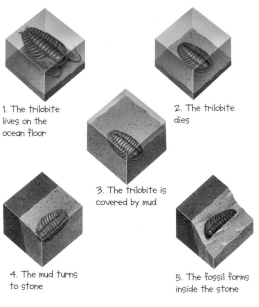

1. The trilobite lives on the ocean floor

2. The trilobite dies

3. The trilobite is covered by mud

4. The mud turns to stone

5. The fossil forms inside the stone

▲ Many fossils of trilobites, small ocean–dwelling creatures, have been found.

Some fossils look like coiled snakes but are really shellfish. These are ammonites. An ammonite's body was covered by a spiral shell. The body rotted away leaving the shell to become the fossil. Ammonites lived in the seas at the same time as the dinosaurs lived on land.

▲ When this ammonite was alive, tentacles would have stuck out of the uncoiled end of the shell.

Dinosaurs did not just leave fossil bones. Some left whole skeletons behind while others are known from only a few bones. Fossilized teeth, skin, eggs and droppings have been found. When dinosaurs walked across mud they left tracks behind that became fossils. By looking at these, scientists have discovered how dinosaurs walked and how fast they could run.

Electricity in your home may have been made by burning fossils. About 300 million years ago the land was covered by forests and swamps. When plants died they fell into the swamps and did not rot away. Over time, their remains were squashed and heated so much that they turned to coal. Today, coal is used to work generators that make electricity.

I DON'T BELIEVE IT!

Some fossils of bacteria are three and a half billion years old.

▶ Coal was formed by trees and plants growing near water. When the trees died the waterlogged ground stopped them rotting away, and peat formed

Dead trees are buried and squashed to form peat

The peat hardens to form coal

Rocks that change

When a rock forms in the crust it may soon be changed again. There are two main ways this can happen. In one way, the rock is heated by hot rocks moving up through the crust. In another way the crust is squashed and heated as mountains form. Both of these ways make crystals in the rock change to form new types of rocks.

▶ Under the ground are layers of rock and some of them can be changed by heat.

Layers of rock beneath the sea

The rocks dip down away from the coast to make the deep ocean

Squashed rock can become folded

If mudstone is squashed and heated it changes to slate. Crystals begin to line up in layers. This makes it easy to split the rock into thin sheets. Slate makes a good roof material. The smooth sheets are also used to make the bases of pool tables.

Rock can become stripy when it is heated and folded. It becomes so hot, it almost melts. Minerals that make up the rock form layers that appear as coloured stripes. These stripes may be wavy, showing the way the rock has been folded. This rock is called gneiss (sounds like 'nice').

Some hot rock travels to the surface through the pipe in a volcano

▲ The stripes in gneiss are formed by layers of different minerals.

Layers of rock away from the heat remain unchanged

Hot rock trapped in the crust can change the rock around it

If limestone is cooked in the crust it turns to marble. The shells which make up limestone break up when they are heated strongly and form marble, a rock which has a sugary appearance. The surface of marble can be polished to make it look attractive and it is used to make statues and ornaments.

QUIZ

1. If a sandstone has red, round, smooth grains, where was the sand made?
2. Which rocks are made from seashells and tiny sea creatures?
3. Name six kinds of dinosaur fossil.
4. Which rock changes into slate?

Answers:
1. The desert 2. Limestone and chalk
3. Bones, teeth, skin, eggs, droppings, tracks
4. Mudstone

Massive mountains

The youngest mountains on Earth are the highest. Highest of all is Mount Everest, which formed 15 million years ago. Young mountains have jagged peaks because softer rocks on the mountain top are broken down by the weather. These pointy peaks are made from harder rocks that take longer to break down. In time, even these hard rocks are worn away. This makes an older mountain shorter and gives its top a rounded shape.

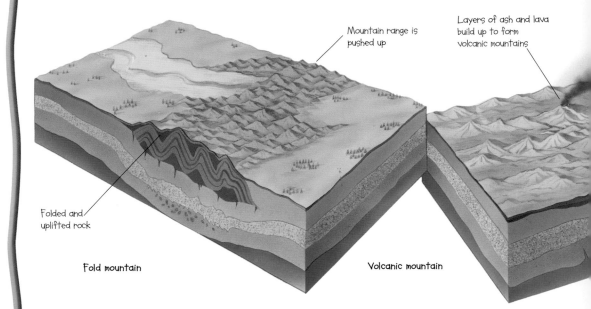

Mountain range is pushed up

Layers of ash and lava build up to form volcanic mountains

Folded and uplifted rock

Fold mountain

Volcanic mountain

When plates in the Earth's crust crash together, mountains are formed. When two continental plates crash together, the crust at the edge of the plates crumples and folds, pushing up ranges of mountains. The Himalayan Mountains in Asia formed in this way.

Some of the Earth's highest mountains are volcanoes. These are formed when molten rock (lava) erupts through the Earth's crust. As the lava cools, it forms a rocky layer. With each new eruption, another layer is added.

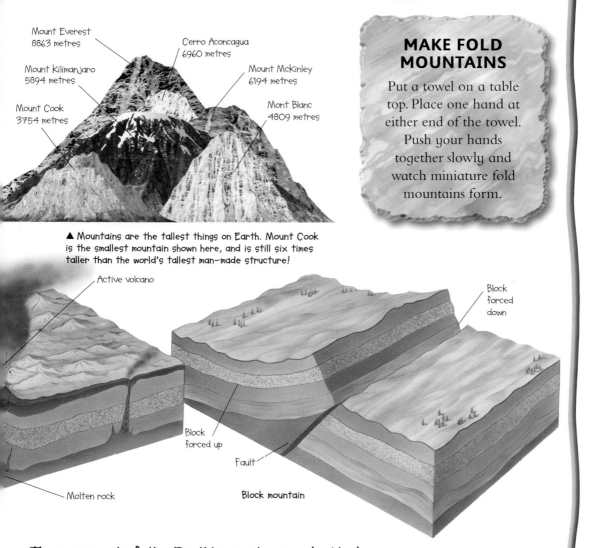

Mount Everest
8863 metres

Cerro Aconcagua
6960 metres

Mount Kilimanjaro
5894 metres

Mount Mckinley
6194 metres

Mount Cook
3754 metres

Mont Blanc
4809 metres

▲ Mountains are the tallest things on Earth. Mount Cook is the smallest mountain shown here, and is still six times taller than the world's tallest man-made structure!

Active volcano

Block forced down

Block forced up

Fault

Molten rock

Block mountain

MAKE FOLD MOUNTAINS

Put a towel on a table top. Place one hand at either end of the towel. Push your hands together slowly and watch miniature fold mountains form.

The movement of the Earth's crust can make blocks of rock pop up to make mountains. When the plates in the crust push together, they make heat which softens the rock, letting it fold. Farther away from this heat, cooler rock snaps when it is pushed. The snapped rock makes huge cracks called faults in the crust. When a block of rock between two faults is pushed by the rest of the crust, it rises to form a block mountain.

▲ It takes millions of years for mountains to form and the process is happening all the time. A group of mountains is called a range. The biggest ranges are the Alps in Europe, the Andes in South America, the Rockies in North America and the highest of all – the Himalayas in Asia.

81

Shaking the Earth

An earthquake is caused by violent movements in the Earth's crust. Most occur when two plates in the crust rub together. An earthquake starts deep underground at its 'focus'. Shock waves move from the focus in all directions, shaking the rock. Where the shock waves reach the surface is called the epicentre. This is where the greatest shaking occurs.

The power of an earthquake can vary. Half a million earthquakes happen every year but hardly any can be felt by people. About 25 earthquakes each year are powerful enough to cause disasters. Earthquake strength is measured by the Richter Scale. The higher the number, the more destructive the earthquake.

▼ Earthquakes can make buildings collapse and cause cracks in roads. Fire is also a hazard, as gas mains can break and catch alight.

1. Lights swing at level 3

4. Bridges and buildings collapse at level 7

2. Windows break at level 5

3. Chimneys topple at level 6

▲ The Richter Scale measures the strength of the shock waves and energy produced by an earthquake. The shock waves can have little effect, or be strong enough to topple buildings.

Shock waves from the focus

Earthquakes under the sea are called seaquakes. These can cause enormous waves called tsunamis. As the tsunami rushes across the ocean, it stays quite low. As it reaches the coast, it rises to form a huge wall of water. The wave rushes onto the land, destroying everything in its path.

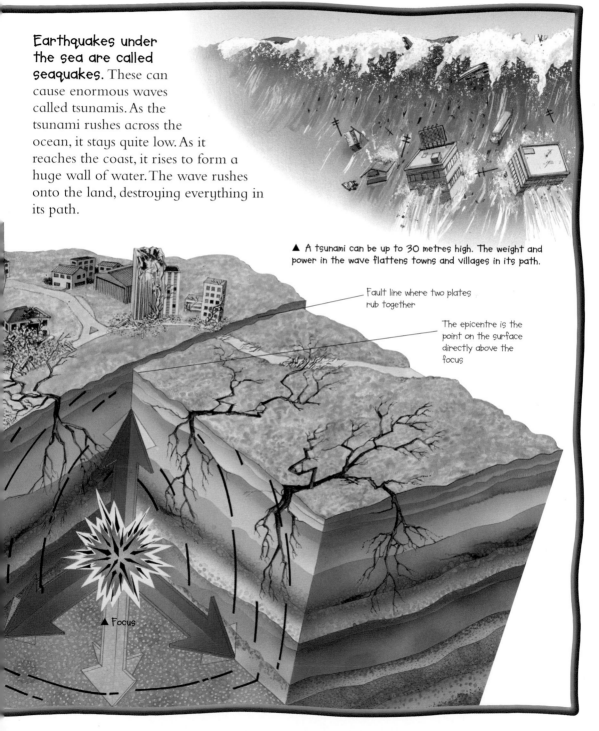

▲ A tsunami can be up to 30 metres high. The weight and power in the wave flattens towns and villages in its path.

Fault line where two plates rub together

The epicentre is the point on the surface directly above the focus

▲ Focus

Cavernous caves

Some caves are made from a tube of lava. As lava moves down the side of a volcano, its surface cools down quickly. The cold lava becomes solid but below, the lava remains warm and keeps on flowing. Under the solid surface a tube may form in which liquid lava flows. When the tube empties, a cave is formed.

▲ A cave made by lava is so large that people can walk through it without having to bend down

Waterfall in a shaft

Waterfall in a sink hole

1. Water seeps through cracks in rock

▶ Water runs through the caves in limestone rock and makes pools and streams. In wet weather it may flood the caves.

▼ Water flows through the cracks in limestone and makes them wider to form caves. The horizontal caves are called galleries and the vertical caves are called shafts

When rain falls on limestone it becomes a cave—maker. Rainwater can mix with carbon dioxide to form an acid strong enough to attack limestone and make it dissolve. Underground, the action of the rainwater makes caves in which streams and lakes can be found.

2. Underground stream carves into rock

3. Large cave system develops

Gallery

Cave opening

I DON'T BELIEVE IT!
The longest stalactite is 59 metres long. The tallest stalagmite is 32 metres tall.

Dripping water in a limestone cave makes rock spikes. When water drips from a cave roof it leaves a small piece of limestone behind. A small spike of rock begins to form. This rock spike, called a stalactite, may grow from the ceiling. Where the drops splash onto the cave floor, tiny pieces of limestone gather. They form a spike which points upwards. This is a stalagmite. Over long periods of time, the two spikes may join together to form a column of rock.

The Earth's treasure

Gold may form small grains, large nuggets or veins in the rocks. When the rocks wear away, the grains may be found in the sand of river beds. Silver forms branching wires in rock. It does not shine like jewellery but is covered in a black coating called tarnish.

▲ Gold nuggets like this one can be melted and moulded to form all kinds of jewellery.

Most metals are found in rocks called ores. An ore is a mixture of different substances, of which metal is one. Each metal has its own ore. For example, aluminium is found in a yellow ore called bauxite. Heat is used to get metals from their ores. We use metals to make thousands of different things, ranging from watches to jumbo jets.

◀ Silver is used for making jewellery and ornaments.

Beautiful crystals can grow in lava bubbles. Lava contains gases which form bubbles. When the lava cools and becomes solid, the bubbles form balloon-shaped spaces in the rock. These are called geodes. Liquids seep into them and form large crystals. The gemstone amethyst forms in this way.

▲ This is bauxite, the ore of aluminium. Heat, chemicals and electricity are used to get the metal out of the rock. Aluminium is used to make all kinds of things, from kitchen foil to aeroplanes.

▶ Inside a geode there is space for crystals, such as amethyst crystals, to spread out, grow and form perfect shapes.

Beryl

Emerald

Diamond

Topaz

Garnet

Gemstones are coloured rocks which are cut and polished to make them sparkle. People have used them to make jewellery for thousands of years. Gems such as topaz, emerald and garnet formed in hot rocks which rose to the Earth's crust and cooled. Most are found as small crystals, but a gem called beryl can have a huge crystal – the largest ever found was 18 metres long! Diamond is a gemstone and is the hardest natural substance found on Earth.

▲ There are more than 100 different kinds of gemstone. Some are associated with different months of the year and are known as 'birthstones'. For example, the birthstone for September is sapphire.

MAKE CRYSTALS FROM SALT WATER

You will need:

table salt
a magnifying glass
a dark-coloured bowl

Dissolve some table salt in some warm water. Pour the salty water into a dark-coloured bowl. Put the bowl in a warm place so the water can evaporate. After a few days, you can look at the crystals with a magnifying glass.

Wild weather

Exosphere

Thermosphere

Mesosphere

Stratosphere

Troposphere

The Earth is wrapped in layers of gases called the atmosphere. The weather takes place in the lowest layer, the troposphere. The layer above is the stratosphere. Aeroplanes fly here to avoid bad weather. The mesosphere is the middle layer and above it is the thermosphere. The exosphere is about 700 kilometres above your head.

▲ As you travel from the planet surface into space, you pass through five layers of the atmosphere.

▼ Water moves between the ocean, air and land in the water cycle.

Water falling as rain

Rain flows into rivers

Water vapour rising from plants

Clouds are made in the air above the oceans. When the Sun shines on the water's surface, some evaporates. A gas called water vapour rises into the air. As the vapour cools, it forms clouds which are blown all over the Earth's surface. The clouds cool as they move inland, and produce rain. Rain falls on the land, then flows away in rivers back to the oceans. We call this process the water cycle.

Water vapour rising from the ocean

▶ A hurricane forms over the surface of a warm ocean but it can move to the coast and onto the land.

A hurricane is a destructive storm which gathers over a warm part of the ocean. Water evaporating from the ocean forms a vast cloud. As cool air rushes in below the cloud, it turns like a huge spinning wheel. The centre of the hurricane (the eye) is completely still. But all around, winds gust at speeds of 300 kilometres an hour. If it reaches land the hurricane can blow buildings to pieces.

Snowflakes form in the tops of clouds. It is so cold here that water freezes to make ice crystals. As the snowflakes get larger, they fall through the cloud. If the cloud is in warm air, the snowflakes melt and form raindrops. If the cloud is in cold air, the snowflakes reach the ground and begin to settle.

▼ The ice crystals in a snowflake usually form six arms.

A tornado is the fastest wind on Earth — it can spin at speeds of 500 kilometres an hour. Tornadoes form over ground that has become very warm. Fast-rising air makes a spinning funnel which acts as a vacuum cleaner. It can devastate buildings and lift up cars and traffic, flinging them to the ground.

I DON'T BELIEVE IT!
Every day there are 45,000 thunderstorms on the Earth.

Lands of sand and grass

The driest places on Earth are deserts. In many deserts there is a short period of rain every year, but some deserts have dry weather for many years. The main deserts of the world are shown on the map.

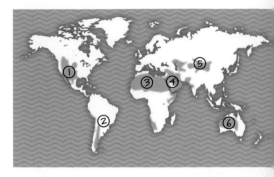

▲ ① North American deserts – Great Basin and Mojave ② Atacama ③ Sahara ④ Arabian ⑤ Gobi ⑥ Australian deserts – Great Sandy, Gibson, Great Victoria, Simpson.

Deserts are not always hot. It can be as hot as 50°C in the day-time but at night the temperature falls quickly. Deserts near the Equator have hot days all year round but some deserts farther from the Equator have very cold winters.

Ridges of sand being blown into dunes

Barchan dune

Rock beneath the desert

I DON'T BELIEVE IT!

The camel has broad feet that stop it sinking in the sand.

Sand dunes are made by the winds blowing across a desert. If there is only a small amount of sand on the desert floor, the wind blows crescent-shaped dunes called barchans. If there is plenty of sand, it forms long, straight dunes called transverse dunes. If the wind blows in two directions, it makes long wavy dunes called seif dunes.

An oasis is a pool of water in the desert. It forms from rainwater that has seeped into the sand then collected in rock. The water then moves through the rock to where the sand is very thin and forms a pool. Trees and plants grow around the pool and animals visit the pool to drink.

Oasis

▼ Plants and animals can thrive at an oasis in the middle of a desert.

A desert cactus stores water in its stem. The grooves on the stem let it swell with water to keep the plant alive in dry weather. The spines stop animals biting into the cactus for a drink.

Grasslands are found where there is too much rain for a desert and not enough rain for a forest. Tropical grasslands near the Equator are hot all year round. Grasslands farther from the Equator have warm summers and cool winters.

Large numbers of animals live on grasslands. In Africa zebras feed on the top of grass stalks, gnu feed on the middle leaves and gazelles feed on the new shoots. This allows all the animals to feed together. Other animals such as lions feed on plant eaters.

▼ Three types of animals can live together by eating plants of different heights. Zebras ① eat the tall grass. Gnu ② eat the middle shoots and gazelle ③ browse on the lowest shoots.

91

Fantastic forests

There are three main kinds of forest. They are coniferous, temperate and tropical forests. The main forest regions are shown on the world map opposite.

▲ This map shows the major areas of forest in the world:
① Coniferous forest ② Temperate forest
③ Tropical forest

Coniferous trees form huge forests around the northern part of the planet. They have long, green, needle-like leaves covered in wax. These trees stay in leaf throughout the year. In winter, the wax helps snow slide off the leaves so that sunlight can reach them to keep them alive. Coniferous trees produce seeds in cones. These are eaten by squirrels.

Large numbers of huge trees grow close together in a rainforest. They have broad, evergreen leaves and branches that almost touch. These form a leafy roof over the forest called a canopy. It rains almost every day in a rainforest and the vegetation is so thick, it can take a raindrop ten minutes to fall to the ground. Three-quarters of all known species of animals and plants live in rainforests. They include huge hairy spiders, brightly coloured frogs and spotted jungle cats.

Most trees in temperate forests have flat, broad leaves and need large amounts of water to keep them alive. In winter, the trees cannot get enough water from the frozen ground, so they lose their leaves and grow new ones in spring. Deer, rabbits, foxes and mice live on the woodland floor while squirrels, woodpeckers and owls live in the trees.

QUIZ

1. What forms at the top of a cloud?

2. What shape is a barchan sand dune?

3. In which kind of forest would you find brightly coloured frogs?

Answers:
1. Snow flake 2. Crescent 3. Tropical

Rivers and lakes

A mighty river can start from a spring. This is a place where water flows from the ground. Rain soaks into the ground, through the soil and rock, until it gushes out on the side of a hill. The trickle of water from a spring is called a stream. Many streams join together to make a river.

Water wears rocks down to make a waterfall.
When a river flows off a layer of hard rock onto softer rock, it wears the softer rock away. The rocks and pebbles in the water grind the soft rock away to make a cliff face. At the bottom of the waterfall they make a deep pool called a plunge pool.

Oxbow lake

Meander

Delta

▶ High in the mountains, streams join to form the headwater of a river. From here the river flows through the mountains then more slowly across the plains to the sea.

A river changes as it flows to the sea.
Rivers begin in hills and mountains. They are narrow and flow quickly there. When the river flows through flatter land it becomes wider and slow-moving. It makes loops called meanders which may separate and form oxbow lakes. Where the river meets the sea is the river mouth. It may be a wide channel called an estuary or a group of sandy islands called a delta.

◀ Waterfalls may only be a few centimetres high, or come crashing over a cliff with a massive drop. Angel Falls in Venezuela form the highest falls in the world. One of the drops is an amazing 807 metres.

Headwater

Lakes form in hollows in the ground. The hollows may be left when glaciers melt or when plates in the crust split open. Some lakes form when a landslide makes a dam across a river.

▲ A landslide has fallen into the river and blocked the flow of water to make a lake.

▼ A volcano can sometimes form in a lake inside a crater.

A lake can form in the crater of a volcano. A few crater lakes have formed in craters left by meteorites that hit Earth long ago.

▼ Most lakes are just blue but some are green, pink, red or even white. The Laguna Colorado in Chile is red due to tiny organisms (creatures) that live in the water.

Some lake water may be brightly coloured. The colours are made by tiny organisms called algae or by minerals dissolved in the water.

World of water

There is so much water on our planet that it could be called 'Ocean' instead of Earth. Only about one third of the planet is covered by land. The rest is covered by four huge areas of water called oceans. A sea is a smaller area of water in an ocean. For example the North Sea is part of the Atlantic Ocean and the Malayan Sea is part of the Pacific Ocean.

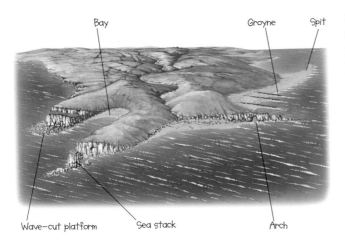

Bay

Groyne   Spit

Wave-cut platform   Sea stack   Arch

Coasts are always changing. Where the sea and land meet is called the coast. In many places waves crash onto the land and break it up. Caves and arches are punched into cliffs. In time, the arches break and leave columns of rock called sea stacks.

◀ The rocks at the coast are broken up by the action of the waves.

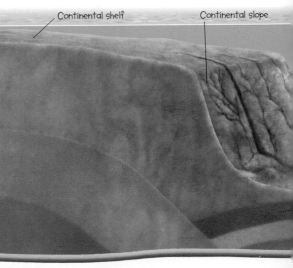

Continental shelf   Continental slope

The oceans are so deep that mountains are hidden beneath them. If you paddle by the shore, sea water is quite shallow. Out in the ocean it can be up to eight kilometres deep. The ocean floor is a flat plain with mountain ranges rising across it. They mark where two places in the crust meet. Nearer the coast may be deep trenches where the edges of two plates have moved apart. Extinct volcanoes form mountains called sea mounts.

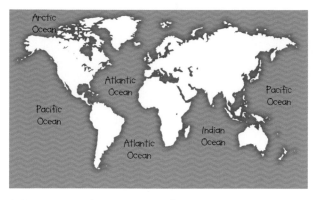

▲ This map shows the major oceans of the world.

There are thousands of icebergs floating in the oceans. They are made from glaciers and ice sheets which have formed at the North and South Poles. Only about a tenth of an iceberg can be seen above water. The rest lies below and can sink ships that sail too close.

▲ Under every iceberg is a huge amount of ice, usually much bigger than the area visible from the surface.

▲ Corals only grow in tropical or sub-tropical waters. They tend to grow in shallow water where there is lots of sunlight.

Tiny creatures can make islands in the oceans. Coral have jelly-like bodies and they live together in their millions. They make rocky homes from minerals in sea water which protects them from feeding fish. Coral builds up to create islands around extinct volcanoes in the Pacific and Indian Oceans.

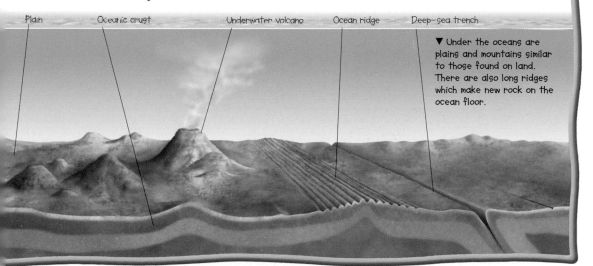

Plain   Oceanic crust   Underwater volcano   Ocean ridge   Deep-sea trench

▼ Under the oceans are plains and mountains similar to those found on land. There are also long ridges which make new rock on the ocean floor.

The planet of life

There are millions of different kinds of life forms on Earth. So far, life has not been found anywhere else. Living things survive here because it is warm, there is water and the air contains oxygen. If we discover other planets with these conditions, there may be life on them too.

Many living things on the Earth are tiny. They are so small that we cannot see them. A whale shark is the largest fish on the planet, yet it feeds on tiny shrimp-like creatures. These in turn feed on even smaller plant-like organisms called plankton, which make food from sunlight and sea water. Microscopic bacteria are found in the soil and even on your skin.

▲ Despite being the biggest fish in the oceans, the mighty whale shark feeds on tiny shrimp-like creatures and plankton (right).

Animals cannot live without plants. A plant makes food from sunlight, water, air and minerals in the soil. Animals cannot make their own food so many of them eat plants. Others survive by eating the plant-eaters. If plants died out, all the animals would die too.

◀ This caterpillar eats as much plant-life as possible before beginning its change to a butterfly.

The air can be full of animals.
On a warm day, midges and gnats
form clouds close to the ground. In
spring and autumn flocks of birds
fly to different parts of the world
to nest. On summer evenings bats
hunt for midges flying in the air.

**The surface of the ground is home
to many small animals.** Mice scurry
through the grass. Larger animals
such as deer hide in bushes. The
elephant is the largest land animal.
It does not need to hide because few
animals would attack it.

**If you dig into the ground you can find
animals living there.** The earthworm is a
common creature found in the soil. It feeds
on rotting plants that it pulls into the soil.
Earthworms are eaten by moles that dig
their way underground.

I DON'T BELIEVE IT!
The star-nosed mole has
feelers on the
end of its nose.
It uses them
to find food.

Caring for the planet

Many useful materials come from the Earth.
These make clothes, buildings, furniture and
containers such as cans. Some materials, like
those used to make buildings, last a long time.
Others, such as those used to make cans, may
be used up on the day they are bought.

We may run out of some materials
in the future. Metals are found in
rocks called ores. When all the ore has
been used up we will not be able to
make new metal. Wood is a material
that we may not run out of as new
trees are always being planted. We
must still be careful not to use too
much wood, because new trees may
not grow fast enough for our needs.

1. Old bottles
are collected
from bottle
banks

2. The glass or plastic are
re-cycled to make raw materials

3. The raw
materials are
re-used to
make new
bottles

▲ The waste collected at a recycling centre is changed
back into useful materials to make many of the things we
frequently use.

Exhaust fumes from traffic
clog up the atmosphere

We can make materials last longer by
recycling them. Metal, glass and plastic
are thrown away after they have been
used, buried in tips and never used again.
Today more people recycle materials. This
means sending them back to factories to
be used again.

Factories pump out chemicals that can cause acid rain. They also dump polluted water in rivers and seas.

▼ Here are some of the ways in which we are harming our planet today. We must think of better ways to treat the Earth in the future.

Cutting down trees can devastate forests and wildlife

Rubbish is dumped in rivers

Air and water can be polluted by our activities. Burning coal and oil makes fumes which can make rainwater acidic. This can kill trees and damages soil. When we make materials, chemicals are often released into rivers and seas, endangering wildlife.

Living things can be protected. Large areas of land have been made into national parks where wildlife is protected. People can come to study both plants and animals.

The Earth is nearly five billion years old. From a ball of molten rock it has changed into a living, breathing planet. We must try to keep it that way. Switching off lights to save energy and picking up litter are small things we can all do.

We use huge amounts of fuel to make energy. The main fuels are coal and oil, which are used in power stations to make electricity. Oil is also used in petrol for cars. In time, these fuels will run out. Scientists are trying to develop ways of using other energy sources such as the wind and wave power. Huge windmills are already used to make electricity.

I DON'T BELIEVE IT!
30 to 50 percent of all living species may be extinct by the middle of the 21st century.

WEATHER

Discover a world of ever-changing weather,
and how it can affect life on Earth.

Duststorms • Rain • Clouds • Floods • Snow
Avalanches • Ice • Winds • Hurricanes • Typhoons
Climates • Seasons • Monsoons • Tropics • Droughts
Tornadoes • Thunderstorms • Lightning • Seasons
Waterspouts • Rainbows • Weather charts

What is weather?

Rain, sunshine, snow and storms are all types of weather. These help us decide what clothes we wear, what food we eat, and what kind of life we lead. Weather also affects how animals and plants survive. Different types of weather are caused by what is happening in the atmosphere, the air above our heads. In some parts of the world, the weather changes every day, in others, it is nearly always the same.

Equator

Tropical, temperate and polar are all types of climate. Climate is the name we give to patterns of weather over a period of time. Near the Equator, the weather is mostly hot and steamy. We call this a tropical climate. Near the North and South Poles, ice lies on the ground year-round and there are biting-cold blizzards. This is a polar climate. Most of the world has a temperate climate, with a mix of cold and warm seasons.

Tropical

Tropical forest

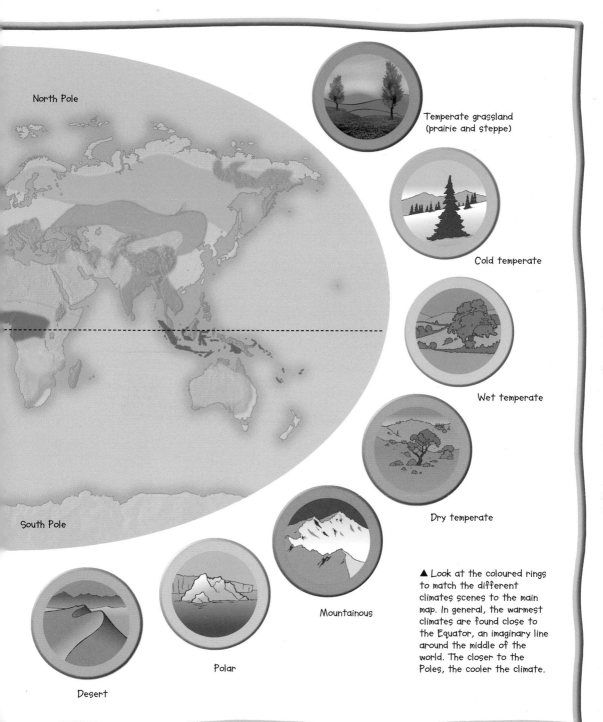

North Pole

Temperate grassland
(prairie and steppe)

Cold temperate

Wet temperate

Dry temperate

South Pole

Mountainous

▲ Look at the coloured rings
to match the different
climates scenes to the main
map. In general, the warmest
climates are found close to
the Equator, an imaginary line
around the middle of the
world. The closer to the
Poles, the cooler the climate.

Polar

Desert

The four seasons

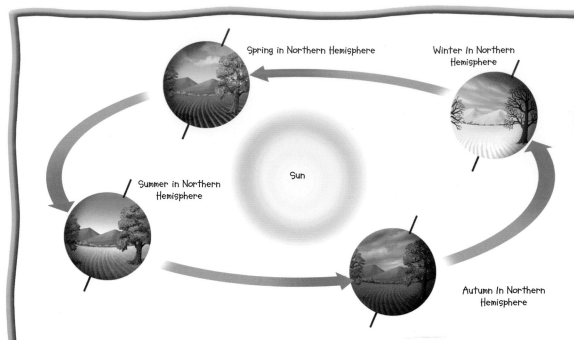

Spring in Northern Hemisphere

Winter In Northern Hemisphere

Summer in Northern Hemisphere

Sun

Autumn In Northern Hemisphere

The reason for the seasons lies in space. Our planet Earth plots a path through space that takes it around the Sun. This path, or orbit, takes one year. The Earth is tilted, so over the year first one and then the other Pole leans towards the Sun, giving us seasons. In June, for example, the North Pole leans towards the Sun. The Sun heats the northern half of Earth and there is summer.

◀ Northern winter and southern summer happen when the Southern Hemisphere is tilted towards the Sun.

When it is summer in Argentina, it is winter in Canada. In December, the South Pole leans towards the Sun. Places in the southern half of the world, such as Argentina, have summer. At the same time, places in the northern half, such as Canada, have winter.

A day can last 21 hours! Night and day happen because Earth is spinning as it circles the Sun. At the height of summer, places near the North Pole are so tilted towards the Sun that it is light almost all day long. In Stockholm, Sweden, Midsummer's Eve lasts 21 hours because the Sun disappears below the horizon for only three hours.

▲ At the North Pole, the Sun never disappears below the horizon at Midsummer's Day.

▼ Deciduous trees like these lose their leaves in autumn, but evergreens keep their leaves all year round.

I DON'T BELIEVE IT !

When the Sun shines all day in the far north, there is 24-hour night in the far south.

Forests change colour in the autumn. Autumn comes between summer and winter. Trees prepare for the cold winter months ahead by losing their leaves. First, though, they suck back the precious green chlorophyll, or dye, in their leaves, making them turn glorious shades of red, orange and brown.

Fewer seasons

Monsoons are winds that carry heavy rains. The rains fall in the tropics in summer during the hot, rainy season. The Sun warms up the sea, which causes huge banks of cloud to form. Monsoons then blow these clouds towards land. Once the rains hit the continent, they can pour for weeks.

▶ When the rains are especially heavy, they cause chaos. Streets turn to rivers and sometimes people's homes are even washed away.

I DON'T BELIEVE IT !

In parts of monsoon India, over 26,000 millimetres of rain have fallen in a single year!

Monsoons happen mainly in Asia. However, there are some parts of the Americas that are close to the Equator that also have a season that is very rainy. Winds can carry such heavy rain clouds that there are flash floods in the deserts of the southwestern United States. The floods happen because the land has been baked hard during the dry season.

Many parts of the tropics have two seasons, not four. They are the parts of the world closest to the Equator, an imaginary line around the middle of the Earth. Here it is always hot, as these places are constantly facing the Sun. However, the movement of the Earth affects the position of a great band of cloud. In June, the tropical areas north of the Equator have the strongest heat and the heaviest rain storms. In December, it is the turn of the areas south of the Equator.

Tropic of Cancer

Equator

Tropic of Capricorn

▲ The tropics lie either side of the Equator, between lines of latitude called the Tropic of Cancer and the Tropic of Capricorn.

In a tropical rainforest, you need your umbrella every day! Rainforests have rainy weather all year round – but there is still a wet and a dry season. It is just that the wet season is even wetter!

▼ Daily rainfall feeds the lush rainforest vegetation.

What a scorcher!

All our heat comes from the Sun. The Sun is a star, a super-hot ball of burning gases. It gives off heat rays that travel 150 million kilometres through space to our planet. Over the journey, the rays cool down, but they can still scorch the Earth.

The Sahara is the sunniest place. This North African desert once had 4300 hours of sunshine in a year! People who live there, such as the Tuareg Arabs, cover their skin to avoid being sunburnt.

The hottest place on Earth is Al Aziziyah in Libya. It is 58°C in the shade – hot enough to fry an egg!

▶ Desert peoples wear headdresses to protect their skin and eyes from the sun and sand.

▼ A mirage is just a trick of the light. It can make us see something that is not really there.

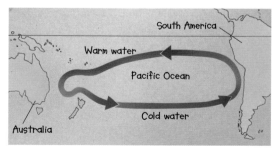

The Sun can trick your eyes. Sometimes, as sunlight passes through our atmosphere, it hits layers of air at different temperatures. When this happens, the air bends the light and can trick our eyes into seeing something that is not there. This is a mirage. For example, what looks like a pool of water might really be part of the sky reflected on to the land.

Too much sun brings drought. Clear skies and sunshine are not always good news. Without rain crops wither, and people and their animals go hungry.

One terrible drought made a 'Dust Bowl'. Settlers in the American Mid-West were ruined by a long drought during the 1930s. As crops died, there were no roots to hold the soil together. The dry earth turned to dust and some farms simply blew away!

▲ The 'Dust Bowl' was caused by strong winds and dust storms. These destroyed huge areas of land.

South America

Warm water

Pacific Ocean

Cold water

Australia

▲ El Niño has been known to cause violent weather conditions. It returns on average every four years.

A sea current can set forests alight. All sorts of things affect our weather and climate. The movements of a sea current called El Niño have been blamed for causing terrible droughts – which led to unstoppable forest fires.

Our atmosphere

Our planet is wrapped in a blanket of air. We call this blanket the atmosphere. It stretches hundreds of kilometres above our heads. The blanket keeps in heat, especially at night when part of the planet faces away from the Sun. During the day, the blanket becomes a sunscreen instead. Without an atmosphere, there would be no weather.

Most weather happens in the troposphere. This is the layer of atmosphere that stretches from the ground to around 10 kilometres above your head. The higher in the troposphere you go, the cooler the air. Because of this, clouds are most likely to form here. Clouds with flattened tops show just where the troposphere meets the next layer, the stratosphere.

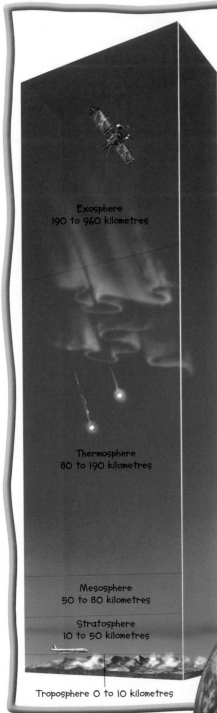

Exosphere
190 to 960 kilometres

Thermosphere
80 to 190 kilometres

Mesosphere
50 to 80 kilometres

Stratosphere
10 to 50 kilometres

Troposphere 0 to 10 kilometres

◀ The atmosphere stretches right into space. Scientists have split it into five layers, or spheres, such as the troposphere.

▼ The Earth is surrounded by the atmosphere. It acts as a blanket, protecting us from the Sun's fierce rays.

Air just cannot keep still. Tiny particles in air, called molecules, are always bumping into each other! The more they smash into each other, the greater the air pressure. Generally, there are more smashes lower in the troposphere, because the pull of gravity makes the molecules fall towards the Earth's surface. The higher you go, the lower the air pressure, and the less oxygen there is in the air.

▶ At high altitudes there is less oxygen. That is why mountaineers often wear breathing equipment.

High pressure

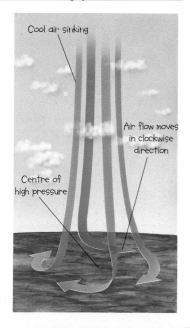

Cool air sinking

Air flow moves in clockwise direction

Centre of high pressure

Low pressure

Warm air rising

Air flow moves in anticlockwise direction

Centre of low pressure

Warmth makes air move. When heat from the Sun warms the molecules in air, they move faster and spread out more. This makes the air lighter, so it rises in the sky, creating low pressure. As it gets higher, the air cools. The molecules slow down and become heavier again, so they start to sink back to Earth.

◀ A high pressure weather system gives us warmer weather, while low pressure gives us cooler more unsettled weather.

Clouds and rain

Rain comes from the sea. As the Sun heats the surface of the ocean, some seawater turns into water vapour and rises into the air. As it rises, it cools and turns back into water droplets. Lots of water droplets make clouds. The droplets join together to make bigger and bigger drops that eventually fall as rain. Some rain is soaked up by the land, but a lot finds its way back to the sea. This is called the water cycle.

▶ The water cycle involves all the water on Earth. Water vapour rises from lakes, rivers and the sea to form clouds in the atmosphere.

RAIN GAUGE

You will need:

jam jar waterproof marker pen
ruler notebook pen

Put the jar outside. At the same time each day, mark the rainwater level on the jar with your pen. At the end of a week, empty the jar. Measure and record how much rain fell each day and over the whole week.

Some mountains are so tall that their summits (peaks) are hidden by cloud. Really huge mountains even affect the weather. When moving air hits a mountain slope it is forced upwards. As it travels up, the temperature drops, and clouds form.

◀ Warm, rising air may be forced up the side of a mountain. At a certain level, lower temperatures make the water form clouds.

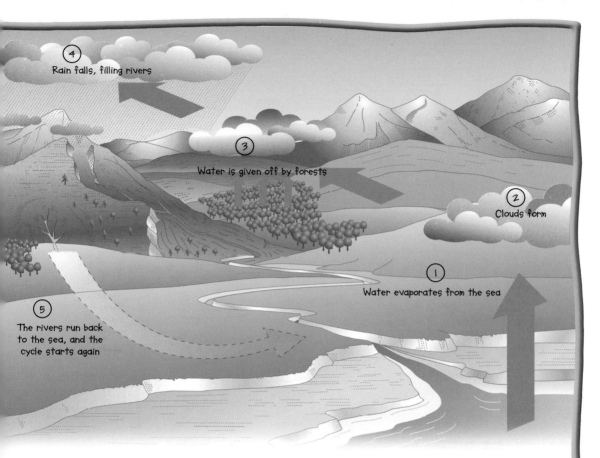

④ Rain falls, filling rivers

③ Water is given off by forests

② Clouds form

① Water evaporates from the sea

⑤ The rivers run back to the sea, and the cycle starts again

▼ Virga happens when rain reaches a layer of dry air. The rain droplets turn back into water vapour in mid–air, and seem to disappear.

Some rain never reaches the ground. The raindrops turn back into water vapour because they hit a layer of super-dry air. You can actually see the drops falling like a curtain from the cloud, but the curtain stops in mid-air. This type of weather is called virga.

Clouds gobble up heat and keep the Earth's temperature regular. From each 2-metre-square patch of land, clouds can remove the equivalent energy created by a 60-Watt lightbulb.

Not just fluffy

Clouds come in all shapes and sizes. To help recognize them, scientists split them into ten basic types. The type depends on what the cloud looks like and where it forms in the sky. Cirrus clouds look like wisps of smoke. They form high in the troposphere and rarely mean rain. Stratus clouds form in flat layers and may produce drizzle or a sprinkling of snow. All types of cumulus clouds bring rain. Some are huge cauliflower shapes. They look soft and fluffy – but would feel soggy to touch.

Cumulonimbus clouds give heavy rain showers

▶ The main classes of cloud – cirrus, cumulus and stratus – were named in the 1800s. An amateur British weather scientist called Luke Howard identified the different types.

Not all clouds produce rain. Cumulus humilis clouds are the smallest heap-shaped clouds. In the sky, they look like lumpy, cotton wool sausages! They are too small to produce rain but they can grow into much bigger, rain-carrying cumulus clouds. The biggest cumulus clouds, cumulus congestus, bring heavy showers.

Cumulus clouds bring rain

Cirrus clouds occur at great heights from the ground

Contrails are the white streaks created by planes

Cirrostratus

Not all clouds are made by nature. Contrails are streaky clouds that a plane leaves behind it as it flies. They are made of water vapour that comes from the plane's engines. The second it hits the cold air, the vapour turns into ice crystals, leaving a trail of white snow cloud.

Sometimes the sky is filled with white patches of cloud that look like shimmering fish scales. These are called mackerel skies. It takes lots of gusty wind to break the cloud into these little patches, and so mackerel skies are usually a sign of changeable weather.

MIX AND MATCH

Can you match the names of these five types of clouds to their meanings?

1. Altostratus   a. heap
2. Cirrus   b. layer
3. Cumulonimbus   c. high + layer
4. Cumulus   d. wisp
5. Stratus   e. heap + rain

Answers:
1.C 2.D 3.E 4.A 5.B

Stratus clouds can bring drizzle or appear as fog

Flood warning

▲ Flooding can cause great damage to buildings and the countryside.

Too much rain brings floods. There are two different types of floods. Flash floods happen after a short burst of heavy rainfall, usually caused by thunderstorms. Broadscale flooding happens when rain falls steadily over a wide area – for weeks or months – without stopping. When this happens, rivers slowly fill and eventually burst their banks. Tropical storms, such as hurricanes, can also lead to broadscale flooding.

There can be floods in the desert. When a lot of rain falls very quickly on to land that has been baked dry, it cannot soak in. Instead, it sits on the surface, causing flash floods.

◄ A desert flash flood can create streams of muddy brown water. After the water level falls, vegetation bursts into life.

There really was a Great Flood. The Bible tells of a terrible flood, and how a man called Noah was saved. Recently, explorers found the first real evidence of the Flood – a sunken beach 140 metres below the surface of the Black Sea. There are ruins of houses, dating back to 5600BC. Stories of a huge flood in ancient times do not appear only in the Bible – the Babylonians and Greeks told of one, too.

▲ In the Bible story, Noah survived the Great Flood by building a huge wooden boat called an ark.

Mud can flood. When rain mixes with earth it makes mud. On bare mountainsides, there are no tree roots to hold the soil together. An avalanche of mud can slide off the mountain. The worst ever mudslide happened after flooding in Colombia, South America in 1985. It buried 23,000 people from the town of Armero.

▼ Mudslides can devastate whole towns and villages, as the flow of mud covers everything it meets.

I DON'T BELIEVE IT!

The ancient Egyptians had a story to explain the yearly flooding of the Nile. They said the goddess Isis filled the river with tears, as she cried for her lost husband.

Deep freeze

Snow is made of tiny ice crystals.
When air temperatures are very
cold – around 0°C – the water
droplets in the clouds freeze
to make tiny ice crystals.
Sometimes, individual crystals
fall, but usually they clump
together into snowflakes.

I DON'T BELIEVE IT!

Antarctica is the coldest place on Earth. Temperatures of –89.2°C have been recorded there.

▲ Falling snow is made worse by strong winds, which can form deep drifts.

No two snowflakes are the same.
This is because snowflakes are made
up of ice crystals, and every ice crystal
is as unique as your fingerprint. Most
crystals look like six-pointed stars, but
they come in other shapes too.

▶ Ice crystals seen under a microscope. A snowflake that is several centimetres across will be made up of lots of crystals like these.

▶ An avalanche gathers speed as it thunders down the mountainside.

Avalanches are like giant snowballs. They happen after lots of snow falls on a mountain. The slightest movement or sudden noise can jolt the pile of snow and start it moving down the slope. As it crashes down, the avalanche picks up extra snow and can end up large enough to bury whole towns.

Marksmen shoot at snowy mountains. One way to prevent deadly avalanches is to stop too much snow from building up. In mountain areas, marksmen set off mini avalanches on purpose. They make sure people are out of the danger zone, then fire guns to trigger a snowslide.

Ice can stay frozen for millions of years. At the North and South Poles, the weather never warms up enough for the ice to thaw. When fresh snow falls, it presses down on the snow already there, forming thick sheets. Some ice may not have melted for a million years or more.

▼ Antarctica is a frozen wilderness. The ice piles up to form amazing shapes, like this arch.

Black ice is not really black. Drizzle or rain turns to ice when it touches freezing-cold ground. This 'black' ice is see-through, and hard to spot against a road's dark tarmac. It is also terribly slippery – like a deadly ice rink.

When the wind blows

Wind is moving air.
Winds blow because air
is constantly moving from
areas of high pressure to
areas of low pressure. The
bigger the difference in
temperature between the
two areas, the faster the
wind blows.

▶ These trees have
been forced into
strange shapes
by the wind.

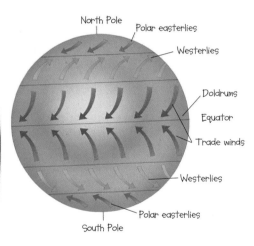

North Pole
Polar easterlies
Westerlies
Doldrums
Equator
Trade winds
Westerlies
Polar easterlies
South Pole

▲ This map shows the pattern of the world's
main winds.

Winds have names. World wind patterns
are called global winds. The most famous
are the trade winds that blow towards the
Equator. There are also well-known local
winds, such as the cold, dry mistral that
blows down to southern France, or the hot,
dry sirroco that blows north of the Sahara.

**Trade winds blow one way north
of the Equator, and another way
in the south.** Trade winds blow in
the tropics, where air is moving to an
area of low pressure at the Equator.
Their name comes from their
importance to traders, when goods
travelled by sailing ship.

QUIZ

1. At what temperature
does water freeze?

2. What does the Beaufort Scale
measure?

3. What are the mistral
and sirroco?

4. How many sides does an ice
crystal usually have?

Answers:
1. 0°C 2. Wind strength
3. Local winds 4. Six

You can tell how windy it is by looking at the leaves on a tree. Wind ranges from light breezes to hurricanes. Its strength is measured on the Beaufort Scale, named after the Irish admiral who devised it. The scale ranges from Force 0, meaning total calm, to Force 12, which is a hurricane

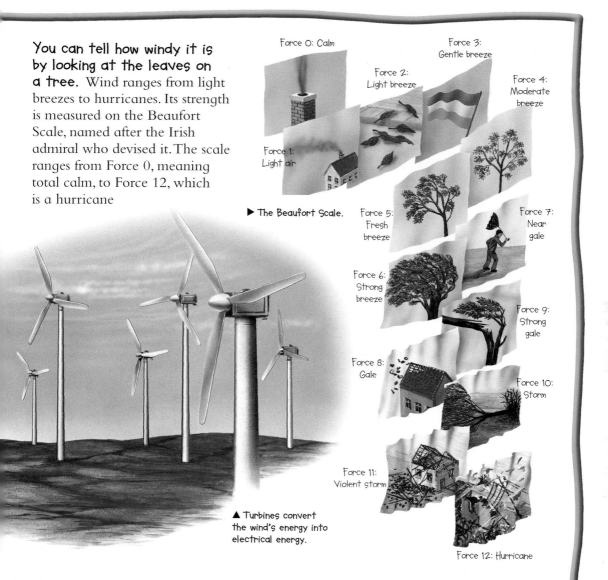

▶ The Beaufort Scale.

Force 0: Calm

Force 1: Light air

Force 2: Light breeze

Force 3: Gentle breeze

Force 4: Moderate breeze

Force 5: Fresh breeze

Force 6: Strong breeze

Force 7: Near gale

Force 8: Gale

Force 9: Strong gale

Force 10: Storm

Force 11: Violent storm

Force 12: Hurricane

▲ Turbines convert the wind's energy into electrical energy.

Wind can turn on your TV. People can harness the energy of the wind to make electricity for our homes. Tall turbines are positioned in windy spots. As the wind turns the turbine, the movement powers a generator and produces electrical energy.

Wind can make you mad! The Föhn wind, which blows across Switzerland, Austria and Bavaria in southern Germany, brings with it changeable weather. This has been blamed for road accidents and even bouts of madness!

Thunderbolts and lightning

Thunderstorms are most likely in summer.
Hot weather creates warm, moist air that
rises and forms towering cumulonimbus
clouds. Inside each cloud, water droplets and
ice crystals bang about, building up positive
and negative electrical charges. Electricity
flows between the charges, creating a flash
that heats the air around it. Lightning is so
hot that it makes the air expand, making a
loud noise or thunderclap.

▼ Cloud–to–cloud lightning is called sheet
lightning, while lightning travelling from the
cloud to the ground is called fork lightning.

Lightning comes in different colours.
If there is rain in the thundercloud, the
lightning looks red; if there's hail, it looks
blue. Lightning can also be yellow or white.

▼ Lightning conductors
absorb the shock and
protect tall buildings.

▶ Dramatic lightning
flashes light up the sky.

Tall buildings are protected from lightning. Church
steeples and other tall structures are often struck by bolts
of lightning. This could damage the building, or give
electric shocks to people inside,
so lightning conductors are
placed on the roof. These
channel the lightning
safely away.

**A person can
survive a lightning
strike.** Lightning is
very dangerous and can
give a big enough shock
to kill you. However, an
American park ranger called
Roy Sullivan survived being
struck seven times.

HOW CLOSE?

Lightning and thunder
happen at the same time, but
light travels faster than sound.
Count the seconds between the
flash and the clap and divide
them by three. This is how
many kilometres away the
storm is.

▼ A sudden hail storm can
leave the ground littered
with small chunks of ice.

**Hailstones can be as big as
melons!** These chunks of ice can fall
from thunderclouds. The biggest ever fell
in Gopaljang, Bangladesh, in 1986
and weighed 1 kilogram each!

125

Eye of the hurricane

Some winds travel at speeds of more than 120 kilometres an hour. Violent tropical storms happen when strong winds blow into an area of low pressure and start spinning very fast. They develop over warm seas and pick up speed until they reach land, where there is no more moist sea air to feed them. Such storms bring torrential rain.

The centre of a hurricane is calm and still. This part is called the 'eye'. As the eye of the storm passes over, there is a pause in the terrifying rains and wind.

I DON'T BELIEVE IT !
Tropical storms are called different names. Hurricanes develop over the Atlantic, typhoons over the Pacific, and cyclones over the Indian Ocean.

▼ This satellite photograph of a hurricane shows how the storm whirls around a central, still 'eye'.

▶ A Hurricane Hunter heads into the storm.

Hurricane Hunters fly close to the eye of a hurricane. These are special weather planes that fly into the storm in order to take measurements. It is a dangerous job for the pilots, but the information they gather helps to predict the hurricane's path – and saves lives.

▲ A hurricane brings battering rain and massive waves.

Hurricanes have names. One of the worst hurricanes was Hurricane Andrew, which battered the coast of Florida in 1992. Perhaps there is a hurricane named after you!

Hurricanes whip up wild waves. As the storm races over the ocean, the winds create giant waves. These hit the shore as a huge sea surge. In 1961, the sea surge following Hurricane Hattie washed away Belize City in South America.

Typhoons saved the Japanese from Genghis Khan. The 13th-century Mongol leader made two attempts to invade Japan – and both times, a terrible typhoon battered his fleet and saved the Japanese!

▶ A typhoon prevented Genghis Khan's navy from invading Japan.

Wild whirling winds

Tornadoes spin at speeds of 480 kilometres an hour!
These whirling columns of wind, also known as twisters, are some of the most destructive storms on Earth. They form in strong thunderstorms, when the back part of the thundercloud starts spinning. The spinning air forms a funnel that reaches down towards the Earth. When it touches the ground, it becomes a tornado.

A tornado can be strong enough to lift a train! The spinning tornado whizzes along the ground like an enormous, high-speed vacuum cleaner, sucking up everything in its path. It rips the roofs off houses, and even tosses buildings into the air. In the 1930s, a twister in Minnesota, USA, threw a train carriage full of people more than eight metres through the air!

▶ A tornado can cause great damage to anything in its path.

Tornado Alley is a twister hotspot in the American Mid-West. This is where hot air travelling north from the Gulf of Mexico meets cold polar winds travelling south, and creates huge thunderclouds. Of course, tornadoes can happen anywhere in the world when the conditions are right.

▲ The shaded area shows Tornado Alley, where there are hundreds of tornadoes each year.

A pillar of whirling water can rise out of a lake or the sea. Waterspouts are spiralling columns of water that can be sucked up by a tornado as it forms over a lake or the sea. They tend to spin more slowly than tornadoes, because water is much heavier than air.

I DON'T BELIEVE IT !

Loch Ness in Scotland is famous for sightings of a monster nicknamed Nessie. Perhaps people who have seen Nessie were really seeing a waterspout.

▲ Waterspouts can suck up fish living in a lake!

Dust devils are desert tornadoes. They shift tonnes of sand and cause terrible damage – they can strip the paintwork from a car in seconds!

▶ A whirling storm of sand in the desert.

129

Pretty lights

Rainbows are made up of seven colours. They are caused by sunlight passing through falling raindrops. The water acts like a glass prism, splitting the light. White light is made up of seven colours – red, orange, yellow, green, blue, indigo and violet – so these are the colours, from top to bottom, that make up the rainbow.

REMEMBER IT!

Richard Of York Gave Battle In Vain

The first letter of every word of this rhyme gives the first letter of each colour of the rainbow – as it appears in the sky:

**Red Orange Yellow
Green Blue
Indigo Violet**

Two rainbows can appear at once. The top rainbow is a reflection of the bottom one, so its colours appear the opposite way round, with the violet band at the top and red at the bottom.

Some rainbows appear at night. They happen when falling raindrops split moonlight, rather than sunlight. This sort of rainbow is called a moonbow.

▲ Although a fogbow is colourless, its inner edge may appear slightly blue and its outer edge slightly red.

It is not just angels that wear halos! When you look at the Sun or Moon through a curtain of ice crystals, they seem to be surrounded by a glowing ring of light called a halo.

Three suns can appear in our sky! 'Mock suns' are two bright spots that appear on either side of the Sun. They often happen at the same time as a halo, and have the same cause – light passing through ice crystals in the air.

▼ An aurora – the most dazzling natural light show on Earth!

Some rainbows are just white. Fogbows happen when sunlight passes through a patch of fog. The water droplets in the fog are too small to work like prisms, so the arching bow is white or colourless.

▲ A halo looks like a circle of light surrounding the Sun or Moon.

▲ Mock suns are also known as parhelia or sundogs.

Auroras are curtains of lights in the sky. They happen in the far north or south of the world when particles from the Sun smash into molecules in the air – at speeds of 1600 kilometres an hour. The lights may be blue, red or yellow.

Made for weather

Camels can go for two weeks without a drink. These animals are adapted to life in a hot, dry climate. They do not sweat until their body temperature hits 40°C, which helps them to save water. The humps on their backs are fat stores, which are used for energy when food and drink is scarce.

Lizards lose salt through their noses. Most animals get rid of excess salt in their urine, but lizards, such as iguanas and geckos, live in dry parts of the world. They need to lose as little water from their bodies as possible.

Camel

Even toads can survive in the desert. The spadefoot toad copes with desert conditions by staying underground in a burrow for most of the year. It only comes to the surface after a shower of rain.

Iguana

Banded gecko

◄ These animals have adapted to life in very dry climates. However, they live in different deserts around the world.

Spadefoot toad

▶ Beneath its gleaming-white fur, the polar bear's skin is black to absorb heat from the Sun.

Polar bears have black skin. These bears have all sorts of special ways to survive the polar climate. Plenty of body fat and thick fur keeps them snug and warm, while their black skin soaks up as much warmth from the Sun as possible.

Acorn woodpeckers store nuts for winter. Animals in temperate climates have to be prepared if they are to survive the cold winter months. Acorn woodpeckers turn tree trunks into larders. During autumn, when acorns are ripe, the birds collect as many as they can, storing them in holes that they bore into a tree.

▶ Storing acorns helps this woodpecker survive the cold winter months.

Weather myths

People once thought the Sun was a god. The sun god was often considered to be the most important god of all, because he brought light and warmth and ripened crops. The ancient Egyptians built pyramids that pointed up to their sun god, Re, while the Aztecs believed that their sun god, Huitzilpochtli, had even shown them where to build their capital city.

The Vikings thought a god brought thunder. Thor was the god of war and thunder, worshipped across what is now Scandinavia. The Vikings pictured Thor as a red-bearded giant. He carried a hammer that produced bolts of lightning. Our day, Thursday, is named in Thor's honour.

◄ In Scandinavian mythology, Thor was the god of thunder.

▲ The Egyptian sun god, Re, was often shown with the head of a falcon.

Hurricanes are named after a god. The Mayan people lived in Central America, the part of the world that is most affected by hurricanes. Their creator god was called Huracan.

Totem poles honoured the Thunderbird.
Certain tribes of Native American Indians
built tall, painted totem poles, carved in the
image of the Thunderbird. They wanted to
keep the spirit happy, because they thought
it brought rain to feed the plants.

▶ A Native American
Indian totem pole
depicting the spirit
of the Thunderbird.

**People once danced for
rain.** In hot places such
as Africa, people developed
dances to bring rain. These
were performed by
the village shaman
(religious woman or
man), using wooden
instruments such as
bullroarers. Sometimes water
was sprinkled on the
ground. Rain dances
are still performed
in some countries
today.

◀ Shamans wore a
special costume for
their rain dance.

MAKE A
BULLROARER

You will need:
a wooden ruler   some string
Ask an adult to drill a hole in one end
of the ruler. Thread through the string,
and knot it, to stop it slipping through
the hole. In an open space, whirl the
instrument above your head to
create a wind noise!

135

Rain or shine?

▲ Kelp picks up any moisture in the air, so it is a good way of telling how damp the atmosphere is.

Seaweed can tell us if rain is on the way. Long ago, people looked to nature for clues about the weather. One traditional way of forecasting was to hang up strands of seaweed. If the seaweed stayed slimy, the air was damp and rain was likely. If the seaweed shrivelled up, the weather would be dry.

'Red sky at night is the sailor's delight'. This is one of the most famous pieces of weather lore and means that a glorious sunset is followed by a fine morning. The saying is also known as 'shepherd's delight'. There is no evidence that the saying is true, though.

I DON'T BELIEVE IT!

People used to say that cows lay down when rain was coming – but there is no truth in it! They lie down whether rain is on the way or not!

Groundhogs tell the weather when they wake. Of course, they don't really, but in parts of the USA, Groundhog Day is a huge celebration. On 2 February, people gather to see the groundhog come out. If you see the creature's shadow, it means there are six more weeks of cold to come.

Groundhog

▼ A blood—red sunset is delightful to look at, but it can't help a sailor to predict the next day's weather.

▲ The Moon is clearly visible in a cloudless night sky. Its light casts a silvery glow over the Earth.

'Clear moon, frost soon'. This old saying does have some truth in it. If there are few clouds in the sky, the view of the Moon will be clear – and there will also be no blanket of cloud to keep in the Earth's heat. That makes a frost more likely – during the colder months, at least.

The earliest weather records are over 3000 years old. They were found on a piece of tortoiseshell and had been written down by Chinese weather watchers. The inscriptions describe when it rained or snowed and how windy it was.

◀ Records of ancient weather were scratched on to this piece of shell.

Instruments and inventors

The Tower of Winds was built 2000 years ago. It was an eight-sided building and is the first known weather station. It had a wind vane on the roof and a water clock inside.

▲ This is how the Tower of Winds looks today. It was built by Andronicus of Cyrrhus in Athens around 75BC. Its eight sides face the points of the compass: north, northeast, east, southeast, south, southwest, west and northwest.

The first barometer was made by one of Galileo's students. Barometers measure air pressure. The first person to describe air pressure – and to make an instrument for measuring it – was an Italian, Evangelista Torricelli. He had studied under the great scientist Galileo. Torricelli made his barometer in 1643.

◄ Torricelli took a bowl of mercury and placed it under the open end of a glass tube, also filled with mercury. It was the weight, or pressure, of air on the mercury in the bowl that stopped the mercury in the tube from falling.

Weather cocks have a special meaning. They have four pointers that show the directions of north, south, east and west. The cockerel at the top swivels so that its head always shows the direction of the wind.

► Weather cocks are often placed on top of church steeples.

A weather house really can predict the weather.
It is a type of hygrometer – an instrument that detects how much moisture is in the air. If there is lots, the rainy-day character comes out of the door!

► Weather houses have two figures. One comes out when the air is damp and the other when the air is dry.

Fahrenheit made the first thermometer in 1714.
Thermometers are instruments that measure temperature. Gabriel Daniel Fahrenheit invented the thermometer using a blob of mercury sealed in an airtight tube. The Fahrenheit scale for measuring heat was named after him. The Centigrade scale was introduced in 1742 by the Swedish scientist Anders Celsius.

◄ This early thermometer shows both the Fahrenheit and the Celsius temperature scales.

QUIZ

1. What is another name for the liquid metal, mercury?

2. What does an anemometer measure?

3. What does a wind vane measure?

4. On the Fahrenheit scale, at what temperature does water freeze?

Answers:
1. Quicksilver 2. Wind speed
3. Wind direction 4. 32°F

World of weather

Working out what the weather will be like is called forecasting. By looking at changes in the atmosphere, and comparing them to weather patterns of the past, forecasters can make an accurate guess at what the weather will be tomorrow, the next day, or even further ahead than that. But even forecasters get it wrong sometimes!

The first national weather offices appeared in the 1800s. This was when people realized that science could explain how weather worked – and save people from disasters. The first network of weather stations was set up in France, in 1855. This was after the scientist Le Verrier showed how a French warship, sunk in a storm, could have been saved. Le Verrier explained how the path of the storm could have been tracked, and the ship sailed to safety.

A cold front is shown by a blue triangle

A warm front is shown by a red semi-circle

Look for the black lines with red semi-circles and blue triangles – they represent an occluded front, where a cold front meets a warm front

These white lines are isobars – they connect places where air pressure is the same

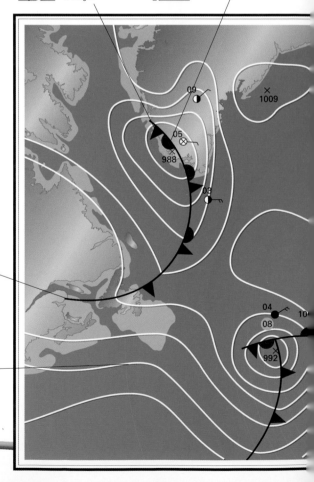

WEATHER SYMBOLS

Learn how to represent the weather on your own synoptic charts. Here are some of the basic symbols to get you started. You may come across them in newspapers or while watching television. Can you guess what they mean?

Nations need to share weather data.
By 1865, nearly 60 weather stations across Europe were swapping information. These early weather scientists, or meteorologists, realized that they needed to present their information using symbols that they could all understand. To this day, meteorologists plot their findings on maps called synoptic charts. They use lines called isobars to show which areas have the same air pressure. The Internet makes it easier for meteorologists to access information.

This symbol shows the strength of the wind – the circle shows how much cloud cover there is

This symbol shows that the wind is very strong – look at the three lines on the tail

This shows an area of calm, with lots of cloud cover

◄ Meteorologists call their weather maps synoptic charts. They use the same symbols, which make up a common language for weather scientists all around the world.

Weather watch

Balloons can tell us about the weather. Weather balloons are hot-air balloons that are sent high into the atmosphere. As they rise, onboard equipment takes readings. These find out air pressure, and how moist, or humid, the air is, as well as how warm. The findings are radioed back to meteorologists on the ground, using a system called radiosonde. Hundreds of balloons are launched around the world every day.

▶ A weather balloon carries its scientific instruments high into the atmosphere.

Some planes hound the weather.

Weather planes provide more atmospheric measurements than balloons can. *Snoopy* is the name of one of the British weather planes. The instruments are carried on its long, pointy nose, so they can test the air ahead of the plane.

▼ *Snoopy's* long nose carries all the equipment needed to monitor the weather.

Satellites help save lives. Their birds'-eye view of the Earth allows them to take amazing pictures of our weather systems. They can track hurricanes as they form over the oceans. Satellite-imaging has helped people to leave their homes and get out of a hurricane's path just in time.

I DON'T BELIEVE IT!

Some of the best weather photos have been taken by astronauts in space.

Some weather stations are all at sea. Weather buoys float on the surface of the oceans, measuring air pressure, temperature and wind direction. They are fitted with transmitters that beam information to satellites in space – which bounce the readings on to meteorologists. Tracking the buoys is just as important. They are carried along by ocean currents, which have a huge effect on our weather systems.

▲ A weather satellite takes photographs of Earth's weather systems from space.

▶ Currents carry the floating weather buoys around the oceans.

Changing climate

Climate change destroyed the dinosaurs – but no one can agree on what caused it. The best explanation is that a huge piece of space rock, called a meteorite, smashed into Earth. It threw up a giant cloud of dust that blocked out the Sun, plunging the world into cold and dark.

▶ Could a meteorite have crashed to Earth and changed the climate? A meteorite crater found in the Gulf of Mexico dates to 65 million years ago – exactly the time that the dinosaurs died out. Perhaps the impact changed the warm climate the dinosaurs were so used to.

Greenland used to be green! This island lies in the Arctic Ocean and is mostly covered by a huge ice sheet. Even in Viking times, Greenland was cold, but Viking settlers built at least two farming colonies there. These died out around the 1400s, after the climate cooled.

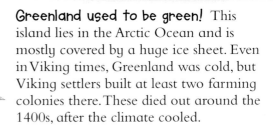

◀ Vikings settled on Greenland's coastline. Inland areas were covered in ice.

A volcano can change the climate!

Big volcanic explosions can create dust that blots out the Sun, just as a meteorite impact can. Dust from the 1815 eruption of a volcano called Tambora did this. This made many crops fail around the world and many people starved.

Tree—felling is affecting our weather.

In areas of Southeast Asia and South America, rainforests are being cleared for farming. When the trees are burned, the fires release carbon dioxide – a greenhouse gas which helps to blanket the Earth and keep in the heat. Unfortunately, high levels of carbon dioxide raise the temperature too much.

◄ Like all plants, rainforest trees take in carbon dioxide and give out oxygen. As rainforests are destroyed, the amount of carbon dioxide in the atmosphere increases.

Air temperatures are rising.

Scientists think the average world temperature may increase by around 1.5°C this century. This may not sound like much, but the extra warmth will mean more storms, including hurricanes and tornadoes, and more droughts too.

QUIZ

1. What may have caused the death of the dinosaurs?

2. Which settlers once lived along the coast of Greenland?

3. Which gas do plants take in?

Answers:
1. Meteorite impact 2. Vikings
3. Carbon dioxide

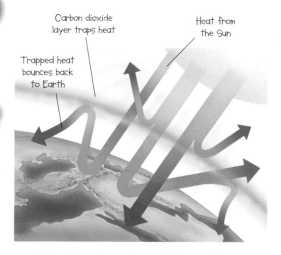

Carbon dioxide layer traps heat

Heat from the Sun

Trapped heat bounces back to Earth

▶ Too much carbon dioxide in the atmosphere creates a 'greenhouse effect'. Just as glass traps heat, so does carbon dioxide. This means more storms and droughts.

OCEANS

Find out fascinating facts about oceans, including all kinds of life and beautiful underwater landscapes.

Underwater volcanoes • Islands • Tides • Shores
Rock pools • Coral reefs • Fish • Sharks • Whales
Dolphins • Seals • Turtles • Sea snakes • Tubeworms
Lobsters • Seabirds • Penguins • Fishing • Boats
Ships • Pirates • Submarines • Divers • Surfers

Water world

Oceans cover more than two-thirds of the Earth's rocky surface. Their total area is about 362 million square kilometres, which means there is more than twice as much ocean as land! Although all the oceans flow into each other, we know them as four different oceans – the Pacific, Atlantic, Indian and Arctic. Our landmasses, the continents, rise out of the oceans.

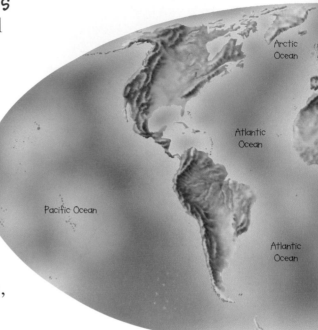

Arctic Ocean

Atlantic Ocean

Pacific Ocean

Atlantic Ocean

The largest, deepest ocean is the Pacific. It covers nearly half of our planet and is almost as big as the other three oceans put together! In places, the Pacific is so deep that the Earth's tallest mountain, Everest, would sink without a trace.

The deepest parts of the Pacific would cover Mount Everest without trace

▶ Mount Everest is the highest point on Earth, rising to 8848 metres. Parts of the Pacific Ocean are deeper than 10,000 metres.

Light hits the surface of the water

▶ A cup of sea water appears see-through. It is only when you look at a large area of sea that it has colour.

Scattered blue and green

Oceans can look blue, green or grey. This is because of the way light hits the surface. Water soaks up the red parts of light but scatters the blue-green parts, making the sea look different shades of blue or green.

Seas can be red or dead. A sea is a small part of an ocean. The Red Sea, for example, is the part of the Indian Ocean between Egypt and Saudi Arabia. Asia's Dead Sea isn't a true sea, but a landlocked lake. We call it a sea because it is a large body of water.

Indian Ocean

▲ The world's oceans cover most of our planet. Each ocean is made up of smaller bodies of water called seas.

I DON'T BELIEVE IT!
97 percent of the world's water is in the oceans. Just a fraction is in freshwater lakes and rivers.

There are streams in the oceans. All the water in the oceans is constantly moving, but in some places it flows as currents, which take particular paths. One of these is the warm Gulf Stream, that travels around the edge of the Atlantic Ocean.

Ocean features

There are plains, mountains and valleys under the oceans, in areas called basins. Each basin has a rim (the flat continental shelf that meets the shore) and sides (the continental slope that drops away from the shelf). In the ocean basin there are flat abyssal plains, steep hills, huge underwater volcanoes called seamounts, and deep valleys called trenches.

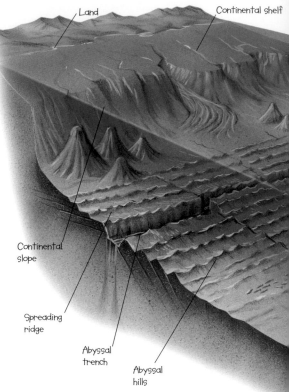

▲ Under the oceans there is a landscape similar to that found on land.

▼ Magma (molten rock) escapes from the seabed to form a ridge. This ridge has collapsed to form a rift valley.

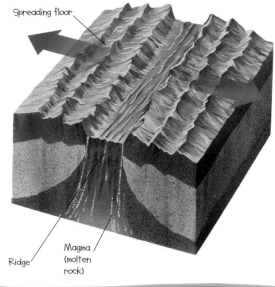

The ocean floor is spreading.

Molten (liquid) rock inside the Earth seeps from holes on the seabed. As the rock cools, it forms new sections of floor that creep slowly out. Scientists have proved this fact by looking at layers of rock on the ocean floor. There are matching stripes of rock either side of a ridge. Each pair came from the same hot rock eruption, then slowly spread out.

▼ An atoll is a ring-shaped coral reef that encloses a deep lagoon. It can form when a volcanic island sinks underwater.

1. Coral starts to grow

4. Coral atoll is left behind

2. Lagoon appears around volcano

3. Volcano disappears

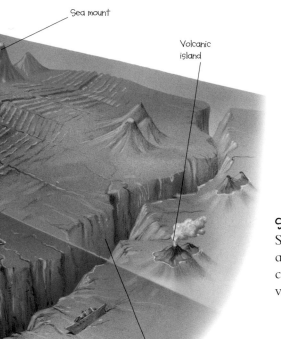

Sea mount

Volcanic island

Ocean trench

Some islands are swallowed by the ocean. Sometimes, a ring-shaped coral reef called an atoll marks where an island once was. The coral reef built up around the island. After the volcano blew its top, the reef remained.

I DON'T BELIEVE IT!

The world's longest mountain chain is under the ocean. It is the Mid-Ocean range and stretches around the middle of the Earth.

► There are more Hawaiian islands still to come – Loihi is just visible beneath the water's surface.

New islands are born all the time. When an underwater volcano erupts, its lava cools in the water. Layers of lava build up, and the volcano grows in size. Eventually, it is tall enough to peep above the waves. The Hawaiian islands rose from the sea like this.

Tides and shores

The sea level rises and falls twice each day along the coast. This is known as high and low tides. Tides happen because of the pull of the Moon, which lifts water from the part of the Earth's surface facing it.

▼ At high tide, the sea rises up the shore and dumps seaweed, shells and drift wood. Most coasts have two high tides and two low tides every day.

High tides happen at the same time each day on opposite sides of the Earth

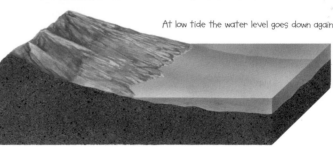

At high tide the water level rises

At low tide the water level goes down again

Spring tides are especially high. They occur twice a month, when the Moon is in line with the Earth and the Sun. Then, the Sun's pulling force joins the Moon's and seawater is lifted higher than usual. The opposite happens when the Moon and Sun are at right angles to the Earth. Then, their pulling powers work against each other causing weak neap tides – the lowest high tides and low tides.

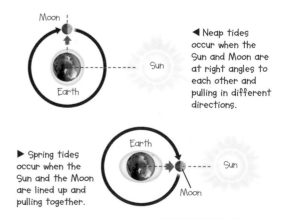

◄ Neap tides occur when the Sun and Moon are at right angles to each other and pulling in different directions.

► Spring tides occur when the Sun and the Moon are lined up and pulling together.

The sea is strong enough to carve into rock.
Pounding waves batter coastlines and erode, or
wear away, the rock.

▶ Waves can create
amazing shapes such
as pillars called
sea stacks.

Sea stack

Arch

▲ A tsunami can travel
faster than a jumbo jet.

**Tidal waves are the most
powerful waves.** Also known
as tsunamis, they happen when
underwater earthquakes trigger
tremendous shock waves. These
whip up a wall of water that
travels across the sea's surface.

**Sand is found on bars and spits, as well as
beaches.** It is made up of grains of worn-down
rock and shell. Sand collects on shorelines and
spits, but also forms on offshore beaches called
sand bars. Spits are narrow ridges of worn sand
and pebbles.

**I DON'T
BELIEVE IT!**
The biggest tsunami was taller
than five Statues of Liberty!
It hit the Japanese Ryuku
Islands in 1771.

Some shores are swampy.
This makes the border
between land and sea
hard to pinpoint. Muddy
coastlines include tropical
mangrove swamps that are
flooded by salty water
from the sea.

▶ The stilt-like roots of mangrove
trees take in both air and water.

153

Life in a rock pool

Rock pools are teeming with all kinds of creatures. Limpets are a kind of shellfish. They live on rocks and in pools at shorelines. Here, they eat slimy, green algae, but they have to withstand the crashing tide. They cling to the rock with their muscular foot, only moving when the tide is out.

Some anemones fight with harpoons. Beadlet anemones will sometimes fight over a feeding ground. Their weapon is the poison they usually use to stun their prey. They shoot tiny hooks like harpoons at each other until the weakest one gives in.

▲ Anemones are named after flowers, because of their petal-like arms.

Starfish can grow new arms. They may have as many as 40 arms, or rays. If a predator grabs hold of one, the starfish abandons the ray, and uses the others to make its getaway!

◄ Starfish are relatives of brittle stars, sea urchins and sea cucumbers.

Hermit crabs do not have shells.
Most crabs shed their shells as they outgrow them, but the hermit crab does not have a shell. It borrows the leftover shell of a dead whelk or other mollusc – whatever it can squeeze into to protect its soft body. These crabs have even been spotted using a coconut shell as a home!

▶ Hermit crabs protect their soft bodies in a borrowed shell.

FIND THE SHELL

Can you find the names of four shells in the puzzle below ?

**1. alcm   2. lesmus
3. teroys   4. hewkl**

Answers:
1. Clam 2. Mussel
3. Oyster 4. Whelk

Sea urchins wear a disguise.
Green sea urchins sometimes drape themselves with bits of shell, pebble and seaweed. This makes the urchin more difficult for predators, or hunters, to spot.

◀ There are about 4500 different types of sponge in the sea.

Sponges are animals!
They are very simple creatures that filter food from sea water. The natural sponge that you might use in the bath is a long-dead, dried-out sponge.

Colourful coral

Tiny animals build huge underwater walls. These are built up from coral, the leftover skeletons of sea creatures called polyps. Over millions of years, enough skeletons pile up to form huge, wall-like structures called reefs. Coral reefs are full of hidey-holes and make brilliant habitats for all sorts of amazing, colourful sea life.

The world's biggest shellfish lives on coral reefs. Giant clams grow to well over one metre long – big enough for you to bathe in its shell!

Seahorse dads have the babies. They don't exactly give birth, but they store the eggs in a pouch on their belly. When the eggs are ready to hatch, a stream of miniature seahorses billows out from the dad's pouch.

▶ Baby seahorses stream out of their father's pouch and into the sea.

Parrot fish

Giant clam

Clownfish

Some fish go to the cleaners. Cleaner wrasse are little fish that are paid for cleaning! Larger fish, such as groupers and moray eels visit the wrasse, which nibble all the parasites and other bits of dirt off the bigger fishes' bodies – what a feast!

Clownfish are sting-proof. Most creatures steer clear of an anemone's stinging tentacles. But the clownfish swims among the stingers, where it's safe from predators. Strangely, the anemone doesn't seem to sting the clownfish.

I DON'T BELIEVE IT!

You can see the Great Barrier Reef from space! At over 2000 km long, it is the largest structure ever built by living creatures.

Lion fish

Cleaner wrasse fish

Some fish look like stones. Stone fish rest on the seabed, looking just like the rocks that surround them. If they are spotted, the poisonous spines on their backs can stun an attacker in seconds.

Stone fish

▲ Tropical coral reefs are the habitat of an amazing range of marine plants and creatures.

Swimming machines

There are over 21,000 different types of fish in the sea. They range from huge whale sharks to tiny gobies. Almost all are covered in scales and use fins and a muscular tail to power through the water. Like their freshwater cousins, sea fish have slits called gills that take oxygen from the water so they can breathe.

The oarfish is bigger than an oar – it is as long as four canoes! It is the longest bony fish and is found in all the world's oceans. Oarfish are handsome creatures – they have a striking red fin along the length of their back.

◀ People once thought oarfish swam horizontally through the water. Now they know they swim upright.

▶ At over 3 metres long, sunfish are the biggest bony fish in the oceans. They feed on plankton.

Sunfish like sunbathing! Ocean sunfish are very large, broad fish that can weigh as much as a tonne. They are named after their habit of sunbathing on the surface of the open ocean.

▶ Flying fish feed near the surface so they are easy to find. Their gliding flight helps them escape most hunters.

Flying fish cannot really fly. Fish can't survive out of water, but flying fish sometimes leap above the waves when they are travelling at high speeds. They use their wing-like fins to keep them in the air for as long as 30 seconds.

▲ In a large group called a school, fish like these yellow snappers have less chance of being picked off by a predator.

QUIZ

1. Which fish like to sunbathe?
2. How many types of fish live in the sea?
3. How does a fish breathe?
4. Can flying fish really fly?

Answers:
1. Sunfish 2. 21,000 3. With its gills 4. No

Not all fish are the same shape. Cod or mackerel are what we think of as a normal fish shape, but fish come in all shapes and sizes. Flounder and other flatfish have squashed-flat bodies. Eels are so long and thin that the biggest types look like snakes, while tiny garden eels resemble worms! And of course, seahorses and seadragons look nothing like other fish at all!

▶ The flounder's flattened shape and dull colouring help to camouflage (hide) it on the seabed.

Shark!

Great whites are the scariest sharks in the oceans. These powerful predators have been known to kill people and can speed through the water at 30 kilometres per hour. Unlike most fish, the great white is warm-blooded. This allows its muscles to work well, but also means the shark has to feed on plenty of meat.

▲ Great white sharks are fierce hunters. They will attack and eat almost anything, but prefer to feed on seals.

▼ Basking sharks eat enormous amounts of plankton. They sieve through around 1000 tonnes of water every hour.

Most sharks are meat—eaters. Herring are a favourite food for sand tiger and thresher sharks, while a hungry tiger shark will gobble up just about anything! Strangely, some of the biggest sharks take the smallest prey. Whale sharks and basking sharks eat tiny sea creatures called plankton.

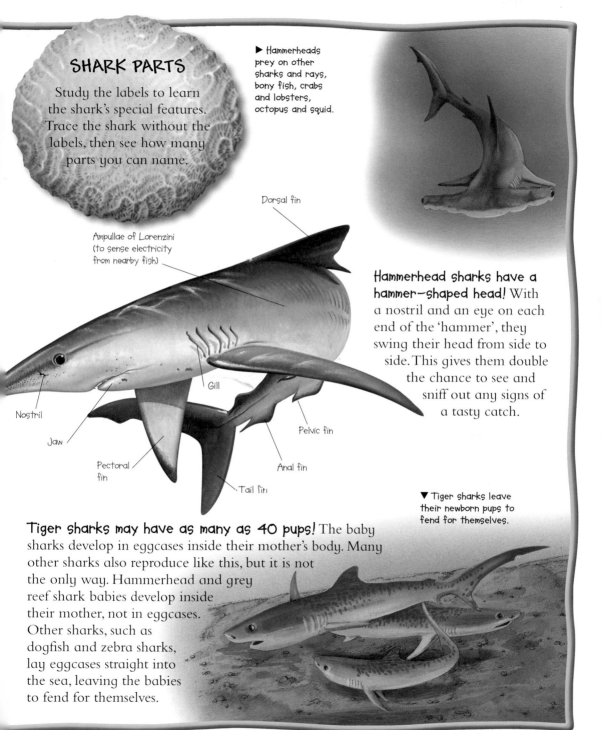

SHARK PARTS

Study the labels to learn the shark's special features. Trace the shark without the labels, then see how many parts you can name.

▶ Hammerheads prey on other sharks and rays, bony fish, crabs and lobsters, octopus and squid.

Dorsal fin

Ampullae of Lorenzini (to sense electricity from nearby fish)

Gill

Nostril

Jaw

Pectoral fin

Pelvic fin

Anal fin

Tail fin

Hammerhead sharks have a hammer—shaped head! With a nostril and an eye on each end of the 'hammer', they swing their head from side to side. This gives them double the chance to see and sniff out any signs of a tasty catch.

▼ Tiger sharks leave their newborn pups to fend for themselves.

Tiger sharks may have as many as 40 pups! The baby sharks develop in eggcases inside their mother's body. Many other sharks also reproduce like this, but it is not the only way. Hammerhead and grey reef shark babies develop inside their mother, not in eggcases. Other sharks, such as dogfish and zebra sharks, lay eggcases straight into the sea, leaving the babies to fend for themselves.

Whales and dolphins

The biggest animal on the planet lives in the oceans. It is the blue whale, measuring about 28 metres in length and weighing up to 190 tonnes. It feeds by filtering tiny, shrimp-like creatures called krill from the water – about four tonnes of krill a day! Like other great whales, it has special, sieve-like parts in its mouth called baleen plates.

▲ As the sperm whale surfaces, it pushes out stale air through its blowhole. It fills its lungs with fresh air and dives down again.

Whales and dolphins have to come to the surface for air. This is because they are mammals, like we are. Sperm whales hold their breath the longest. They have been known to stay underwater for nearly two hours.

▲ Blue whale calves feed on their mother's rich milk until they are around eight months old.

Killer whales play with their food.
They especially like to catch baby seals, which they toss into the air before eating. Killer whales are not true whales, but the largest dolphins. They have teeth for chewing, instead of baleen plates.

▲ Killer whales carry the baby seals out to sea before eating them.

▶ The beluga is a type of white whale. It makes a range of noises – whistles, clangs, chirps and moos!

Dolphins and whales sing songs to communicate. The noisiest is the humpback whale, whose wailing noises can be heard for hundreds of kilometres. The sweetest is the beluga – nicknamed the 'sea canary'. Songs are used to attract a mate, or just to keep track of each other.

Moby Dick was a famous white whale.
It starred in a book by Herman Melville about a white sperm whale and a whaler called Captain Ahab.

The narwhal has a horn like a unicorn's. This Arctic whale has a long, twirly tooth that spirals out of its head. The males use their tusks as a weapon when they are fighting over females.

I DON'T BELIEVE IT!

Barnacles are shellfish. They attach themselves to ships' hulls, or the bodies of grey whales and other large sea animals.

▲ The narwhal's 3 metre tusk seems too long for its body.

Sleek swimmers

Whales and dolphins are not the only sea mammals.
Seals, sea lions and walruses are warm-blooded
mammals that have adapted to ocean life.
These creatures are known as pinnipeds,
meaning 'fin feet'. They have flippers
instead of legs – far more useful for
swimming! They also have
streamlined bodies and a layer
of fatty blubber under the
skin, to keep them warm
in chilly waters.

▶ Most seals live
in cold waters.
Crabeater, leopard
and Weddell seals
live in Antarctica.
The northern seals,
that live around
the Arctic, include
harp and bearded
seals.

**Elephant seals are well-named – they
are truly enormous!** Southern elephant
seal males can weigh over three and a half
tonnes, while their northern cousins weigh
at least two. During their three month-long
breeding season, males stay ashore to fight
off any rivals. Unable to hunt for fish, some
lose as much as half their body weight.

Sea otters anchor themselves when they sleep. These playful creatures live off the Pacific coast among huge forests of giant seaweed called kelp. When they take a snooze, they wrap a strand of kelp around their body to stop them being washed out to sea.

▲ Anchored to the kelp, a sea otter is free to crack open a crab shell – and snack!

Walruses seem to change colour!
When a walrus is in the water, it appears pale brown or even white. This is because blood drains from the skin's surface to stop the body losing heat. On land, the blood returns to the skin and walruses can look reddish brown or pink!

▼ Walruses use their tusks as weapons. They are also used to break breathing holes in the ice, and to help the walrus pull itself out of the water.

I DON'T BELIEVE IT!

Leopard seals sing in their sleep! These seals, found in the Antarctic, chirp and whistle while they snooze.

Ocean reptiles

Marine iguanas are the most seaworthy lizards. Most lizards prefer life on land, where it is easier to warm up their cold-blooded bodies, but marine iguanas depend on the sea for their food. They dive underwater to graze on the algae and seaweed growing on rocks.

▲ Marine iguanas are found around the Galapagos Islands in the Pacific. When they are not diving for food, they bask on the rocks that dot the island coastlines. The lizards' dark skin helps to absorb the Sun's heat.

Turtles come ashore only to lay their eggs. Although they are born on land, turtles head for the sea the minute they hatch. Females return to the beach where they were born to dig their nest. After they have laid their eggs, they go straight back to the water. Hawksbill turtles may lay up to 140 eggs in a clutch, while some green turtle females clock up 800 eggs in a year!

▲ In a single breeding season, a female green turtle may lay as many as ten clutches, each containing up to 80 eggs!

There are venomous (poisonous) snakes in the sea. Most stay close to land and come ashore to lay their eggs. Banded sea snakes, for example, cruise around coral reefs in search of their favourite food, eels. But the yellow-bellied sea snake never leaves the water. It gives birth to live babies in the open ocean.

▼ Banded sea snakes use venom (poison) to stun prey, but the yellow-bellied sea snake has a sneakier trick. Once its colourful underside has attracted some fish, it darts back – so the fish are next to its open mouth! The venom of sea snakes is more powerful than that of any land snake.

Banded sea snake

Yellow-bellied sea snake

MIX AND MATCH

Can you match these sea turtles to their names?
1. Green 2. Hawksbill
3. Leatherback 4. Loggerhead

Answers:
1C 2B 3D 4A

a.

b.

c.

d.

▼ Leatherbacks are the biggest turtles in the world and can grow to four metres in length.

Leatherbacks dive up to 1200 metres for dinner. These turtles hold the record for being the biggest sea turtles and for making the deepest dives. Leatherbacks feed mostly on jellyfish but their diet also includes molluscs, crabs and lobsters, starfish and sea urchins.

Icy depths

Few creatures can survive in the dark, icy–cold ocean depths. Food is so hard to come by, the deep-sea anglerfish does not waste energy chasing prey — it has developed a clever fishing trick. A stringy 'fishing rod' with a glowing tip extends from its dorsal fin or hangs above its jaw. This attracts smaller fish to the anglerfish's big mouth.

▼ Anglerfish are black or brown for camouflage. Only their glowing 'fishing rod' is visible in the gloom.

▼ The light created by deep–sea fish, or by bacteria living on their bodies, is known as biological light, or bioluminescence.

Lantern fish

Cookiecutter shark

Dragon fish

Some deep–sea fish glow in the dark. As well as tempting prey, light also confuses predators. About 1500 different deep-sea fish give off light. The lantern fish's whole body glows, while the dragon fish has light organs dotted along its sides and belly. Just the belly of the cookiecutter shark gives off a ghostly glow. Cookiecutters take biscuit-shaped bites out of their prey's body!

Black swallowers are greedy-guts!
These strange fish are just 25 centimetres
long but can eat fish far bigger than
themselves. Their loose jaws unhinge to
fit over the prey. Then the stretchy body
expands to take in their enormous meal.

▶ The viperfish is named for its long, snake-like fangs.

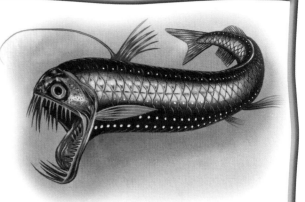

▼ Like many deep-sea fish, black swallowers have
smooth, scaleless skin.

**Viperfish have teeth which are invisible
in the dark.** They swim around with their
jaws wide open. Deep-sea shrimp often see
nothing until they are right inside the
viperfish's mouth.

▼ Tubeworms grow around deep-sea volcanoes called
black smokers.

**I DON'T
BELIEVE IT!**
Female deep-sea anglerfish
grow to 120 centimetres in
length, but the males are a tiny
six centimetres!

**On the seabed, there are worms as
long as cars!** These are giant tubeworms
and they cluster around hot spots on the
ocean floor. They feed on tiny particles
that they filter from the water.

Amazing journeys

Many ocean animals travel incredible distances.
Spiny lobsters spend the summer feeding off the
coast of Florida, but head south in autumn to
deeper waters. They travel about 50 kilometres
along the seabed, in columns that may be
more than 50-strong. They keep together
by touch, using their long, spiky
antennae (feelers).

▲ In spring, spiny lobsters return to shallower
waters. They spawn (lay their eggs) around the
coral reefs off the Straits of Florida.

Arctic terns are the long-distance
flying champs. These seabirds fly farther
than any other bird. After nesting in the
Arctic, they head south for the Antarctic.
In its lifetime, one bird might cover more
than 1,250,000 kilometres!

◄ In a single year,
an Arctic tern may
fly more than
40,000 kilometres!

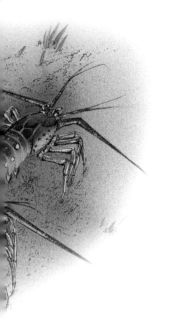

Grey whales migrate, or travel, farther than any other mammal. There are two main grey whale populations in the Pacific. One spends summer off the Alaskan coast. In winter they migrate south to Mexico to breed. The whales may swim nearly 20,000 kilometres in a year. The other grey whale group spends summer off the coast of Russia, then travels south to Korea.

▶ Grey whales spend summer in the Bering Sea, feeding on tiny, shrimp-like creatures called amphipods. They spend their breeding season, December to March, in the warmer waters off Mexico.

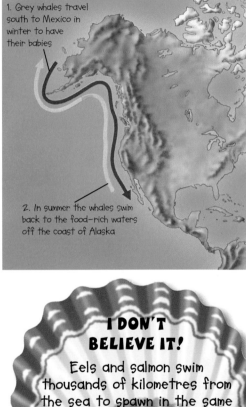

1. Grey whales travel south to Mexico in winter to have their babies

2. In summer the whales swim back to the food-rich waters off the coast of Alaska

Baby loggerhead turtles make a two-year journey. They are born on beaches in Japan. The hatchlings hurry down to the sea and set off across the Pacific to Mexico, a journey of 10,000 kilometres. They spend about five years there before returning to Japan to breed.

▼ Not all loggerhead hatchlings make it to the sea. As they race down the beach, some are picked off by hungry gulls or crabs.

I DON'T BELIEVE IT!

Eels and salmon swim thousands of kilometres from the sea to spawn in the same river nurseries where they were born.

171

On the wing

Wandering albatrosses are the biggest seabirds.
An albatross has a wingspan of around three metres – about the length of a family car! These sea birds are so large, they take off by launching from a cliff. Albatrosses spend months at sea. They are such expert gliders that they even sleep on the wing. To feed, they land on the sea, where they sit and catch creatures such as squid.

◄ A gannet dives and captures a fishy meal in its beak.

Gannets wear air–bag shock absorbers. The gannet's feeding technique is to plummet headfirst into the ocean and catch a fish in its beak. It dives at high-speed and hits the water hard. Luckily, the gannet's head is protected with sacs of air that absorb most of the shock.

Puffins nest in burrows. While many birds jostle for space on a high cliff ledge, puffins dig a burrow on the clifftop. Here, they lay a single egg. Both parents feed the chick for the first six weeks.

▼ Puffins often scrape their own burrows, or they may take over an abandoned rabbit hole.

Boobies dance to attract a mate. There are two types of booby, blue or red-footed. The dancing draws attention to the male's colourful feet. Perhaps this stops the females from mating with the wrong type of bird.

▼ Boobies are tropical seabirds that nest in colonies.

Frigate birds puff up a balloon for their mate. Male frigate birds have a bright-red pouch on their throat. They inflate, or blow up, the pouch as part of their display to attract a female.

▲ A frigate bird shows off to its mate.

Perfect penguins

Macaroni, chinstrap, jackass and emperor are all types of penguin. There are 17 different types in total, and most live around the Antarctic. Penguins feed on fish, squid and krill. Their black-and-white plumage is important camouflage. Seen from above, a penguin's black back blends in with the water. The white belly is hard to distinguish from the sunlit surface of the sea.

Chinstrap penguin

Penguins can swim, but not fly. They have oily, waterproofed feathers and flipper-like wings. Instead of lightweight, hollow bones – like a flying bird's – some penguins have solid, heavy bones. This enables them to stay underwater longer when diving for food. Emperor penguins can stay under for 15 minutes or more.

I DON'T BELIEVE IT!

The fastest swimming bird is the gentoo penguin. It has been known to swim at speeds of 27 kilometres per hour!

▶ Penguins have a layer of fat under their feathers to protect them in the icy water.

Gentoo penguin

Adélie penguin

King penguin

Emperor penguin

Emperor penguin dads balance an egg on their feet. They do this to keep their egg off the Antarctic ice, where it would freeze. The female leaves her mate with the egg for the whole two months that it takes to hatch. The male has to go without food during this time. When the chick hatches, the mother returns and both parents help to raise it.

► A downy emperor penguin chick cannot find its own food in the sea. It must wait until it has grown its waterproof, adult plumage.

▲ An Adélie penguin builds its nest from stones and small rocks.

Some penguins build stone circles. This is the way that Adélie and gentoo penguins build nests on the shingled shores where they breed. First, they scrape out a small dip with their flippered feet and then they surround the hollow with a circle of pebbles.

Harvests from the sea

◄ Fishermen attach buoys to their lobster pots, so they can remember where to find them again.

Oysters come from beds – and lobsters from pots!

The animals in the oceans feed other sea creatures, and they feed us, too! To gather oysters, fishermen raise them on trays or poles in the water. First, they collect oyster larvae, or babies. They attract them by putting out sticks hung with shells. Lobster larvae are too difficult to collect, but the adults are caught in pots filled with fish bait.

Some farmers grow seaweed. Seaweed is delicious to eat, and is also a useful ingredient in products such as ice cream and plant fertilizer. In shallow, tropical waters, people grow their own on plots of seabed.

▲ The harvested seaweed can be dried in the sun to preserve it.

▶ The oil platform's welded—steel legs rest on the seabed. They support the platform around 15 metres above the surface of the water.

Derrick

Crane

Flare

Helicopter landing pad

Oil processing area

Sea minerals are big business. Minerals are useful substances that we mine from the ground — and oceans are full of them! The most valuable are oil and gas, which are pumped from the seabed and piped ashore or transported in huge supertankers. Salt is another important mineral. In hot, low-lying areas, people build walls to hold shallow pools of sea water. The water dries up in the sun, leaving behind crystals of salt.

There are gemstones under the sea. Pearls are made by oysters. If a grain of sand is lodged inside an oyster's shell, it irritates its soft body. The oyster coats the sand with a substance called nacre, which is also used to line the inside of the shell. Over the years, more nacre builds up and the pearl gets bigger.

QUIZ

1. What are the young of lobster called?
2. What substances are pumped from the seabed?
3. Is seaweed edible?
4. Which gemstone is made by oysters?

Answers:
1. Larvae 2. Oil and gas
3. Yes 4. Pearl

▶ Pearl divers carry an oyster knife for prising open the oyster's shell.

First voyages

The first boats were made from tree trunks. Early people hollowed out tree trunks to craft their own dug-outs. For several hundred years, the Maori peoples of New Zealand made log war canoes, decorating them with beautiful carvings.

▼ Maori war canoes were usually carved out of kauri pine trunks.

▶ A painted eye on the trireme's hull was believed to protect the boat from evil spirits.

Greek warships were oar—some!
The ancient Greeks used people-power and sails to move their ships through the water. Triremes were warships rowed by three layers of oarsmen. In battle, the trireme was steered straight at an enemy ship like a battering ram.

▼ Viking longboats were clinker–built, which means that they were made of overlapping planks of wood.

Boats found the way to a new world.

The 1400s were an amazing time of exploration and discovery. One explorer, Christopher Columbus, set sail from Spain in 1492 with a fleet of three ships. He hoped to find a new trade route to India, but instead he found the Americas! Before then, they were not even on the map!

Dragons guarded Viking longboats.

Scandinavian seafarers decorated their boats' prows with carvings of dragons and serpents to terrify their enemies. Built from overlapping planks, Viking longboats were very seaworthy. Leif Ericson was the first Viking to cross the Atlantic Ocean to Newfoundland, in North America just over 1000 years ago.

▶ Columbus's fleet consisted of the *Niña*, the *Pinta* and the *Santa Maria*.

It is thought that Chinese navigators made the first compass–like device about 2500 years ago.

Compasses use the Earth's magnetism to show the directions of north, south, east and west. They are used at sea, where there are no landmarks. The navigators used lodestone, a naturally magnetic rock, to magnetize the needle.

▶ Early compasses were very simple. During the 1300s compasses became more detailed.

BOAT SCRAMBLE!

Unscramble the letters to find the names of six different types of boat.

1. leacvar 2. chenroos
3. rarlewt 4. coclear
5. leglay 6. pecpril

Answers:
1. Caravel 2. Schooner
3. Trawler 4. Coracle
5. Galley 6. Clipper

Pirates!

Pirates once ruled the high seas.
Pirates are sailors who attack and board other ships to steal their cargoes. Their golden age was during the 1600s and 1700s. This was when heavily laden ships carried treasures, weapons and goods back to Europe from colonies in the Americas, Africa and Asia. Edward Teach, better known as Blackbeard, was one of the most terrifying pirates. He attacked ships off the coast of North America during the early 1700s. To frighten his victims, it is said that he used to set fire to his own beard!

There were women pirates, too.
Piracy was a man's world, but some women also took to the high seas. Mary Read and Anne Bonny were part of a pirate crew sailing around the Caribbean. They wore men's clothes and used fighting weapons, including daggers, cutlasses and pistols.

▼ Pirate weapons had often been stolen on previous raids. The men fought to the death.

There are still pirates on the oceans. Despite police patrols who watch for pirates and smugglers, a few pirates still operate. Luxury yachts are an easy target and in the South China Sea, pirate gangs on motor boats even attack large merchant ships.

▼ Divers have found some extraordinary hoards of treasure on board sunken galleons.

There is treasure lying under the sea. Over the centuries, many ships sunk in storms or hit reefs. They include pirate ships loaded with stolen booty. Some ships were deliberately sunk by pirates. The bed of the Caribbean Sea is littered with the remains of Spanish galleons, many of which still hold treasure!

PIRATE FLAG!

You will need:

paper   paints   brushes

The skull-and-crossbones is the most famous pirate flag, but it was not the only one. Copy one of these designs!

Going under

A submarine has dived deeper than 10,000 metres. The two-person *Trieste* made history in 1960 in an expedition to the Mariana Trench in the Pacific, the deepest part of any ocean. It took the submarine five hours to reach the bottom, a distance of 10,911 metres. On the way down, the extreme water pressure cracked part of the craft, but luckily, the two men inside returned to the surface unharmed.

▲ *Trieste* spent 20 minutes at the bottom of the Mariana Trench. The trench is so deep, you could stack the world's tallest building, the CN Tower, inside it 19 times (left)!

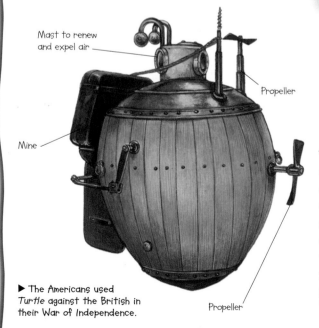

Mast to renew and expel air

Propeller

Mine

Propeller

▶ The Americans used *Turtle* against the British in their War of Independence.

The first combat submarine was shaped like an egg! *Turtle* was a one-person submarine that made its test dive in 1776. It was the first real submarine. It did not have an engine – it was driven by a propeller that was turned by hand! *Turtle* was built for war. It travelled just below the surface and could fix bombs to the bottom of enemy ships.

Divers have a spare pair of lungs.
Scuba divers wear special breathing
apparatus called 'aqua lungs'. French
divers, Jacques Cousteau and Emile
Gagnan, came up with the idea of a
portable oxygen supply. This meant that
divers were able to swim freely for the
first time, rather than wearing a heavy
suit and helmet.

I DON'T BELIEVE IT!

In 1963 Jacques Cousteau built a village on the bed of the Red Sea. Along with four other divers, he lived there for a whole month.

◀ Divers control their breathing to make their oxygen supply last as long as possible.

**The biggest submarines weighed
26,500 tonnes.** They were Russian
submarines called *Typhoons*, built in the
1970s and 1980s. As well as being the
biggest subs, they were also the fastest,
able to top 40 knots.

Periscope

Rudder

Living quarters

Torpedo firing tube

Engine room

▲ The *Typhoons* did not
need to come up to refuel
because they were
nuclear-powered.

Diving plane

Superboats

Some ships are invisible.
Stealth warships are not really
invisible, of course, but they
are hard to detect using radar.
There are already materials
being used for ships that can
absorb some radar signals.
Some paints can soak up
radar, too, and signals are
also bounced off in confusing
directions by the ships' strange,
angled hulls.

The world's biggest ship is nearly
half a kilometre long. It is a
supertanker called *Jahre Viking*.
Supertankers carry cargoes of
oil around the world. They
move slowly because they are
so huge and heavy.

▲ An angled, sloping hull gives very little
radar echo. This makes the stealth ship's
location hard to pinpoint.

▼ The giant supertanker *Jahre
Viking* is just over 458 metres long.

Not all boats ride the waves. Hovercrafts sit slightly above the water. They have a rubbery skirt that traps a cushion of air for them to ride on. Without the drag of the water to work against, hovercraft can cross the water much faster.

◄ Hovercraft can travel at up to 65 knots, the equivalent of 120 kilometres per hour.

▼ *Freedom Ship* will be over 1300 metres long. Aircraft 'taxis' will be able to take off and land on its rooftop runway.

Ships can give piggy-backs! Heavy-lift ships can sink part of their deck underwater, so a smaller ship can sail aboard for a free ride. Some ships carry planes. Aircraft carriers transport planes that are too small to carry enough fuel for long distances. The deck doubles up as a runway, where the planes take off and land.

Freedom Ship will resemble a floating city. It will be one of the first ocean cities, with apartments, shopping centres, a school and a hospital. The people who live on *Freedom* will circle the Earth once every two years. By following the Sun, they will live in constant summertime!

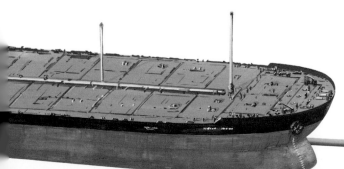

Riding the waves

The first sea sport was surfing. It took off in the 1950s, but was invented centuries earlier in Hawaii. Hawaii is still one of the best places to surf – at Waimea Bay, surfers catch waves that are up to 11 metres high. The record for the longest rides, though, are made off the coast of Mexico, where it is possible to surf for more than 1.5 kilometres.

▶ Modern surfboards are made of super–light materials. This means they create little drag in the water – and the surfer can reach high speeds!

A single boat towed 100 waterskiers! This record was made off the coast of Australia in 1986 and no one has beaten it yet. The drag boat was a cruiser called *Reef Cat*.

◀ Water skiing is now one of the most popular of all water sports.

QUIZ

1. What was the name of the fastest hydroplane?
2. When did jetskis go on sale?
3. Where is Waimea Bay?
4. What is a trimaran?

Answers:
1. Spirit of Australia
2. 1973 3. Hawaii
4. A three-hulled boat

Jetskiers can travel at nearly 100 kilometres per hour. Jetskis were developed in the 1960s. Their inventor was an American called Clayton Jacobsen who wanted to combine his two favourite hobbies, motorbikes and waterskiing. Today, some jetskiers are professional sportspeople.

◄ Jetskis first went on sale in 1973.

◄ Trimarans have three hulls, while catamarans have two.

Three hulls are sometimes better than one. Powerboating is an exciting, dangerous sport. Competitors are always trying out new boat designs that will race even faster. Multi-hulled boats minimize drag, but keep the boat steady. Trimarans have three slender, streamlined hulls that cut through the water.

▶ Hydroplanes are motor boats that skim across the surface of the water.

Hydroplanes fly over the waves. They are a cross between a boat and a plane. Special 'wings' raise the hull two metres above the water. The fastest hydroplane ever was *Spirit of Australia*. Driven by Kenneth Warby, it sped along at more than 500 kilometres per hour above the surface of the water!

Ocean stories

▼ Jason and the Argonauts steer their ship between two huge moving cliffs called the Cyanean Rocks. They faced many dangers on their journey.

The Greek hero Jason made an epic sea voyage. The ancient Greeks made up lots of sea adventure stories, probably because they lived on scattered islands. In the legend of the Argonauts, a hero called Jason sets off in a boat called the *Argos* with a band of brave men. He goes on a quest to find the Golden Fleece, a precious sheepskin guarded by a fierce dragon.

Neptune (or Poseidon) was an undersea god. Poseidon was the name used by the ancient Greeks and Neptune by the ancient Romans. Both civilizations pictured their god with a fork called a trident. They blamed their gods for the terrible storms that wrecked boats in the Mediterranean.

► Neptune raises his trident and whips up a storm.

▲ The beautiful goddess Aphrodite emerges from the sea.

The Greek goddess of love was born in the sea. Aphrodite, said to be the daughter of Zeus, was born out of the foam of the sea. The Romans based their love goddess, Venus, on the same story. Lots of artists have painted her rising from the waves in a giant clam shell.

I DON'T BELIEVE IT!

A mermaid's purse is the name given to the eggcases of the dog shark. They look a little bit like handbags!

Long ago, people believed in a giant sea monster, called the kraken. The stories were used to explain the dangers of the sea. Sightings of the giant squid might have inspired these tales.

▶ Mistaken for a monster! The 15 metre-long giant squid has eyes as big as dinner plates.

Mermaids lured sailors to their deaths on the rocks. Mythical mermaids were said to be half-woman, half-fish. Folklore tells how the mermaids confused sailors with their beautiful singing – with the result that their ships were wrecked on the rocks.

▼ Mermaids were said to have a fishy tail instead of legs.

189

INSECTS & SPIDERS

Explore the creepy–crawly world and discover
a huge variety of insects, bugs and spiders.

Dragonflies • Mosquitoes • Grasshoppers
Flies • Ladybirds • Butterflies • Moths • Bees
Wasps • Ants • Beetles • Caterpillars • Crickets
Webs • Wolf spiders • Black Widows • Scorpions
Cockroaches • Termites • Locusts • Tarantulas

Insects or spiders?

Insects are among the most numerous and widespread animals on Earth. They form the largest of all animal groups, with millions of different kinds, or species, that live almost everywhere in the world. But not all creepy-crawlies are insects. Spiders belong to a different group called arachnids, and millipedes are in yet another group!

Tortoiseshell butterfly

Spiny green nymph

Cricke

Tarantula

Pink-winged stick insect

Dragonfly

Cockchafer beetle

Stag beetle

Honeybee

Honeybee

Millipede

Giant longhorn beetle

Tarantula hawk wasp

Wood ants

193

Insects everywhere!

The housefly is one of the most common, widespread and annoying insects. There are many other members of the fly group, such as bluebottles, horseflies, craneflies ('daddy longlegs') and fruitflies. They all have two wings. Most other kinds of insects have four wings.

Housefly

Ladybird

The ladybird is a noticeable insect with its bright red or yellow body and black spots. It is a member of the beetle group. This is the biggest of all insect groups, with more than half a million kinds, from massive goliath and rhinoceros beetles to tiny flea-beetles and weevil-beetles.

The white butterfly is not usually welcome in the garden. Their young, known as caterpillars, eat the leaves of the gardener's precious flowers and vegetables. There are thousands of kinds of butterflies and even more kinds of their night-time cousins, the moths.

White butterfly feeding from a flower

The earwig is a familiar insect in the park, garden, garage, shed – and sometimes house. Despite their name, earwigs do not crawl into ears or hide in wigs. But they do like dark, damp corners. Earwigs form one of the smaller insect groups, with only 1300 different kinds.

▲ This earwig is being threatened, so it raises its tail to try to make itself look bigger.

Ants are fine in the garden or wood, but are pests in the house. Ants, bees and wasps make up a large insect group with some 300,000 different kinds. Most can sting, although many are too small to hurt people. However, some, such as bulldog ants, have a painful bite.

SPOT THE INSECTS!

Have you seen any insects so far today? Maybe a fly whizzing around the house or a butterfly flitting among the flowers? On a warm summer's day you probably see many kinds of insects. On a cold winter's day there are fewer insects about. Most are hiding away or have not yet hatched out of their eggs.

◄ Insects like these white butterflies do not have a bony skeleton inside their bodies like we do. Their bodies are covered by a series of horny plates. This is called an exoskeleton

The scorpionfly has a nasty looking sting on a long curved tail. It flies or crawls in bushes and weeds during summer. Only the male scorpionfly has the red tail. It looks like the sting of a scorpion but is harmless.

How insects grow

All insects begin life inside an egg. The female insect usually lays her eggs in an out-of-the-way place, such as under a stone, leaf or bark, or in the soil.

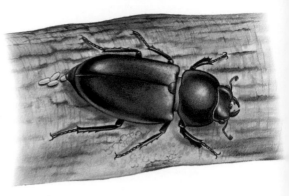

▲ This female stag beetle does not have huge jaws for fighting like the male does. However, her bite is much more powerful than the male's.

When some types of insects hatch, they do not look like their parents. A young beetle, butterfly or fly is very different from a grown-up beetle, butterfly or fly. It is soft-bodied, wriggly and worm-like. This young stage is called a larva. There are different names for various kinds of larvae. A fly larva is called a maggot, a beetle larva is a grub and a butterfly larva is a caterpillar.

A female insect mates with a male insect before she can lay her eggs. The female and male come together to check that they are both the same kind of insect, and they are both healthy and ready to mate. This is known as courtship. Butterflies often flit through the air together in a 'courtship dance'.

▶ Large caterpillars always eat into the centre of the leaf from the edge. Caterpillars grasp the leaf with their legs, while their specially developed front jaws chew at their food.

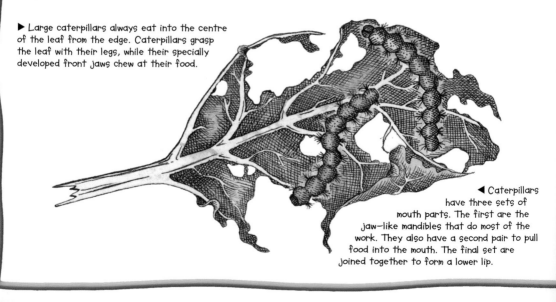

◀ Caterpillars have three sets of mouth parts. The first are the jaw-like mandibles that do most of the work. They also have a second pair to pull food into the mouth. The final set are joined together to form a lower lip.

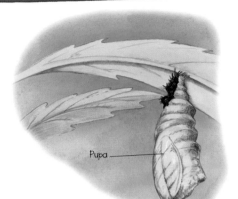

Pupa

The larva eats and eats. It sheds its skin several times so it can grow. Then it changes into the next stage of its life, called a pupa. The pupa has a hard outer case that stays still and inactive. But, inside, the larva is changing body shape. This change is known as metamorphosis.

▲ This peacock butterfly has just emerged from its pupal case and is stretching its wings for the first time.

At last the pupa's case splits open and the adult insect crawls out. Its body, legs and wings spread out and harden. Now the insect is ready to find food and also find a mate.

Some kinds of insects change shape less as they grow up. When a young cricket or grasshopper hatches from its egg, it looks similar to its parents. However it may not have any wings yet.

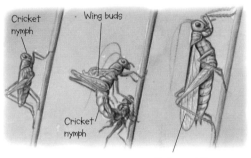

Cricket nymph

Wing buds

Cricket nymph

Mature adult

The young cricket eats and eats, and sheds or moults its skin several times as it grows. Each time it looks more like its parent. A young insect which resembles the fully grown adult like this is called a nymph. At the last moult it becomes a fully formed adult, ready to feed and breed.

I DON'T BELIEVE IT!

Courtship is a dangerous time for the hunting insect called the praying mantis. The female is much bigger than the male, and as soon as they have mated, she may eat him!

Air aces

Most kinds of insects have two pairs of wings and use them to fly from place to place. One of the strongest fliers is the Apollo butterfly of Europe and Asia. It flaps high over hills and mountains, then rests on a rock or flower in the sunshine.

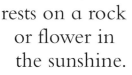

Apollo butterfly

A fast and fierce flying hunter is the dragonfly. Its huge eyes spot tiny prey such as midges and mayflies. The dragonfly dashes through the air, turns in a flash, grabs the victim in its legs and whirrs back to a perch to eat its meal.

Some insects flash bright lights as they fly. The firefly is not a fly but a type of beetle. Male fireflies 'dance' in the air at dusk, the rear parts of their bodies glowing on and off about once each second. Female fireflies stay on twigs and leaves and glow in reply as part of their courtship.

Dragonfly

The smallest fliers include gnats, midges and mosquitoes. These are all true flies, with one pair of wings. Some are almost too tiny for us to see. Certain types bite animals and people, sucking their blood as food.

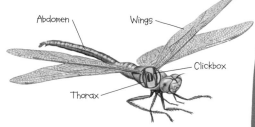

Abdomen

Wings

Clickbox

Thorax

An insect's wings are attached to the middle part of its body, the thorax. This is like a box with strong walls, called a clickbox. Muscles inside the thorax pull to make the walls click in and out, which makes the wings flick up and down. A large butterfly flaps its wings once or twice each second. Some tiny flies flap almost 1000 times each second.

MAKE A FLAPPING FLY

You will need:

some stiff card   round-ended scissors
tissue paper   sticky tape

1. Ask an adult for help. Carefully cut out the card to make a box with two open ends as shown.

2. Use strips of stiff card to make struts for the wings and attach these to the side walls of the box. Make the rest of the wings from tissue paper.

3. Hold the box as shown. Move the top and bottom walls in, then out. This bends the side walls and makes the wings flap, just like a real insect.

A few insects lack wings. They are mostly very small and live in the soil, such as bristletails and springtails. One kind of bristletail is the silverfish—a small, shiny, fast-running insect.

199

Champion leapers

Many insects move around mainly by hopping and jumping, rather than flying. They have long, strong legs and can leap great distances, especially to avoid enemies and escape from danger. Grasshoppers are up to 15 centimetres long. Most have very long back legs and some types can jump more than 3 metres. Often the grasshopper opens its brightly patterned wings briefly as it leaps, giving a flash of colour.

The champion leaping insects, for their body size, are fleas. They are mostly small, just 2–3 millimetres long. But they can jump over 30 centimetres, which is more than 100 times their body size. Fleas suck blood or body fluids from warm-blooded animals, mainly mammals but also birds.

Flea

Grasshopper

An insect leaper that jumps with its tail, rather than its legs, is the springtail. Springtails are tiny, 1–3 millimetres long, or as long as this letter 'l'! Some types can leap more than 5 centimetres.

The click beetle, or skipjack, is another insect leaper. This beetle is about 12 millimetres long. When in danger it falls on its back and pretends to be dead. But it slowly arches its body and then straightens with a jerk and a 'click'. It can flick itself about 25 centimetres into the air!

QUIZ

Which type of insect can jump farthest?

Put these insects in order of how far they can leap.
Grasshopper   Flea
Click beetle   Springtail

Now put them in order of how far they can leap compared to their sizes.

Answers:
The grasshopper can jump farthest, then the flea, click beetle and finally the springtail. The flea can jump farthest for its size, then the click beetle, the springtail and finally the grasshopper.

Click beetle

▲ The 'tail' rear part of the springtail's body, is shaped like a V or Y. It is usually folded under the body and held in place by a trigger-like flap. When the flap moves aside the 'tail' flicks down and flips the insect through the air.

Super sprinters

Some insects rarely fly or leap. They prefer to run, and run, and run… all day, and even all night too. Among the champion insect runners are cockroaches. They are tough and adaptable, with about 3600 different kinds. A few burrow in soil or live in caves. But most scurry speedily across the ground on their long legs.

▲ Cockroaches have low, flat bodies and can dart into narrow crevices, under logs and stones and bricks, and into cupboards, furniture – and beds!

Green tiger beetle

The green tiger beetle is an active hunter that races over open ground almost too fast for our eyes to follow. It chases smaller creatures such as ants, woodlice, worms and little spiders. It has huge jaws for its size and soon rips apart any victim.

▲ The stonefly nymph, the larva of the stonefly, runs around on the bed of its river home searching for food.

One of the busiest insect walkers is the devil's coach-horse, a type of beetle with a long body that resembles an earwig. It belongs to the group known as rove beetles which walk huge distances to find food. The devil's coach-horse has powerful mouthparts and tears apart dead and dying small caterpillars, grubs and worms.

Devil's coach-horse

Some insects walk not only across the ground, but also up smooth, shiny surfaces such as walls and even windows. They have wide feet with many tiny hooks or sticky pads. These grip bumps that are too small to see in substances such as glossy, wet leaves or window glass.

Stunning swimmers

Many kinds of insects live underwater in ponds, streams, rivers and lakes. Some walk about on the bottom, such as the young forms or nymphs of dragonflies and damselflies. Others swim strongly using their legs as oars to row through the water. The great diving beetle hunts small water creatures such as tadpoles and baby fish. It can give a person a painful bite in self-defence.

Some water insects, such as the great silver water beetle, breathe air. So they must come to the surface for fresh supplies. The hairs on the beetle's body trap tiny bubbles of air for breathing below.

Gills

Mayfly nymphs

Damselfly nymph

Some insects even walk on water. The pondskater has a slim, light body with long, wide-splayed legs. It glides across the surface 'skin' or film caused by the feature of water known as surface tension. It is a member of the bug group of insects and eats tiny animals that fall into the pond.

The nymphs of dragonflies, damselflies, stoneflies and mayflies have tails with feathery gills. These work like the gills of a fish, for breathing underwater. These young insects never need to go to the surface until they change into adults.

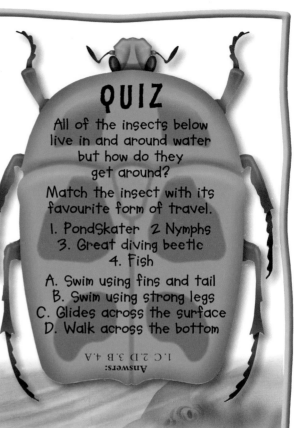

QUIZ

All of the insects below live in and around water but how do they get around?

Match the insect with its favourite form of travel.

1. PondSkater 2 Nymphs
3. Great diving beetle
4. Fish

A. Swim using fins and tail
B. Swim using strong legs
C. Glides across the surface
D. Walk across the bottom

Answers:
1.C 2.D 3.B 4.A

Pond skater

Great diving beetle

Dragonfly nymph

Brilliant burrowers

Soil teems with millions of creatures – and many are insects. Some are the worm-like young forms of insects, called larvae or grubs, as shown below. Others are fully grown insects, such as burrowing beetles, ants, termites, springtails and earwigs. These soil insects are a vital source of food for all kinds of larger animals from spiders and shrews to moles and many types of birds.

The larva of the click beetle is shiny orange, up to 25 millimetres long and called a wireworm. It stays undergound, feeding on plant parts, for up to five years. Then it changes into an adult and leaves the soil. Wireworms can be serious pests of cereal crops such as barley, oats and wheat. They also eat beet and potatoes that you would find underground.

◀ The European mole burrows and feeds on the insects and worms that live in the soil.

Cranefly

Cranefly larva, leatherjacket

However, insects in the soil can also cause great damage to plants, especially farm crops. They eat roots and other underground parts, especially crops such as potatoes and carrots.

▶ Many insects pose a threat to farmers' crops. Farmers can use pesticides, chemicals to kill the insects, but many people think that this harms other plants and animals.

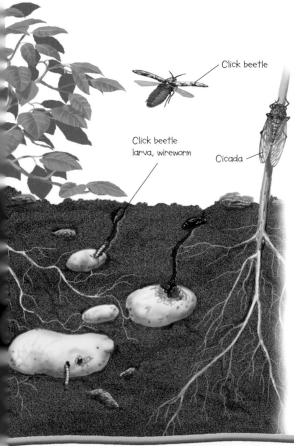

The larva of the cranefly ('daddy long–legs') is called a leatherjacket after its tough, leathery skin. Leatherjackets eat the roots of grasses, including cereal crops such as wheat. They hatch from their eggs in late summer, feed in the soil through autumn and winter and spring, and change into pupae and then adults the next summer.

Click beetle

Click beetle larva, wireworm

Cicada

QUIZ

Sort out the following items into three groups:
A Larger animals which eat insect larvae
B Insect larvae
C Plants eaten by larvae

1. Crow
2. Potato
3. Wireworm
4. Mole
5. Cicada grub
6. Carrot

Answers:
A. 1 and 4. B. 3 and 5.
C. 2 and 6.

The larva of the cicada may live underground for more than ten years. Different types of cicadas stay in the soil for different periods of time. The American periodic cicada is probably the record-holder, taking 17 years to change into a pupa and then an adult. Cicada larvae suck juices from plant roots. Grown-up cicadas make loud chirping or buzzing sounds.

Cicada larva

Bloodthirsty bugs

Most insects may be small, but they are among the fiercest and hungriest hunters in the animal world. Many have mouthparts shaped like spears or saws, which are relatively big compared to their bodies, for grabbing and tearing up victims. Some actively chase after prey. Others lie in wait and surprise the prey.

Antenna detects smells

Jaws used for digging and cutting up food

Gold Wasp's head

The lacewing looks delicate and dainty as it sits on a leaf by day or flies gently at night. However, it is a fearsome hunter of smaller creatures, especially aphids such as greenfly and blackfly. It chews the aphid and drinks its body fluids. It may also have a sip of sweet, sugary nectar from a flower.

One of the most powerful insect predators is the preying mantis. It is also called the praying mantis since it holds its front legs folded, like a person with hands together in prayer. But the front legs have sharp spines and snap together like spiky scissors to grab caterpillars, moths and similar food.

Lacewing eating an aphid

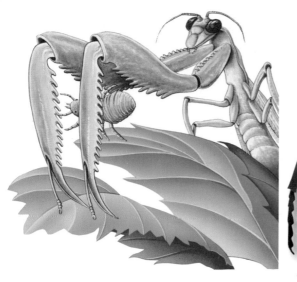

▲ The mantis stays perfectly still, camouflaged by its body colouring that blends in with the leaf or flower where it waits. When a victim comes near – SNAP!

QUIZ

1. What does a wasp use its jaws for?

2. What is the lacewing's favourite food?

3. Finish the name of this insect predator: the preying...?

4. The larva of which animal digs a dangerous trap for ants?

Answers:
1. Digging and cutting up food.
2. Aphids such as greenfly and blackfly.
3. Mantis. 4. Ant-lion

Ant–lions are insects that resemble lacewings. The ant-lion larva lives in sand or loose soil. It digs a small pit and then hides below the surface at the bottom. Small creatures wander past, slip and slide into the pit, and the ant–lion larva grasps them with its fang-like mouthparts.

▲ The ant–lion larva sits in a small hole at the bottom of its pit, waiting for an unwary ant.

209

Veggie bugs

About 9 out of 10 kinds of insects eat some kind of plant food. Many feed on soft, rich, nutritious substances. These include the sap in stems and leaves, the mineral-rich liquid in roots, the nectar in flowers and the soft flesh of squashy fruits and berries.

Solid wood may not seem very tasty, but many kinds of insects eat it. They usually consume the wood when they are larvae or grubs, making tunnels as they eat their way through trees, logs, and timber structures such as bridges, fences, houses and furniture.

Elm beetle

Elm beetle larva

Mealy-bug

Furniture beetle

Woodworm (Furniture beetle larva)

Flowerbug

Insects even feed on old bits of damp and crumbling wood, dying trees, brown and decaying leaves and smelly, rotting fruit. They are not fussy eaters! This is nature's way of recycling goodness and nutrients in old plant parts, and returning them to the soil so new trees and other plants can grow.

Capsid bug

Shield bug

Fruitfly

Lacebug

I DON'T BELIEVE IT!

Animal droppings are delicious and tasty to many kinds of insects. Various types of beetles lay their eggs in warm and steamy piles of droppings. The larvae soon hatch out and eat the dung!

Unwelcome guests

Insects may be small, but some have very powerful bites and poison stings. A few can even kill people. The hornet is a large type of wasp and has a jagged sting on its rear end. It does not use this often. But when it does, it can cause great pain to a person and easily deal death to a small animal.

Hornet

Sting

Bee

Sting

Like wasps, bees also have a poison sting at their rear end. After the wasp jabs its sting into an enemy, the sting comes out and the wasp can fly away and use it again. It's like stabbing with a dagger. But when a bee does this, the sting has a hook or barb and stays in the enemy. As the bee flies away the rear part of its body tears off and the bee soon dies.

Bird-eating spider

Bird-eating spiders really do eat birds! They inject their venom, or poison, into their prey with large fangs. As well as birds, they eat lizards, frogs and even small poisonous snakes. It can take as much as a day to suck the body of a snake dry!

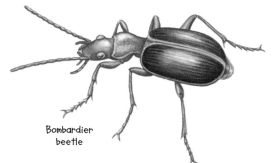

Bombardier beetle

The bombardier beetle squirts out a spray of horrible liquid from its rear end, almost like a small spray-gun! This startles and stings the attacker and gives the small beetle time to escape.

QUIZ

Do you know which of these insects is most poisonous or harmful to a person, and which is the least dangerous?

Hornet   Earwig
Grasshopper Bulldog ant
Bee   Moth

Answers:
From the most to least dangerous: hornet (powerful sting), bee (less powerful sting), bulldog ant (stinging bite), moth (a few types have stinging hairs on the body), grasshopper (might scratch when it kicks) earwig (pretty much totally harmless)

One army ant can give a small bite. But 10,000 are much more dangerous. These ants are mainly from South America and do not stay in a nest like other ants. They crawl in long lines through the forest, eating whatever they can bite, sting and overpower, from other insects to large spiders, lizards and birds. They rest at night before marching on the next day.

Towns for termites

Some insects live together in huge groups called colonies — which are like insect cities. There are four main types of insects which form colonies. One is the termites. The other three are all in the same insect subgroup and are bees, wasps and ants.

Inside the termite 'city' there are various groups of termites, with different kinds of work to do. Some tunnel into the soil and collect food such as tiny bits of plants. Others guard the entrance to the nest and bite any animals which try to enter. Some look after the eggs and young forms, or larvae.

Some kinds of termites make their nests inside a huge pile of mud and earth called a termite mound. The termites build the mound from wet mud which goes hard in the hot sun. The main part of the nest is below ground level. It has hundreds of tunnels and chambers where the termites live, feed and breed.

▶ Termites mounds are incredibly complex constructions. They can reach 10 metres tall, and have air conditioning shafts built into them. These enable the termites to control the temperature of the nest to within 1 degree.

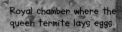

Royal chamber where the queen termite lays eggs

Male termite mates with queen

Courtier workers look after the queen

Nursery termites care for eggs and larvae

Forager termites collect food

Cleaner termites repair the nest and get rid of wastes

214

Wasp nest

A wasp nest will have about 2000 wasps in it, but these are small builders in the insect world! A termite colony may have more than 5,000,000 inhabitants! Other insect colonies are smaller, although most have a similar set-up with one queen and various kinds of workers. Wood-ants form nests of up to 300,000 and honeybees around 50,000. Some bumble-bees live in colonies numbering only 10 or 20.

The queen termite is up to 100 times bigger than the workers. She is the only one in the nest who lays eggs – thousands every day.

Leaf–cutter ants grow their own food! They harvest leaves which they use at the nest to grow fungus, which they eat.

I DON'T BELIEVE IT!

Ants get milk from green cows! The 'cows' are really aphids. Ants look after the aphids. In return, when an ant strokes an aphid, the aphid oozes a drop of 'milk', a sugary liquid called honeydew, which the ant sips to get energy.

▶ When the sections of leaf are taken back to the nest, other ants cut them up into smaller sections. They are then used in gardens to grow the ants' food.

Where am I?

Insects have some of the best types of camouflage in the whole world of animals. Camouflage is when a living thing is coloured and patterned to blend in with its surroundings, so it is difficult to notice. This makes it hard for predators to see or find it. Or, if the insect is a predator itself, camouflage helps it to creep up unnoticed on prey.

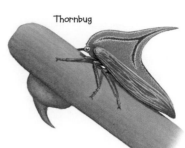

Thornbug

The thornbug has a hard, pointed body casing. It sits still on a twig pretending to be a real thorn. It moves about and feeds at night.

Stick and leaf insects look exactly like sticks and leaves. The body and legs of a stick insect are long and twig-like. The body of a leaf insect has wide, flat parts which are coloured to resemble leaves. Both these types of insects eat plants. When the wind blows they rock and sway in the breeze, just like the real twigs and leaves around them.

Spiny green nymph

Green Indian stick insect

Rajah Brooke's bird-wing butterfly

Shieldbugs have broad, flat bodies that look like the leaves around them. The body is shaped like the shield carried by a medieval knight-in-armour.

Shieldbug

Many butterflies seem too brightly coloured to blend in with their surroundings. But when the wings are held together over the butterfly's back, the undersides show. These are usually brown or green – dark colours like the leaves.

Green Indian stick insect

Rajah Brooke's bird-wing butterfly

MAKE A CAMOUFLAGE SCENE

1. Carefully cut out a butterfly shape from stiff card. Colour it brightly with a bold pattern, such as yellow and brown spots on an orange background, or orange stripes on a blue background.

2. Cut out 10 to 20 leaf shapes from card. Colour them like your butterfly. Stick the leaves on a cardboard branch.

3. Your butterfly may seem far too bright and bold to be camouflaged. But put the butterfly on your branch. See how well its camouflage works now!

The bird-dropping caterpillar looks just like – a pile of bird's droppings! Not many animals would want to eat it, so it survives longer.

Bird-dropping caterpillar

Great pretenders

Some insects pretend to be what they're not – especially other insects. For example, a hoverfly has a body with yellow and black stripes. At first sight it looks very similar to a wasp. But it is not. It is a type of fly and it is harmless. It cannot sting like a real wasp.

A mimic is an animal which, at a glance, looks similar to another animal, but which is really a different kind of creature. The animal which the mimic resembles is known as the model. Usually, the model is dangerous or harmful in some way. It may have a powerful bite or a poisonous sting. Other animals avoid it. Usually, the mimic is harmless. But it looks like the harmful model, so other animals avoid it too. The mimic gains safety or protection by looking like the model.

▲ The harmless hoverfly looks just like a wasp. Like other mimics, it fools other animals into thinking that it is more dangerous than it is.

The hornet-moth is a mimic of the large type of wasp known as the hornet. A hornet has a very painful sting and few other creatures dare to try and eat it. The hornet-moth is harmless but few other creatures dare to eat it either.

Hornet (model)

Hornet moth (mimic)

The monarch butterfly has bright, bold colours on its wings. These warn other animals, such as birds and lizards, that its flesh tastes horrible and is poisonous. The viceroy butterfly is very similar to the monarch but it is a mimic—its flesh is not distasteful. As well as being poisonous, the monarch is also a champion migrating insect.

Monarch butterfly

The bee—fly cannot sting like a real bee. But it looks just like a bee, with a hairy striped body.

The bee—fly avoids predators by looking like a bee.

The ant—beetle resembles an ant, although it does not have a strong bite and a sting like a real ant. The ant-beetle enters the ant's nest and steals ant larvae to eat.

Ant—beetle

QUIZ

Sort these models and mimics into pairs where the harmless mimic looks like the harmful model.

Mimic	Model
Ant-beetle	Hornet
Bee-fly	Ant
Hornet-moth	Bee
Hoverfly	Monarch
Viceroy	Wasp

Answers:
Ant-beetle and ant; bee-fly and bee;
Hornet-moth and hornet; hoverfly
and wasp; viceroy and monarch.

Stay or go?

The cold of winter or the dryness of drought are hard times for most animals, including insects. How can they survive? One answer is to hibernate. Many insects find a safe, sheltered place and go to sleep. Butterflies crawl behind creepers and vines. Ladybirds cluster in thick bushes. Beetles dig into the soil or among tree roots. However, these insects are not really asleep in the way that you go to sleep. They are simply too cold to move. As the weather becomes warmer, they become active again.

▶ Locusts eat massive areas of farm crops and people may be left to starve.

Peacock butterfly

Ladybird

Squash beetle

▲ All these insects hibernate through winter each year.

Some insects migrate, travel long distances to somewhere conditions are better. Some insects do this only when they become too numerous. After a few years of good conditions in Africa, locusts (a type of large grasshopper) increase in numbers so much they form vast swarms of millions. With so many locusts together, they eat all the food in a whole area and fly off to look for more.

I DON'T BELIEVE IT!

Some insects migrate the wrong way! In Australia bogong moths sometimes fly off in search of better conditions. Some keep on flying out over the sea, fall into the water and die.

Some insects migrate every year. These include ladybirds, death's-head hawkmoths, painted lady butterflies and libellula dragonflies.

Death's-head hawkmoth

Some insects migrate every year. In North America, monarch butterflies fly south during autumn. They spend the winter in warm parts of California, USA and Mexico. Millions of monarchs gather there in winter roosts. Next spring they fly north again to feed and breed.

221

Noisy neighbours

The tropical forest is warm and still – but far from quiet. Many insects are making chirps, buzzes, clicks, screeches, hums and other noises. Most are males, making their songs or calls to attract females at breeding time.

Giant wood wasp

Some of the noisiest insects are cicadas, plant-eating bugs with large wings. The male cicada has two thin patches of body casing, one on either side of its abdomen (rear body part). Tiny muscles pull in each patch, then let it go again, like clicking a tin lid in and out. This happens very fast and the clicks merge into a buzzing sound which can be heard one kilometre away.

Great green bush cricket

Great green bush cricket

Mole cricket

Cicada

Garden tiger moth

Deathwatch beetle

Cockchafer

Click beetle

Screech beetle

QUIZ

1. What is a locust?
2. Which butterflies spend the summer in California in the USA and Mexico?
3. Do monarch butterflies hibernate through winter?
4. What do cicadas eat?
5. How did mole-crickets get their name?

Answers:
1. A type of large grasshopper.
2. Monarch butterflies. 3. No, they migrate. 4. Plants. 5. They burrow like moles.

Like most other crickets, the male katydid chirps by rubbing together his wings. The bases of the wings near the body have hard, ridged strips like rows of pegs. These click past each other to make the chirping sound.

The male mole-cricket chirps in a similar way. But he also sits at the entrance to his burrow in the soil. (Mole-crickets get their name from the way they tunnel through soil, like real moles.) The burrow entrance is specially shaped, almost like the loudspeaker of a music system. It makes the chirps sound louder and travel farther.

Meet the family!

Are all minibeasts, bugs and creepy-crawlies truly insects? One way to tell is to count the legs. If a creature has six legs, it's an insect. If it has fewer or more, it's some other kind of animal. However leg-counting only works with fully-grown or adult creatures. Some young forms or larvae, like fly maggots, have no legs at all. But they develop into six-legged flies, and flies are certainly insects.

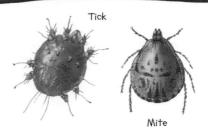
Tick

Mite

Maggots

Mites and ticks have eight legs. They are not insects. Ticks and some mites cling onto larger animals and suck their blood. Some mites are so small that a handful of soil may contain half a million of them. Mites and ticks belong to the group of animals with eight legs, called arachnids. Other arachnids are spiders and scorpions.

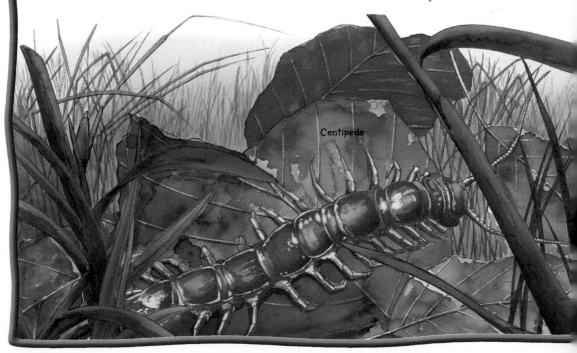
Centipede

A woodlouse has a hard body casing and feelers on its head. But it has more than 10 legs so it is certainly not an insect! It is a crustacean – a cousin of crabs and lobsters.

Woodlouse

Centipedes have lots of legs, far more than six – usually over 30. The centipede has two very long fangs that give a poison bite. It races across the ground hunting for small animals to eat – such as insects.

Millipedes have 50 or 100 legs, maybe even more. They are certainly not insects. Millipedes eat bits of plants such as old leaves, bark and wood.

QUIZ

Which of these minibeasts has a poisonous bite or sting?

Millipede
Scorpion
Woodlouse
Tick
Centipede
Maggot

Answers:
Only the centipede and scorpion have a poisonous bite or sting.

Millipede

Centipede

Silky spiders

A spider has eight legs. So it's not an insect. It's a type of animal called an arachnid. All spiders are deadly hunters. They have large fang-like jaws which they use to grab and stab their prey. The fangs inject a poison to kill or quieten the victim. The spider then tears it apart and eats it, or sucks out its body juices. Like spiders, scorpions and mites and ticks have eight legs. So they are also arachnids.

Several spinnerets produce silk

Spigots produce coarse silk for making webs

Spools produce fine silk for wrapping prey

All spiders can make very thin, fine threads called silk. These come out of the rear of the spider's body, from parts called spinnerets. Spiders spin their silk for many reasons. About half of the 40,000 different kinds of spiders make webs or nets to catch prey. Some spiders wrap up their living victims in silk to stop them escaping, so the spider can have its meal later. Some female spiders make silk bags, called cocoons, where they lay their eggs, and others spin protective silk 'nursery tents' for their babies.

1. A spider starts a web by building a bridge.

2. Then it makes a triangle shape.

3. It adds more threads to make a strong framework.

4. Finally, the spider fills the frame with circular threads.

5. A spider's web is strong enough to catch large insects.

MAKE A SPIDER'S WEB

You will need:

a piece of card   a reel of cotton
round-ended scissors   glue or sticky tape

1. Ask an adult for help. Cut a
large hole out of the card. Stretch
a piece of cotton across the hole
and glue or tape both ends.

2. Do the same again several
times at a different angles.
Make sure all the threads cross
at the centre of the hole.

3. Starting at the centre, glue
a long piece of thread to
one of the cross-pieces, then
to the next cross-piece but slightly
farther away from the centre, and so
on. Work your way round in a
growing spiral until you reach
the edge. That's the way
that real spiders
make webs.

◀ The Australian
redback spider is one
of the most deadly of
a group called widow
spiders. These spiders get
their name because, once they
have mated, the female may well
eat the male!

**Some spiders have very strange
ways of using their silk threads.**
The spitting spider squirts sticky silk
at its victim, like throwing tiny ropes
over it. The bolas spider catches
moths and other insects flying past
with its own kind of fishing line. The
water spider makes a criss-cross sheet
of silk that holds bubbles of air. It
brings the air down from the surface,
so the spider can breathe underwater.

◀ The bolas
spider makes a sticky ball
and sticks it to a length of silk.
It then whirls this rope around like a
lasso and catches insects flying past.

Inventive arachnids

Not all spiders catch their prey using webs. Wolf spiders are strong and have long legs. They run fast and chase tiny prey such as beetles, caterpillars and slugs.

Wolf spider

The trapdoor spider lives in a burrow with a wedge-shaped door made from silk. The spider hides just behind this door. When it detects a small animal passing, it opens the door and rushes out to grab its victim.

Trapdoor spider

▶ This gold leaf crab spider has caught a honeybee. Its venom works fast to paralyse the bee. If it did not, the bee's struggling might harm the spider and draw the attention of the spider's enemies.

The crab spider looks like a small crab, with a wide, tubby body and curved legs. It usually sits on a flower which is the same colour as itself. It keeps very still so it is camouflaged – it merges in with its surroundings. Small insects such as flies, beetles and bees come to the flower to gather food and the crab spider pounces on them.

▼ The eyes of the tiny jumping spider work like a zoom lens on a camera, and help it judge distances very well.

The jumping spider is only 5–10 millimetres long – but it can leap more than 20 times this distance. It jumps onto tiny prey such as ants. The jumping spider's eyes are enormous for its small body, so it can see how far it needs to leap so that it lands on its victim.

Bird–eating spiders, sometimes called 'tarantulas', are huge, hairy spiders from tropical South America and Africa. Stretch out your hand and it still would not be as big as some of these giants. They are strong enough to catch big beetles, grasshoppers, other spiders and even mice, frogs, lizards and small birds.

I DON'T BELIEVE IT!

The name 'tarantula' was first given to a type of wolf spider from Europe. Its body is about 40 millimetres long and it lives in a burrow. Its bite can be very irritating, sore and painful.

▶ This tarantula has caught a katydid, a type of grasshopper.

A sting in the tail

A scorpion has eight legs. It is not an insect. Like a spider, it is an arachnid. Scorpions live in warm parts of the world. Some are at home in dripping rainforests. Others like baking deserts. The scorpion has large, crab-like pincers, called pedipalps, to grab its prey, and powerful jaws like scissors to chop it up.

The scorpion has a dangerous poison sting at the tip of its tail. It may use this to poison or paralyse a victim, so the victim cannot move. Or the scorpion may wave its tail at enemies to warn them that, unless they go away, it will sting them to death!

▶ This scorpion has caught a katydid. It has paralysed it with its sting, and will soon settle down to eat.

The sun–spider or solifuge is another very fierce, eight–legged, spider–like hunter, with a poisonous bite. It lives in deserts and dry places, which is why it's sometimes called the camel-spider.

The false scorpion looks like a scorpion, with big pincers. But it does not have a poisonous sting in its tail. It doesn't even have a tail. And it's tiny – it could fit into this 'o'! It lives in the soil and hunts even smaller creatures.

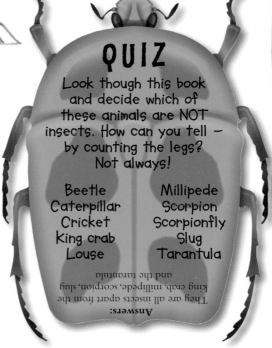

QUIZ

Look though this book and decide which of these animals are NOT insects. How can you tell – by counting the legs? Not always!

Beetle
Caterpillar
Cricket
King crab
Louse

Millipede
Scorpion
Scorpionfly
Slug
Tarantula

Answers:
They are all insects apart from the king crab, millipede, scorpion, slug and the tarantula

King crab

A crab may seem an odd cousin for a spider or scorpion. But the horseshoe or king crab is very unusual. It has eight legs – so it's an arachnid. It also has a large domed shell and strong spiky tail. There were horseshoe crabs in the seas well before dinosaurs roamed the land.

Animals don't have to be big to be dangerous. These spiders are both very poisonous and their bites can even kill people. This is why you should never mess about with spiders or poke your hands into holes and dark places!

Violin spider

Black widow spider

Friends and foes

Some insects are harmful — but others are very helpful. They are a vital part of the natural world. Flies, butterflies, beetles and many others visit flowers to collect nectar and pollen to eat. In the process they carry pollen from flower to flower. This is called pollination and is needed so that the flower can form seeds or fruits.

▲ Spiders are very helpful to gardeners. They catch lots of insect pests, like flies, in their webs.

▼ These bees are busy working in their hive. On the right you can see the young, c-shaped grubs.

Bees make honey, sweet and sticky and packed with energy. People keep honeybees in hives so the honey is easier to collect. Wild bees make honey to feed their larvae and as a food store when conditions are bad. But the honey is eaten by numerous animals such as bears, ratels (honey-badgers) and birds.

Termites

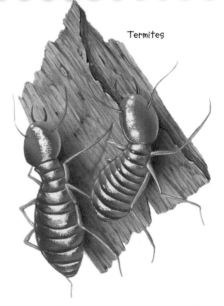

A few kinds of insects are among the most harmful creatures in the world. They do not attack and kill people directly, like tigers and crocodiles. But they do spread many types of dangerous diseases such as malaria.

Some bloodsucking flies, such as mosquitos, carry diseases such as malaria. If the fly bites a person and sucks their blood, it may pass the disease into thier body. As the fly bites another person, a tiny drop of the first person's blood gets into the second person – and the disease is passed on.

Mosquito

Some insects even damage wooden houses, bridges, barns and walkways. Certain kinds of termites make nests in the wood and tunnel inside it. The damage cannot be seen from the outside until the timber is eaten almost hollow. Then it collapses into a pile of dust if anyone even touches it!

REPTILES &
AMPHIBIANS

Discover slithery snakes and jumping toads,
and find out how reptiles and amphibians live.

Crocodiles • Alligators • Caimans • Lizards
Tortoises • Iguanas • Frogs • Toads • Salamanders
Tadpoles • Eggs • Slow worms • Geckos • Chameleons
Newts • Flying snakes • Vipers • Sea snakes

Cold-blooded creatures

Reptiles and amphibians are cold-blooded animals. This means that they cannot control their body temperature like we can. A reptile's skin is dry and scaly, most reptiles spend much of their time on land. Most amphibians live in or around water. The skin of an amphibian is smooth and wet.

Nile crocodiles

Golden arrow–poison frog

Common frog

Spotted salamander

Eastern green mamba snake

Komodo dragon

Indian cobra

Desert tortoise

Jackson's chameleon

Shingleback lizard

Frilled lizard

237

Scales and slime

Reptiles and amphibians can be divided into smaller groups. There are four kinds of reptiles, snakes and lizards, the crocodile family, tortoises and turtles and the tuatara. Amphibians are split into frogs and toads, newts and salamanders, and caecilians.

▲ Crocodiles are the largest reptiles in the world. Their eyes and nostrils are placed high on their heads so that they can stay mostly under water while approaching their prey.

Reptiles do a lot of sunbathing! They do this, called basking, to get themselves warm with the heat from the sun so that they can move about. When it gets cold, at night or during a cold season, they might sleep, or they might hibernate, which means that they go into a very deep sleep.

Most reptiles have dry, scaly, waterproof skin. This stops their bodies from drying out. The scales are made of keratin and may form very thick, tough plates. Human nails are also made of the same sort of material.

▲ This reptile, an agama lizard from Africa, gets itself warm by lying, or basking, in the sun.

The average amphibian has skin that is moist, fairly smooth and soft.
Oxygen can pass easily through their skin, which is important because most adult amphibians breathe through their skin as well as with their lungs. Reptiles breathe only through their lungs.

Amphibians' skin is kept moist by special glands just under the surface.
These glands produce a sticky substance called mucus. Many amphibians also keep their skin moist by making sure that they are never far away from water.

QUIZ

1. Are reptiles warm— or cold–blooded?
2. Are amphibians warm or cold–blooded?
3. Can you think how these creatures might warm up?
4. How do reptiles breathe?
5. How do amphibians breathe?

Answers:
1. Cold-blooded.
2. Cold-blooded.
3. By a spot of sunbathing!
4. Through their lungs.
5. Through their skin and lungs.

▶ Oxygen passes in through the skin and into the blood, while carbon dioxide passes out.

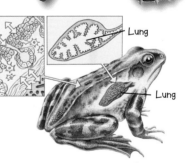

Lung

Lung

Some amphibians have no lungs.
Humans breathe with their lungs to get oxygen from the air and breathe out carbon dioxide. Most amphibians breathe through their skin and lungs, but lungless salamanders breathe only through their skin and the lining of the mouth.

Sun worshippers

Most reptiles live in warm or hot habitats. Many are found in dry, burning-hot places such as deserts and dry grassland. They have various clever ways of surviving in these harsh conditions.

Even reptiles can get too hot sometimes! When this happens, they hide in the shade of a rock or bury themselves in the sand. Some escape the heat by being nocturnal – coming out mostly at night.

Common iguana

Banded gecko

Desert tortoise

Spadefoot toad

Reptiles need very little food and water. Unlike warm-blooded animals, they don't use food to create body heat, so many can survive in places with scarce food supplies, such as deserts. Their thick skin means that as little water as possible escapes from their bodies.

Reptiles need a certain level of warmth to survive. This is why there are no reptiles in very cold places, such as at the North and South Poles, or at the very tops of mountains.

Banded gecko

Like reptiles, many amphibians live in very hot places. But sometimes it can get too hot and dry for them. The spadefoot toad from Europe, Asia and North America buries itself in the sand to escape the heat and dryness.

Leopard lizard

Zebratail lizard

North American puff adder

Cooler customers

Many amphibians are common in cooler, damper parts of the world. Amphibians like wet places. Most mate and lay their eggs in water.

As spring arrives, amphibians come out of hiding. The warmer weather sees many amphibians returning to the pond or stream where they were born. This may mean a very long journey through towns or over busy roads.

I DON'T BELIEVE IT!

Look out – frog crossing the road! In some countries, signs warn drivers of a very unusual 'hazard' ahead – frogs or toads travelling along the roads to return to breeding grounds.

When the weather turns especially cold, amphibians often hide away. They simply hibernate in the mud at the bottom of ponds or under stones and logs. This means that they go to sleep in the autumn, and don't wake up until spring!

▶ This aquatic, or water–living, salamander is called a mudpuppy. It lives in freshwater lakes, rivers and streams in North America.

Journeys to breeding grounds may be up to 5 kilometres long, a long way for an animal only a few centimetres in length! This is like a man walking to a pond 90 kilometres away without a map! The animals find their way by scent, landmarks, the Earth's magnetic field and the Sun's position.

243

Water babies

Amphibians live in water and on land. Most are born and grow up in fresh water such as ponds, pools, streams and rivers. They move onto dry land when they are adults and return to water to breed.

Adult toad

A froglet loses its tail and grows into an adult frog.

Frog spawn (eggs) float on top of fresh water

Tadpoles hatch from the eggs

Tadpoles grow legs and change into froglets

Adult newt

Feathery gills of the larva of the fire salamander

Most amphibians completely change their appearance as they grow. This kind of change is called metamorphosis.

The young of amphibians are called larvae. For example, tadpoles are the larvae of frogs and toads, and most newts and salamanders. Amphibian larvae can survive in water because they breathe through large, feathery flaps called gills that can take oxygen from the water.

▼ The axolotl lives only in Mexico, in the southern part of North America.

I DON'T BELIEVE IT!

The male South American Surinam toad is quite an acrobat. When mating underwater, he has to press the eggs onto his mate's back. The eggs remain there until they hatch.

The axolotl is an amphibian that has never grown up. This type of water-living salamander has never developed beyond the larval stage. It does, however, develop far enough to be able to breed.

The majority of amphibians lay soft eggs. These may be in a jelly-like string or clump of tiny eggs called spawn, as with frogs and toads. Newts lay their eggs singly.

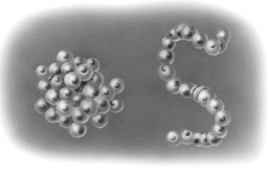

▲ Most amphibians lay their eggs in clumps or strings like these.

A few amphibians give birth to live young instead of laying eggs. The eggs of the fire salamander, for example, stay inside their mother, where the young hatch out and develop. She then gives birth to young that are much like miniature adults.

Land-lubbers

The majority of reptiles spend their whole lives away from water. They are very well adapted for life on dry land. Some do spend time in the water, but most reptiles lay their eggs on land.

▲ This female West African dwarf crocodile is laying her eggs in a hole, dug near to the water.

Most reptile eggs are much tougher than those of amphibians. This is because they must survive life out of the water. Lizards and snakes lay eggs with leathery shells. Crocodile and tortoise eggs have a hard shell rather like birds' eggs.

▲ Alligators lay their eggs in a mound of plants and earth. They lay between 35 and 40 eggs.

▲ A ground python's egg is large compared to its body. A female is about 85 centimetres long, and her eggs are about 12 centimetres long.

▲ A lizard called a Javan bloodsucker lays strange eggs like this. No one knows why their eggs are this very long and thin shape.

▲ Galapagos giant tortoises lay round eggs like this one. They will hatch up to 200 days after they were laid.

The eggs feed and protect the young developing inside them. The egg yolk provides food for the developing young, called an embryo. The shell protects the embryo from the outside world, but also allows vital oxygen into the egg.

INVESTIGATING EGGS

Reptile eggs are rather like birds' eggs. Next time you eat an omelette or boiled egg, rinse out half an empty eggshell, fill it with water, and wait a while. Do you see how no water escapes? Wash your hands well once you're done. Like this bird's eggshell, reptile eggshells stop the egg from drying out, although they let air in and are tough enough to protect the embryo.

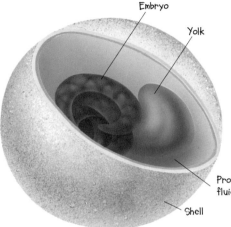

Embryo
Yolk
Protective fluid
Shell

◀ Slow worms are not worms at all. They are legless lizards that live in Europe, Africa and Asia. They are viviparous lizards, which means that they give birth to live young.

Young reptiles hatch out of eggs as miniature adults. They do not undergo a change, or metamorphosis, like amphibians do.

Some snakes and lizards, like slow worms, don't lay eggs. Instead, they give birth to fully developed live young. Animals that do this are called 'viviparous'.

Snake eggs left in the undergrowth

Little and large

Reptiles and amphibians come in every shape and size. There are more than 6500 species (types) of reptiles and 4000 species of amphibians. They range from tiny frogs to giant, dinosaur-like lizards.

Saltwater crocodile

Giant salamander

The largest reptile award goes to the saltwater crocodile from around the Indian and west Pacific Oceans. It measures a staggering 8 metres from nose to tail – an average adult man is not even 2 metres tall! Cold streams in Japan are home to the largest amphibian – a giant salamander that is around 1.5 metres long, and weighs up to 40 kilograms.

▲ The saltwater or estuarine crocodile lives in southern India, Indonesia and North Australia. It is the largest and one of the most dangerous species of crocodile. The giant salamander, though, is mostly harmless and feeds on snails and worms.

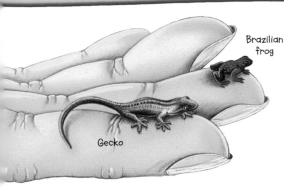

Brazilian frog

Gecko

The world's tiniest reptile is a gecko from the Caribbean Virgin Islands. This lizard measures under 20 millimetres long. A Brazilian frog is among the smallest of amphibians. Its body length is just 9.8 millimetres, that's almost small enough to fit on your thumbnail!

QUIZ

1. Where does the world's smallest reptile come from?

2. What kind of animal is the world's largest amphibian?

3. Where does the world's largest crocodile live?

4. Which group contains more species – reptiles or amphibians?

Answers:
1. The Caribbean Virgin Islands.
2. A Japanese salamander.
3. Australia and India
4. Reptiles.

▼ One type of giant tortoise comes from the Galapagos Islands in the Pacific Ocean, to the west of South America. The tortoise grows up to 1.2 metres long, and can weigh 215 kilograms.

Adaptable animals

Many species have amazing special adaptations to help them live safely and easily in their surroundings. Crocodiles, for example have a special flap in their throats which means that they can open their mouth underwater without breathing in water.

Geckos can climb up vertical surfaces or even upside down. They are able to cling on because they have five wide-spreading toes, each with sticky toe-pads, on each foot. These strong pads are covered with millions of tiny hairs that grip surfaces tightly.

Wide toe-pads covered with tiny hairs

▶ This is a tokay gecko from South and Southeast Asia. It is one of the most common geckos, and also one of the largest, measuring up to 28 centimetres long. It is usually easy to find them because they like to live around houses. The people of Asia and Indonesia believe that it is good luck for a gecko to come and live by or in their house!

Tortoises and turtles have hard, bony shells for protection. They form a suit of armour that protects them from predators (animals who might hunt and eat them) and also from the hot sun.

Chameleon

California newt

Chameleons have adapted very well to their way of life in the trees. They have long toes which can grip branches firmly, and a long tail that can grip branches like another hand. Tails that can grip like this are called 'prehensile'. Chameleons are also famous for being able to change their colour to blend in with their surroundings. This is called 'camouflage', and is something that many other reptiles and amphibians use.

The flattened tails of newts make them expert swimmers. Newts are salamanders that spend most of their lives in water, so they need to be able to get about speedily in this environment.

▶ This is a very close-up view of a small part of a gill. As water flows over the gills, oxygen can pass into the amphibian's blood.

water flows over the gills

READING ABOUT REPTILES

Pick a favourite reptile or amphibian and then find out as much as you can about it. List all the ways you think it is especially well adapted to deal with its lifestyle and habitat.

An amphibian's gills enable it to breathe underwater. Blood flows inside the feathery gills, at the same time as water flows over the outside. As the water flows past the gills, oxygen passes out of the water, straight into the blood of the amphibian.

251

Natural show-offs

▶ Cobras make themselves look more threatening by forming a wide hood of loose skin stretched over flexible ribs.

Certain reptiles and amphibians love to make a show of themselves. Some of this 'display' behaviour is used to attract females when the breeding season comes around. It is also used to make enemies think twice before pouncing.

◀ This great crested newt from Europe is showing its colours.

Male newts go to great lengths to impress during the mating season. Great crested newts develop frills along their backs, black spots over their skin, and a red flush across the breast. Their colourful spring coat also warns off enemies.

Anole lizard

The male anole lizard of Central and South America guards his territory and mates jealously. When rival males come too close, he puffs out a bright red throat pouch at them. Two males may face each other with inflated throats for hours at a time!

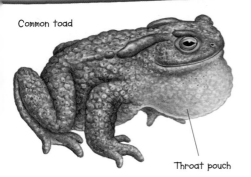

Common toad

Throat pouch

Some male Agamid lizards appear to impress females with a little body–building. They can be seen perched on top of rocks, doing push–ups and bobbing their heads up and down.

Many frogs and toads also puff themselves up. Toads can inflate their bodies to look more frightening. Frogs and toads can puff out their throat pouches. This makes their croaking love-calls to mates, and 'back off' calls to enemies, much louder.

A frilled lizard in full display is an amazing sight. This lizard has a large flap of neck skin that normally lies flat. When faced by a predator, it spreads this out to form a huge, stiff ruff that makes it look bigger and scarier!

▲ The frilled lizard lives in Australia and New Guinea. Its frill can be up to 25 centimetres across, almost half the length of its body!

Male monitor lizards have their own wrestling competitions! At the beginning of the mating season they compete to try to win the females. They rear up on their hind legs and wrestle until the weaker animal gives up.

253

Sensitive creatures

Reptiles and amphibians find out about the world by using their senses such as sight, smell and touch. Some animals have lost senses that they don't need. Worm-like amphibians called caecilians, for example, spend their whole lives underground, so they don't have any use for eyes. However, some animals have developed new senses which are very unusual!

▲ Pit vipers, such as rattlesnakes, can detect the heat given off by their prey even in complete darkness.

Frogs and toads have developed new senses. They have something called Jacobson's organ in the roofs of their mouths. This helps them to 'taste' and 'smell' the outside world. Jacobson's organ is also found in snakes and some lizards.

Snakes have poor hearing and eyesight but they make up for it in other ways. They can find prey by picking up its vibrations travelling through the ground. Some snakes have pits in their faces that detect heat given off by prey. In contrast to snakes, frogs and toads have large and well-developed eardrums and very good hearing.

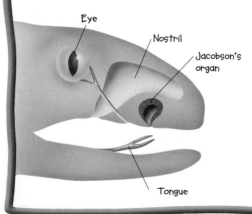

Eye

Nostril

Jacobson's organ

Tongue

Ear of American bullfrog

▼ The Fijian banded iguana lives on the islands of Fiji and Tonga in the Pacific Ocean.

I DON'T BELIEVE IT!

One African gecko has such thin skin over its ear-openings that if you were to look at it with the openings lined up precisely, you would see light coming through from the other side of its head!

Geckos and iguanas have large eyes and very good eyesight. They are a type of lizard that can't blink. Instead of having movable eyelids like humans, they have fixed, transparent 'spectacles' over their eyes. Most lizards have very good sight – they need it to hunt down their small and fast insect prey.

Large eyes give the gecko excellent vision.

Geckos lick their eyes to keep them clean.

▲ This is a web-footed gecko from southwest Africa. It lives in the Namib Desert, where it hardly ever rains. To get the water it needs, it licks dew from the stones, and also licks its own eyes!

255

Expert hunters

All amphibians and most reptiles are meat—eaters. They use a huge variety of ways to do their tracking, trapping and hunting.

▲ Crocodiles and alligators are specially adapted to be able to lie in the water with only their eyes and nostrils showing. They wait in shallow water for animals to come and drink, then leap up and drag their prey under the water.

Long, sticky tongue to catch insects

The chameleon lizard is a highly efficient hunting machine. Each eye moves separately from the other, so the chameleon can look in two directions at once. When a tasty fly buzzes past, the chameleon shoots out an incredibly long tongue in a fraction of a second and draws the fly back into its mouth.

Salamanders creep up slowly before striking. They move gradually towards prey and then suddenly seize it with their tongue or between their sharp teeth.

Crocodiles and snakes can open their fierce jaws extra wide to eat huge dinners! A snake can separate its jaw bones to eat huge eggs or to gulp down animals much larger than its head. A large snake can swallow pigs and deer – whole!

Skull

A snake's lower jaws can work separately. First one side pulls, and then the other, to draw the prey into the throat.

The snake's lower jaws can also detach from its skull to eat large prey.

BE A CHAMELEON!

Like a chameleon, you need two eyes to judge distances easily. Here's an experiment to prove it!

Close one eye. Hold a finger out in front of you, and with one eye open, try to touch this fingertip with the other. It's not as easy as it looks! Now open both eyes and you'll find it a lot easier!

Two eyes give your brain two slightly different angles to look at the object, so it is easier to tell how far away it is!

A snake has to swallow things whole. This is because it has no large back teeth for crushing prey and can't chew.

The chameleon's eyes can move independently to locate a tasty insect!

▶ Once the chameleon has spotted a tasty insect with one eye, it first has to swivel its other eye to look at the prey. This is because it is easier to judge distances with two eyes.

257

Fliers and leapers

Some reptiles and amphibians can take to the air – if only for a few seconds. This helps animals to travel further, escape predators or swoop down on passing prey before it gets away.

Even certain kinds of snake can glide. The flying snake lives in the tropical forests of southern Asia. It can jump between branches or glide through the air in 'S' movements.

▶ Flying snakes can glide between branches of trees to hunt lizards and frogs.

▶ The flying dragon lizard has taken things a step further than the geckos. Its 'wings' are skin stretched out over ribs that can even fold back when they are not in use!

◀ Flying geckos' skills are all important for food. Either they are trying to catch food, or they are trying to avoid becoming food for something else!

Gliding snakes fly by making their bodies into parachutes. They do this by raising their rib-cages so that their bodies flatten out like a ribbon.

Flying geckos form another group of natural parachutes. They have webbed feet and folds of skin along their legs, tail and sides, which together form the perfect gliding machine.

Some frogs can glide. Deep in the steamy rainforests of southeast Asia and South America, tree frogs flit from tree to tree. Some can glide as far as 12 metres, clinging to their landing spot with suckers on their feet.

Frogs and toads use their powerful hind legs for hopping or jumping. The greatest frog leaper comes from Africa. Known as the rocket frog, it has been known to jump up to 4.2 metres.

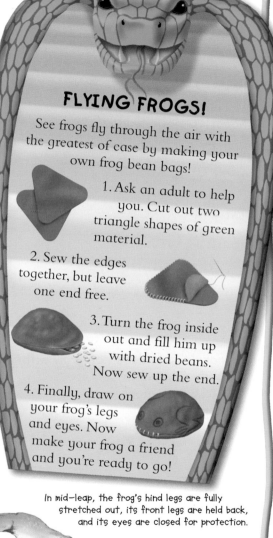

FLYING FROGS!

See frogs fly through the air with the greatest of ease by making your own frog bean bags!

1. Ask an adult to help you. Cut out two triangle shapes of green material.

2. Sew the edges together, but leave one end free.

3. Turn the frog inside out and fill him up with dried beans. Now sew up the end.

4. Finally, draw on your frog's legs and eyes. Now make your frog a friend and you're ready to go!

The powerful muscles in the frog's hind legs push off.

In mid–leap, the frog's hind legs are fully stretched out, its front legs are held back, and its eyes are closed for protection.

As it lands, its body arches and the front legs act as a brake.

Fast and slow

The reptile and amphibian worlds contain their fair share of fast and slow movers. But the slow-coaches are not necessarily at a disadvantage. A predator may be able to seize the slow-moving tortoise, but it certainly can't bite through its armour-plated shell!

▶ The sidewinder snake moves at up to 4 kilometres per hour over the shifting sands of its desert home.

Tortoises never take life in a hurry and are among the slowest animals on Earth. The top speed for a giant tortoise is 5 metres per minute! These giant tortoises live on the small Galapagos islands in the Pacific Ocean, and not anywhere else in the world.

▲ The giant tortoise is definitely a slow mover at only 0.3 kilometres per hour!

Chameleons are also slow—movers. They move slowly through the trees, barely noticeable as they hunt for insects.

▲ The chameleon is a very slow mover, until its tongue pops out to trap a passing fly!

▶ Tuataras live on a few small islands off the coast of New Zealand.

Some lizards can trot off at high speed by 'standing up'. Water dragon lizards from Asia can simply rear up onto their hind legs to make a dash for it – much faster than moving on four legs.

◄ The speedy crested water dragon can run on its back legs to escape predators.

FLAT RACE

Get together a group of friends and hold your own animal race day. Each of you cuts a flat animal shape – a frog or tortoise, say – out of paper or very light card. If you wish, add details with coloured pencils or pens. Now race your animals along the ground to the finishing line by flapping a newspaper or a magazine behind them.

One of the world's slowest animals is the lizard–like tuatara. When resting, it breathes just once an hour, and may still be growing when it is 60 years old! Their slow lifestyle in part means that they can live to be 120 years old! The tuatara is sometimes called a 'living fossil'. This is because it is the only living species of a group of animals that died out millions of years ago. No one knows why only the tuatara survives.

Racerunner lizards, from North and South America, are true to their name. The six-lined racerunner is the fastest recorded reptile on land. In 1941 in South Carolina, USA it was recorded reaching an amazing speed of 29 kilometres per hour!

◄ The six–lined racerunner from America is the fastest reptile on land.

263

Champion swimmers

Amphibians are well-known for their links with water, but some types of reptile are also aquatic (live in the water). Different types of amphibian and reptile have developed all kinds of ways of tackling watery lifestyles.

Hellbender

Rough-skinned newt

Eastern newt

Newts and salamanders swim rather like fish. They make an 'S'-shape as they move. Many have flat tails that help to propel them along in the water.

Great crested newt

Toads and frogs propel themselves by kicking back with their hind legs. They use their front legs as a brake for landing when they dive into the water. Large, webbed feet act like flippers, helping them to push through the water.

Frog draws its legs up

Pushes its feet out to the side

The main kick back with toes spread propels the frog forward through the water

Frog closes its toes and draws its legs in and up for the next kick

A swimming snake may seem unlikely, but most snakes are experts in the water. Sea snakes can stay submerged for five hours and move rapidly through the depths. European grass snakes are also good swimmers. They have to be because they eat animals that live around water.

I DON'T BELIEVE IT!

Floating sea snakes often find themselves surrounded by fish who gather at the snake's tail to avoid being eaten. When the snake fancies a snack, it swims backwards, fooling the unlucky fish into thinking its head is its tail!

Yellow-bellied sea snake

Paddle-like end to the tail

Banded sea snakes

The bands act like camouflage to help break up the outline of the snake's body.

Sea turtles have light, flat shells so they can move along more easily under water. Some have managed speeds of 29 kilometres per hour. Their flipper-like front legs 'fly' through the water. Their back legs form mini-rudders for steering.

▲ The Pacific ridley
turtle lives in warm waters all around the world.
It feeds on shrimp, jellyfish, crabs, sea-snails and fish.

265

Nature's tanks

Tortoises and turtles are like armoured tanks – slow but very well-protected by their shells. Tortoises live on land and eat mainly plants. Some turtles are flesh-eaters that live in the salty sea. Other turtles, some of which are called terrapins, live in freshwater lakes and rivers.

When danger threatens, tortoises can quickly retreat into their mobile homes. They simply draw their head, tail and legs into their shell.

Tortoises and turtles are ancient members of the reptile world. They are the oldest living reptiles, and might have been around with the very first dinosaurs, about 200 million years ago. They also live longer than almost any other animal – some for up to 150 years!

I DON'T BELIEVE IT!

A giant tortoise can support a one tonne weight. This means that it could be used as a jack, to lift up a car – but far kinder and easier simply to go to a local garage!

▶ The matamata turtle lives only in South America. It is one of the strangest of all turtles, as its head is almost flat, and is shaped like a triangle. It lies on the bottom of rivers and eats fish that swim past.

▶ The Indian softshell turtle is also called the narrow-headed turtle because of its long, thin head. It is a very fast swimmer that feeds on fish.

◀ The leopard tortoise lives in Africa. It was named after the yellow and black leopard-style markings of its shell.

▶ The hawksbill turtle lives in warm seas all around the world. Its beautiful shell means that it has been hunted so much that it has nearly died out. It is now protected in many countries.

Some sea turtles are among nature's greatest travellers. The green turtle migrates an amazing 2000 kilometres from its feeding grounds off the coast of Brazil to breeding sites such as Ascension Island, in the South Atlantic.

Green turtle

ATLANTIC OCEAN

AFRICA

Brazil

SOUTH AMERICA

Ascension Island

Dangerous enemies

Animals such as crocodiles, some snakes and snapping turtles make nasty enemies. Snakes are famed for poisoning or strangling prey before gobbling it down. Other reptiles have also found ways of making themselves especially dangerous.

▲ This rat snake has caught its prey, a small meadow vole. It then loops its body around the vole, and stops it breathing by holding it very tight.

▼ The alligator snapping turtle lives in deep rivers and lakes in the USA. To hunt, it opens its mouth so fish can see what looks like a worm, but is actually just bait. When fish come to investigate, the turtle snaps them up!

Bait

Venom
gland

Folding
fangs

Tube for venom
to be injected

**Poisonous snakes inject
venom (poison) into their prey.**
They do this through grooved or
hollow teeth called fangs. Rattlesnakes
are poisonous snakes with a rattle at
the end of their tail that they shake to
frighten predators. Constricting snakes
such as pythons coil themselves around
victims and squeeze them to death.

QUIZ

1. What are a snake's hollow teeth called?
2. What is the other name for snakes that strangle their prey?
3. Why do some amphibians have brightly patterned skin?
4. How did the arrow–poison frog earn its name?

Answers:
1. Fangs. 2. Constrictors.
3. To warn predators that they are poisonous.
4. Because native people tip their spears and arrows in its poison.

▼ The tiger salamander comes from North America. It is the largest land–living salamander in the world, growing up to 40 centimetres long.

▼ The gila monster from the desert areas of North America is one of only two venomous lizards in the world. The gila stores fat in its tail, to live off when it can't find food.

▶ This is the golden arrow–poison frog from Central and South America. It is so poisonous that the native people extract the venom to use on their arrow–tips.

Bright patterns on some amphibians' skin warn predators. Their skin may be foul-tasting or causes irritation. Arrow-poison frogs from South America's rainforests have very bright colours, while fire salamanders have bright yellow spots or stripes.

269

Clever mimics

From crocodiles and tortoises to lizards and frogs, reptiles and amphibians are masters of disguise. Some blend into their surroundings naturally, while others can change their appearance – perfect for avoiding predators or sneaking up on prey.

Green tree frog

Malaysian horned frog

Arum lily frog

Natal ghost frog

Frogs and toads are experts in the art of camouflage (blending with surroundings). Many are coloured shades of green or green-brown, to look just like leaves, grass or tree bark.

African clawed toad

Many lizards have green or brown camouflage colouring, too. The chameleon lizard can also change its colour. If it meets an enemy whilst it is walking along a branch, it can stay very still, crouch down and make itself look like the leaves and bark.

The fire-bellied toad has a bright red tummy! It uses it to distract its enemies. When it's threatened it leaps away to safety, and the quick flash of bright red confuses the attacker, and gives the frog an extra fraction of a second to escape.

▼ This European grass snake is pretending to be dead. It rolls over onto its back, wiggles as if dying, and then lies still with its mouth open and its tongue hanging out!

Some snakes can even pretend to be dead. They lie coiled up with their tongue hanging out, so that predators will look elsewhere for a meal.

The alligator snapper looks like a rough rock as it lies on the ocean floor. This cunning turtle has an extra trick up its sleeve. The tip of its tongue looks like a juicy worm, which it waves at passing prey to lure them into its jaws.

ANIMAL DISGUISE!

Make a mask of your favourite reptile or amphibian from a piece of card or a paper plate. Attach some string or elastic to hold it to your head, cut some eye-holes and then colour it all in. You could also try making felt finger puppets – and have a whole handful of reptiles!

Escape artists

Reptiles and amphibians form food for other animals. They have developed clever ways to escape predators and survive – at least long enough to grow up and breed.

Some salamanders and lizards have detachable tails. If a predator grabs a five-lined tree skink lizard by the tail, it will be left just holding a twitching blue tail! The tail does grow back.

The chuckwalla lizard gets itself into tight corners. It can jam itself into a rock crevice, then puff its body up so that predators cannot pull it out.

A young blue—tongued skink uses colour as a delay tactic. The lizard simply flashes its bright blue tongue and mouth lining at enemies. The startled predator lets its prey slip away.

The Australian shingleback lizard has a tail shaped like a head. By the time a confused predator has worked this one out, the lizard has made its getaway.

▲ The shingleback lizard, which end is its head?

Crocodiles can walk on their tails! If they are being threatened they can move so fast they almost leap out of the water! This is called 'tail-walking'.

Close relatives

An alligator isn't quite the same as a crocodile and a frog isn't quite the same as a toad. These pairs of animals are very similar, but they do have certain differences. If you look carefully, you will be able to spot the small differences between them.

▼ This Nile crocodile lives in Africa. It eats large mammals and birds which it catches from the water's edge while they drink.

Tooth showing

Pointed snout

Alligators are generally smaller than their relations the crocodiles. They have more rounded snouts and are only found in China and America. Crocodiles are larger, with pointed snouts. They also have two large teeth showing when their mouth is shut.

Shorter, more rounded snout

▼ Caimans are part of the same family as crocodiles and alligators, but are more closely related to alligators. The spectacled caiman gets its name from the ridge between its eyes. This looks like the bridge of a pair of spectacles!

▲ This American alligator lives in the the southeastern United States. It reaches up to 5.5 metres long.

Crocodiles and alligators also have some other, very special and rather surprising close relations. They are the closest living relatives of the dinosaurs! The dinosaurs were also reptiles that lived millions of years ago. No one knows why, but all of the dinosaurs died out about 65 million years ago. For some reason, certain other animals that were also around at this time, like crocodiles, alligators and also turtles, survived.

I DON'T BELIEVE IT!

Whether a baby alligator is a girl or boy depends on temperature. A boy will develop in a warm egg, but a girl will develop in a cold one. For crocodiles, it's the other way around!

Short skull

Long legs will become shorter as Protosuchus evolves.

▼ Protosuchus is one of the ancestors of the crocodiles. It lived about 225 million years ago during the Triassic Period. It had quite a short skull, which shows that it had not yet adapted fully for eating fish. It probably ate small lizards.

Most frogs live in damp places. Their bodies suit this environment. They tend to have strongly webbed feet, long back legs and smooth skin.

Tree frog

Most toads spend their time on dry land. They don't have strongly webbed feet and their skin is warty and quite dry. Toads are normally shorter and squatter than frogs, with shorter legs.

Giant toad

Scary monsters

Early explorers told amazing tales of dragons living in faraway lands that few people had visited. It may be that these explorers had somehow seen flying lizards or giant monitor lizards such as the Komodo dragon. Perhaps this is how myths about dragons started.

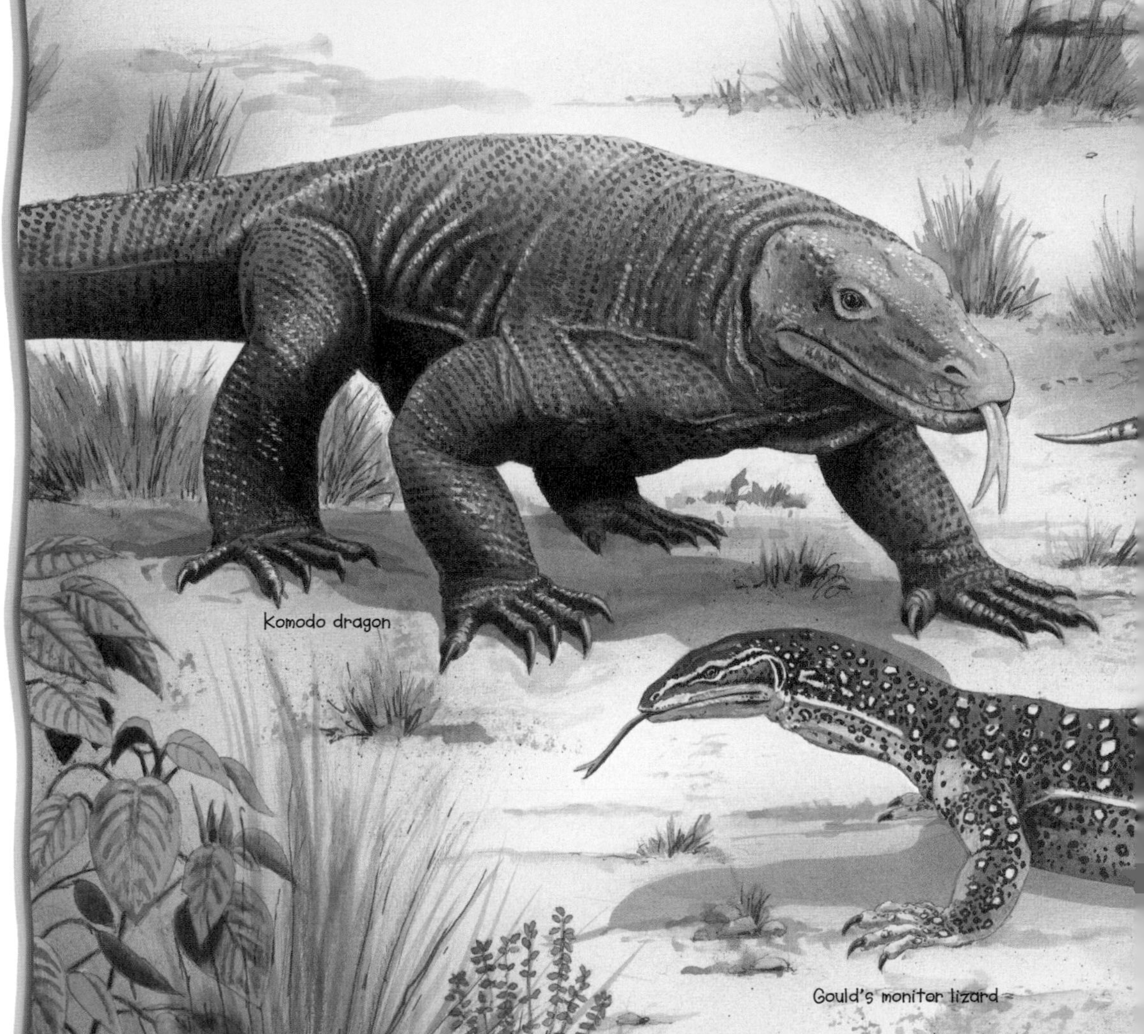

Komodo dragon

Gould's monitor lizard

Flying dragon

Nile monitor lizard

QUIZ

1. What is usually larger, a crocodile or an alligator?

2. Alligators have two large teeth showing when their mouth is shut. True or false?

3. What is the largest monitor lizard alive today?

Answers:
1. Crocodiles are usually larger. 2. False, crocodiles have their teeth showing. 3. The Komodo dragon

Monitor lizards are long-necked reptiles from Australia, Asia and Africa. The rare Komodo dragon is a monitor from a group of islands in Indonesia, southeast Asia. It is the largest, fiercest lizard alive, up to 4 metres long, weighing 140 kilograms and eating small deer and wild boar.

BIRDS

Explore the world of birds, and discover where
they live and how they raise their young.

Falcons • Roadrunners • Penguins • Gannets
Ostriches • Condors • Hummingbirds • Albatrosses
Peacocks • Birds of paradise • Nightingales • Owls
Eagles • Cuckoos • Geese • Ducks • Vultures • Kiwis
Ravens • Swans • Parrots • Emus • Kingfishers
Pelicans • Woodpeckers • Toucans • Flamingos

What are birds?

A bird has two legs, a pair of wings and a body that is covered with feathers. Birds are, perhaps, the animals we see most often in the wild. They live all over the world — everywhere from Antarctica to the hottest deserts and rainforests. They range in size from the huge ostrich, which stands 2.75 metres tall, a whole metre taller than a man, to the tiny bee hummingbird, which is scarcely bigger than a real bee.

Osprey

Greater flamingo

Mallard

Grey heron

Kingfisher

Greater
honeyguide

Helmeted
hornbill

Masai
ostrich

Lesser
green
broadbill

Blue
peafowl

Red-billed
hornbill

African
jacana

Blue-crowned
hanging parrot

The bird world

There are more than 9000 different types, or species, of bird. These have been organized by scientists into groups called orders, which contain many different species. The largest order is the passerines, also known as perching or song birds.

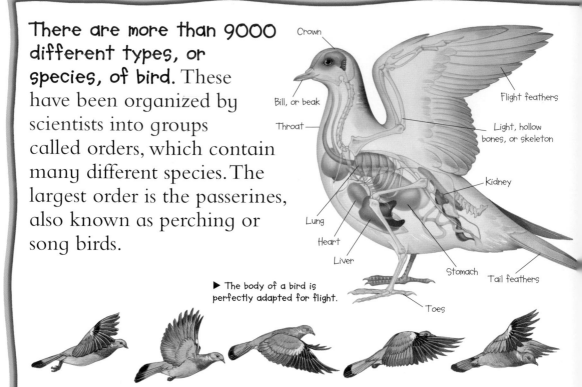

Crown

Bill, or beak

Throat

Lung

Heart

Liver

Flight feathers

Light, hollow bones, or skeleton

Kidney

Stomach

Tail feathers

Toes

▶ The body of a bird is perfectly adapted for flight.

▲ Most doves and pigeons are hunted by predators. Strong wing muscles, that make up a third of their weight, help them to take off rapidly and accelerate to 80 kilometres an hour.

Birds are the only creatures that have feathers. The feathers are made of keratin – the same material as our hair and nails. Feathers keep a bird warm and protect it from the wind and rain. Its wing and tail feathers allow a bird to fly. Some birds also have very colourful feathers which help them to attract mates or blend in with their surroundings. This is called camouflage.

▶ The bird with the most feathers is thought to be the whistling swan, with more than 25,000 feathers.

All birds have wings. These are the bird's front limbs. There are many different wing shapes. Birds that soar in the sky for hours, such as hawks and eagles, have long broad wings. These allow them to make the best use of air currents. Small fast-flying birds such as swifts have slim, pointed wings.

▶ The egg protects the growing young and provides it with food. While the young develops the parent birds, such as this song thrush, keep the egg safe and warm.

All birds lay eggs. It would be impossible for birds to carry their developing young inside their bodies like mammals do – they would become too heavy to fly.

All birds have a beak for eating. The beak is made of bone and is covered with a hard material called horn. Birds have different kinds of beak for different types of food. Insect-eating birds tend to have thin, sharp beaks for picking up their tiny prey. The short, strong parrot's beak is ideal for cracking hard-shelled nuts.

QUIZ

1. How many types of bird are there?

2. How many feathers does the whistling swan have?

3. What are feathers made of?

4. What is the largest order of birds called?

5. What sort of beaks do hunting birds have?

Answers:
1. More than 9000
2. More than 25,000 3. Keratin
4. The passerines
5. Powerful hooked beaks

◀ Hunting birds, such as this goshawk, have powerful hooked beaks for tearing flesh.

Little and large

The world's largest bird is the ostrich. This long-legged bird stands up to 2.75 metres tall and weighs up to 115 kilograms – twice as much as an average adult human. Males are slightly larger than females. The ostrich lives on the grasslands of Africa where it feeds on plant material such as leaves, flowers and seeds.

Ostrich

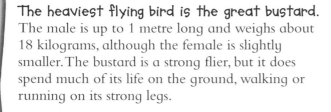

▼ The great bustard lives in southern Europe and parts of Asia.

The heaviest flying bird is the great bustard. The male is up to 1 metre long and weighs about 18 kilograms, although the female is slightly smaller. The bustard is a strong flier, but it does spend much of its life on the ground, walking or running on its strong legs.

Bee hummingbird

The bee hummingbird is the world's smallest bird. Its body, including its tail, is only about 5 centimetres long and it weighs only 2 grams – about the same as a small spoonful of rice. It lives on Caribbean islands and, like other hummingbirds, feeds on flower nectar.

The largest bird of prey is the Andean condor. A type of vulture, this bird measures about 110 centimetres long and weighs up to 12 kilograms. This huge bird of prey soars over the Andes Mountains of South America, hunting for food.

▼ Like most vultures, the condor is a scavenger. It looks for carrion, the carcasses of dead animals and the remains of other hunters' kills.

◀ The wandering albatross only comes to land at breeding time. It lays its eggs on islands in the South Pacific, South Atlantic and Indian Ocean.

QUIZ

1. How much does a bee hummingbird weigh?

2. Where do ostriches live?

3. What does the great bustard eat?

4. How long are the wandering albatross's wings?

5. Where does the collared falconet live?

Answers:
1. 2 grams 2. Africa
3. Insects and seeds 4. 3.3 metres
from tip to tip 5. India and
Southeast Asia

The wandering albatross has the longest wings of any bird. When outstretched, they measure as much as 3.3 metres from tip to tip. The albatross spends most of its life in the air. It flies over the oceans, searching for fish and squid which it snatches from the water surface.

Wilson's storm petrel

Wilson's storm petrel is the smallest seabird in the world. Only 16 to 19 centimetres long, this petrel hops over the water surface snatching up tiny sea creatures to eat. It is very common over the Atlantic, Indian and Antarctic Oceans.

The smallest bird of prey is the collared falconet. This little bird, which lives in India and Southeast Asia, is only about 19 centimetres long. It hunts insects and other small birds.

Collared falconet

Speedy movers

The fastest flying bird is the peregrine falcon. It hunts other birds in the air and makes spectacular high-speed dives to catch its prey. During a hunting dive, a peregrine may move as fast as 180 kilometres an hour. In normal level flight, it flies at about 95 kilometres an hour. Peregrine falcons live almost all over the world.

Ducks and geese are also fast fliers. Many of them can fly at speeds of more than 65 kilometres an hour. The red-breasted merganser and the common eider duck can fly at up to 100 kilometres an hour.

Sword–billed hummingbird

When this hummingbird lands, it has to tilt its head right back to support the weight of its huge bill

Tail feathers spread for landing

A hummingbird's wings beat 50 or more times a second as it hovers in the air. The tiny bee hummingbird may beat its wings at an amazing 200 times a second. When hovering, the hummingbird holds its body upright and beats its wings backwards and forwards, not up and down, to keep itself in one place in the air. The fast-beating wings make a low buzzing or humming sound that gives these birds their name.

FEED THE BIRDS!

In winter, food can be scarce for birds. You can make your own food cake to help them.

You will need:
225g of suet, lard or dripping
500g of seeds, nuts, biscuit crumbs, cake and other scraps

Ask an adult for help. First melt the fat, and mix it thoroughly with the seed and scraps. Pour it into an old yogurt pot or similar container, and leave it to cool and harden. Remove the cake from the container. Make a hole through the cake, put a string through the hole and hang it from a tree outside.

◄ The peregrine falcon does not just fold its wings and fall like many birds, it actually pushes itself down towards the ground. This powered dive is called a stoop.

The swift spends nearly all its life in the air and rarely comes to land. It can catch prey, eat, drink and mate on the wing. After leaving its nest, a young swift may not come to land again for two years, and may fly as far as 500,000 kilometres.

Swifts eat insects that they chase and catch in mid-air!

◄ The spine-tailed swift is thought to fly at speeds of up to 160 kilometres an hour.

Swifts have long, slim wings that are perfect for their life in the air.

The greater roadrunner is a fast mover on land. It runs at speeds of 20 kilometres an hour as it hunts for insects, lizards and birds' eggs to eat. It can fly but seems generally to prefer running.

Roadrunner

Superb swimmers

Penguins are the best swimmers and divers in the bird world. They live in and around the Antarctic, which is right at the very south of the world. They spend most of their lives in water, where they catch fish and tiny animals called krill to eat, but they do come to land to breed. Their wings act as strong flippers to push them through the water, and their tail and webbed feet help them steer. Penguins sometimes get around on land by tobogganing over ice on their tummies!

Emperor penguin

Gentoo penguin

The gentoo penguin is one of the fastest swimming birds. It can swim at up to 27 kilometres an hour – that's faster than most people can run! Mostly, though, penguins probably swim at about 5 to 10 kilometres an hour.

The gannet makes an amazing dive from a height of 30 metres above the sea to catch fish in the sea. This seabird spots its prey as it soars above the ocean. Then with wings swept back and neck and beak held straight out in front, the gannet plunges like a dive-bomber. It enters the water, seizes its prey and surfaces a few seconds later.

QUIZ

1. From how high does a gannet dive?

2. How many kinds of penguin are there?

3. How fast can a gentoo penguin swim?

4. How long can an emperor penguin stay underwater?

5. Where do most kinds of penguin live?

Answers:
1. 30 metres 2. 18
3. 27 kilometres an hour
4. 18 minutes 5. Antarctica

Northern gannet

▼ King penguins and emperor penguins regularly dive deeper than 250 metres. Emperor penguins have been timed making dives lasting more than 18 minutes.

King penguin

◄ There are about 18 different kinds of penguin. Most live in and around Antarctica.

289

Looking good!

At the start of the breeding season male birds try to attract females. Some do this by showing off their beautiful feathers. Others perform special displays or dances. The male peacock has a long train of colourful feathers. When female birds come near, he begins to spread his tail, showing off the beautiful eye-like markings. He dances up and down and shivers the feathers to get the females' attention.

The male bowerbird attracts a mate by making a structure of twigs called a bower. The bird spends many hours making it attractive, by decorating it with berries and flowers. Females choose the males with the prettiest bowers. After mating, the female goes away and makes a nest for her eggs. The male's bower is no longer needed.

The male roller performs a special display flight to impress his mate. Starting high in the air, he tumbles and rolls down to the ground while the female watches from a perch. Rollers are brightly coloured insect-eating birds that live in Africa, Europe, Asia and Australia.

Spotted bowerbird

Fawn breasted bowerbird

Black faced golden bowerbird

◀ Bowerbirds live in Australia and New Guinea.

▼ Female peacocks tend to choose the males with the most attractive feathers.

I DON'T BELIEVE IT!

Water birds called great crested grebes perform a courtship dance together. During the dance they offer each other gifts – beakfuls of water weed!

Cock-of-the-rock

The blue bird of paradise hangs upside-down to show off his wonderful feathers. As he hangs, his tail feathers spread out and he swings backwards and forwards while making a special call to attract the attention of female birds. Most birds of paradise live in New Guinea. All the males have beautiful plumage, but females are much plainer.

Blue bird of paradise

Male cock-of-the-rock dance to attract mates. Some of the most brightly coloured birds in the world, they gather in groups and leap up and down to show off their plumage to admiring females. They live in the South American rainforest.

The nightingale sings its tuneful song to attract females. Courtship is the main reason why birds sing, although some may sing at other times of year. A female nightingale chooses a male for his song rather than his looks.

Night birds

Some birds, such as the poorwill, hunt insects at night when there is less competition for prey. The poorwill sleeps during the day and wakes up at dusk to start hunting. As it flies, it opens its beak very wide and snaps moths out of the air.

▼ As well as moths, the poorwill also catches grasshoppers and beetles on the ground.

Barn owl

The barn owl is perfectly adapted for night-time hunting. Its eyes are very large and sensitive to the dimmest light. Its ears can pinpoint the tiniest sound and help it to locate prey. Most feathers make a sound as they cut through the air, but the fluffy edges of the owl's feathers soften the sound of wing beats so the owl can swoop silently on its prey.

The kakapo is the only parrot that is active at night. It is also a ground-living bird. All other parrots are daytime birds that live in and around trees. During the day the kakapo sleeps in a burrow or under a rock, and at night it comes out to find fruit, berries and leaves to eat. It cannot fly, but it can climb up into trees using its beak and feet. The kakapo only lives in New Zealand.

Kakapo

Like bats, the oilbird uses sounds to help it fly in darkness. As it flies, it makes clicking noises which bounce off objects in the caves in South America where it lives, and help the bird find its way. At night, the oilbird leaves its cave to feed on the fruits of palm trees.

Unlike most birds, the kiwi has a good sense of smell which helps it find food at night. Using the nostrils at the tip of its long beak, the kiwi sniffs out worms and other creatures hiding in the soil. It plunges its beak into the ground to reach its prey.

Kiwi

QUIZ

1. Where are the kiwi's nostrils?

2. Where does the kakapo live?

3. What does the oilbird eat?

4. What's special about the barn owl's feathers?

5. What kind of bird is a poorwill?

Answers:
1. At the end of its beak
2. New Zealand 3. The fruits of palm trees 4. They have fluffy edges
5. It is a type of nightjar

Home sweet home

Birds make nests in which to lay their eggs and keep them safe. The bald eagle makes one of the biggest nests of any bird. The nest is made of sticks and is built in a tall tree or on rocks. It is used year after year. It can grow as large as 2.5 metres across and 3.5 metres deep – big enough for several people to get into!

The female hornbill lays her eggs in prison! The male hornbill walls up his mate and her eggs in a tree hole. He blocks the entrance to the hole with mud, leaving only a small opening. The female looks after the eggs and the male brings food, passing it through the opening. Once the eggs hatch the female has to remain safely in the hole with her young for a few weeks while the male supplies food.

▲ The bald eagle lives in North America. In 1782 the United States adopted the bald eagle as its national bird.

The male weaver bird makes a nest from grass and stems. He knots and weaves the pieces together to make a long nest, which hangs from the branch of a tree. The nest makes a warm, cosy home for the eggs and young, and is also very hard for any predator to get into.

The male weaver bird twists strips of leaves around a branch or twig.

Then, he makes a roof, and an entrance so he can get inside!

When it's finished, the long entrance helps to provide a safe shelter for the eggs.

The cave swiftlet makes a nest from its own saliva or spit. It uses the spit as glue to make a cup-shaped nest of feathers and grass.

Cave swiftlet

The mallee fowl makes a temperature-controlled nest mound. It is made of plants covered with sand. As the plants rot, the inside of the mound gets warmer. The female bird lays her eggs in holes made in the sides of the mound. The male bird then keeps a check on the temperature with his beak. If the mound cools, he adds more sand. If it gets too hot he makes some openings to let warmth out.

Mallee fowl

The cuckoo doesn't make a nest at all – she lays her eggs in the nests of other birds! She lays up to 12 eggs, all in different nests. The owner of the nest is called the host bird. The female cuckoo removes one of the host bird's eggs before she puts one of her own in, so the number in the nest remains the same.

I DON'T BELIEVE IT!

Most birds take several minutes to lay an egg. The cuckoo can lay her egg in 9 seconds! This allows her to pop her egg into a nest while the owner's back is turned.

Great travellers

The Canada goose spends the summer in the Arctic and flies south in winter. This regular journey is called a migration. In summer, the Arctic bursts into bloom and there are plenty of plants for the geese to eat while they lay their eggs and rear their young. In autumn, when the weather turns cold, they migrate, this means they leave to fly to warmer climates farther south. This means that the bird gets warmer weather all year round.

▼ The Canada goose tends to return to its birthplace to breed.

▶ The Arctic tern travels farther than any other bird and sees more hours of daylight each year than any other creature.

The Arctic tern makes one of the longest migrations of any bird. It breeds in the Arctic during the northern summer. Then, as the northern winter approaches, the tern makes the long journey south to the Antarctic – a trip of some 15,000 kilometres – where it catches the southern summer. In this way the tern gets the benefit of long daylight hours for feeding all year round.

◄ The American golden plover is camouflaged in the tundra vegetation by the spectacular patterns on its back.

Every autumn, the American golden plover flies up to 12,800 kilometres from North to South America. It breeds on the North American tundra where it feasts on the insects that fill the air during the brief Arctic summer. When summer is over the plover flies to South America for the winter. This means it has plentiful food supplies all year round.

WHO GOES WHERE?

On this world map are the migration routes of the Canada goose, the Arctic tern and the American golden plover. Each one is a different colour. Can you work out which is which?

Green: American golden plover
Red: Arctic tern
Yellow: Canada goose
Answers:

Desert dwellers

Many desert birds have sandy—brown feathers to blend with their surroundings. This helps them hide from their enemies. The cream-coloured courser lives in desert lands in Africa and parts of Asia. It is hard to see on the ground, but when it flies, the black and white pattern on its wings makes it more obvious. So the courser runs around rather than fly. It feeds on insects and other creatures it digs from the desert sands.

▲ The elf owl is able to catch prey in its feet as it flies.

Cream—coloured courser

The elf owl makes its nest in a hole in a desert cactus. This prickly, uncomfortable home helps to keep the owl's eggs safe from enemies, who do not want to struggle through the cactus' spines. The elf owl is one of the smallest owls in the world and is only about 14 centimetres long. It lives in desert areas in the southwest of the USA.

Birds may have to travel long distances to find water in the desert. But this is not always possible for little chicks. To solve this problem, the male sandgrouse has special feathers on his tummy which act like sponges to hold water. He flies off to find water and thoroughly soaks his feathers. He then returns home where his young thirstily gulp down the water that he's brought.

◄ The sandgrouse lives throughout Asia, often in semi—desert areas.

The cactus wren eats cactus fruits and berries. This little bird hops about among the spines of cactus plants and takes any juicy morsels it can find. It also catches insects, small lizards and frogs on the ground. Cactus wrens live in the southwestern USA.

I DON'T BELIEVE IT!

The lammergeier vulture drops bones onto rocks to smash them into pieces. It then swallows the soft marrow and even splinters of bone, bit by bit. Powerful acids in the bird's stomach allow the bone to be digested.

The lappet–faced vulture scavenges for its food. It glides over the deserts of Africa and the Middle East, searching for dead animals or the left-overs of hunters such as lions. When it spots something, the vulture swoops down and attacks the carcass with its strong hooked bill. Its head and neck are bare so it does not have to spend time cleaning its feathers after feeding from a messy carcass.

▼ The lappet–faced vulture has very broad wings. These are ideal for soaring high above the plains of its African home, searching for food.

Staying safe

Birds have clever ways of hiding themselves from enemies. The tawny frogmouth is an Australian bird that hunts at night. During the day, it rests in a tree where its brownish, mottled feathers make it hard to see. If the bird senses danger it stretches itself, with its beak pointing upwards, so that it looks almost exactly like an old broken branch or tree stump.

Tawny frogmouth

If a predator comes too close to her nest and young, the female killdeer leads the enemy away by a clever trick. She moves away from the nest, which is made on the ground, making sure the predator has noticed her. She then starts to drag one wing as though she is injured and is easy prey. When she has led the predator far enough away from her young she suddenly flies up into the air and escapes.

▶ The killdeer lives in North America.

Guillemots find that there is safety in numbers. Thousands of these birds live together on cliff tops and rocks. They do not build nests but simply lay their eggs on the rock or bare earth. Most land hunters cannot reach the birds on these rocks, and any flying egg thieves are soon driven away by the mass of screeching, pecking birds.

I DON'T BELIEVE IT!

The guillemot's egg is pear-shaped with one end much more pointed than the other. This means that the egg rolls round in a circle if it is pushed or knocked, so does not fall off the cliff.

Safe and sound

A bird's egg protects the developing chick inside. The yellow yolk in the egg provides the baby bird with food while it is growing. Layers of egg white, called albumen, cushion the chick and keep it warm, while the hard shell keeps everything safe. The shell is porous – it allows air in and out so that the chick can breathe. The parent birds keep the egg warm in a nest. This is called incubation.

1. The chick starts to chip away at the egg.

The kiwi lays an egg a quarter of her own size. The egg weighs 420 grams – the kiwi only weighs 1.7 kilograms. This is like a new baby weighing 17.5 kilograms, most weigh about 3.5 kilograms.

The biggest egg in the world is laid by the ostrich. An ostrich egg weighs about 1.5 kilograms – an average hen's egg weighs only about 50 grams. The shell of the ostrich egg is very strong, measuring up to 2 millimetres thick.

The smallest egg in the world is laid by the bee hummingbird. It weighs about 0.3 grams. The bird itself weighs only 2 grams.

Bee hummingbird egg

Ostrich egg

2. The chick uses its egg tooth to break free.

3. The egg splits wide open.

4. The chick is able to wriggle free. Its parents will look after it for several weeks until it can look after itself.

The number of eggs laid in a clutch varies from 1 to more than 20. A clutch is the name for the number of eggs that a bird lays in one go. The number of clutches per year also changes from bird to bird. The grey partridge lays one of the biggest clutches, with an average of 15 to 19 eggs, and the common turkey usually lays 10 to 15 eggs. The emperor penguin lays one egg a year.

Common turkey

QUIZ

1. How thick is the shell of an ostrich egg?

2. How many eggs a year does the emperor penguin lay?

3. How much does the bee hummingbird's egg weigh?

4. For how long does the wandering albatross incubate its eggs?

5. For how long does the great spotted woodpecker incubate its eggs?

Answers:
1. 2 millimetres 2. One 3. 0.3 grams 4. up to 82 days 5. 10 days

The great spotted woodpecker incubates its egg for only 10 days. This is one of the shortest incubation periods of any bird. The longest incubation period is of the wandering albatross, which incubates its eggs for up to 82 days.

Jungle life

Birds of paradise are among the most colourful of all rainforest birds. Only the males have brilliant plumage and decorative feathers; the females are generally much plainer. There are about 42 different kinds of birds of paradise and they all live in the rainforests of New Guinea and northeast Australia. Fruit is their main food but some also feed on insects and spiders.

Harpy eagle

The Congo peafowl was only discovered in 1936. It lives in the dense rainforest of West Africa and has rarely been seen. The male bird has beautiful glossy feathers while the female is mostly brown and black.

Congo peafowl

Hoatzin

The harpy eagle is the world's largest eagle. It is about 90 centimetres long and has huge feet and long sharp claws. It feeds on rainforest animals such as monkeys and sloths, which it catches in the trees.

The hoatzin builds its nest overhanging water. If its chicks are in danger they can escape by dropping into the water and swimming to safety. This strange bird with its ragged crest lives in the Amazon rainforest in South America.

The quetzal has magnificent tail feathers which are up to 90 centimetres long. This beautiful bird lives in the rainforests of Central America. It was worshipped as a sacred bird by the ancient Mayan and Aztec people.

QUIZ

1. When was the Congo peafowl discovered?

2. How long are the quetzal's tail feathers?

3. How many kinds of birds of paradise are there?

4. Where does the scarlet macaw live?

5. How do the hoatzin's chicks escape danger?

Answers:
1. 1936 2. About 90 centimetres
3. About 42 4. South America 5. They
drop out of their nest into the water

Quetzal

The scarlet macaw is one of the largest parrots in the world. This spectacular bird is 85 centimetres long, including its very long tail and lives in the South American rainforest. It moves in flocks of 20 or so that screech loudly as they fly from tree to tree feeding on fruit and leaves.

Scarlet macaw

The junglefowl is the ancestor of the farmyard chicken. This colourful bird lives in the Southeast Asian rainforest, where it feeds on seeds and insects.

Junglefowl

The biggest birds

The fast-running emu is the largest bird in Australia. Like the ostrich it cannot fly, but it can run at speeds of more than 50 kilometres an hour on its long legs as it searches for fruit, berries and insects to eat. In the breeding season the female lays up to 10 eggs in a dip in the ground. The male then takes over and incubates the clutch.

Key
① Emu
② Bennet's Cassowary
③ Kwi
④ Cassowary

▼ These flightless birds are among the largest birds in the world.

▼ The ostrich is the world's fastest two-legged runner. It is specially adapted for speed, and can run at up to 70 kilometres an hour.

Very powerful upper leg muscles

Extra flexible knees

Long, strong legs

Bendy two-toed feet

The rhea lives on the grassy plains of South America. It is a fast-running bird but it cannot fly. It eats mainly grass and other small plants, but it also catches insects and other small creatures such as lizards. In the breeding season, male rheas fight to gather a flock of females. Once he has his flock, the male rhea digs a nest in the ground. Each of the females lays her eggs in this nest. The male incubates the eggs, and he looks after the chicks until they are about six months old.

▼ The rhea can sprint faster than a horse, reaching speeds of up to 50 kilometres an hour.

Cassowaries are flightless birds which live in the rainforests of Australia and New Guinea. There are three species – all are large birds with long, strong legs and big, sharp-clawed feet. On the cassowary's head is a large horny crest, called a casque. Experts think that when the bird is moving through the dense forest, it holds its head down and uses the casque to help it break its way through the tangle of plants.

④

③

I DON'T BELIEVE IT!

One rhea egg is the equivalent to about 12 hen's eggs. It has long been a tasty feast for local people.

Messing about on the river

The jacana can walk on water! It has amazingly long toes that spread the bird's weight over a large area and allow it to walk on floating lily pads as it hunts for food such as insects and seeds. Jacanas can also swim and dive. There are eight different types of jacana, also called lilytrotters. They live in parts of North and South America, Africa and Asia.

Kingfisher

The kingfisher makes its nest in a tunnel in a riverbank. Using their strong beaks, a male and female pair dig a tunnel up to 60 centimetres long and make a nesting chamber at the end. The female lays up to eight eggs which both parents take turns to look after.

Jacana

The heron catches fish and other water creatures. This long-legged bird stands on the shore or in shallow water and reaches forward to grab its prey with a swift thrust of its dagger-like beak.

Heron

A small bird called the dipper is well-adapted to river life. It usually lives around fast-flowing streams and can swim and dive well. It can even walk along the bottom of a stream, snapping up prey such as insects and other small creatures. There are five different types of dipper and they live in North and South America, Asia and Europe.

Dipper

The pelican collects fish in the big pouch that hangs beneath its long beak. When the pelican pushes its beak into the water the pouch stretches and fills with water – and fish. When the pelican then lifts its head up, the water drains out of the pouch leaving any food behind.

The pelican uses its pouch like a net to catch fish.

Osprey

The osprey is a bird of prey which feeds mainly on fish. This bird is found nearly all over the world near rivers and lakes. It watches for prey from the air then plunges into the water with its feet held out in front ready to grab a fish. Special spikes on the soles of its feet help it hold onto its slippery catch.

313

Can I have some more?

The woodpecker uses its special strong beak to bore into tree trunks and catch insects. The bird holds on tightly to a tree trunk with the help of its strong feet and sharp claws. Its stiff tail feathers also help to give it support. It starts to hammer into the trunk, disturbing wood-boring insects that live beneath the tree bark. The insects try to flee, but the woodpecker quickly snaps them up.

▶ There are more than 200 different kinds of woodpecker, including this Eurasian woodpecker. They live in North and South America, Africa, Europe and Asia.

The antbird keeps watch over army ants as they march through the forest. The bird flies just ahead of the ants and perches on a low branch. It then pounces on the many insects, spiders and other small creatures that try to escape from the marching column of ants. Some antbirds also eat the ants themselves. There are about 240 different types of antbirds that live in Central and South America.

Antbird

▼ Honeyguides have been known to lead honey–loving humans to bees' nests.

The honeyguide bird uses the honey badger to help it get food. The honeyguide feeds on bee grubs and honey. It can find the bees' nests but it is not strong enough to break into them. So it looks for the honey badger to help. It leads the badger toward the bees' nest. When the honey badger smashes into the nest, the honeyguide can also eat its fill.

The hummingbird feeds on flower nectar. Nectar is a sweet liquid made by flowers to attract pollinating insects. It is not always easy for birds to reach, but the hummingbird is able to hover in front of the flower while it sips the nectar using its long tongue.

Hummingbird

I DON'T BELIEVE IT!

The hummingbird has to eat lots of nectar to get enough energy to survive. If a human were to work as hard as a hummingbird, he or she would need to eat three times their weight in potatoes each day.

Snow and ice

The coldest places on Earth are the Arctic and the Antarctic. The Arctic is as far north as it is possible to go, and the Antarctic is south, at the bottom of the Earth. The snowy owl is one of the largest birds in the Arctic. Its white feathers hide it in the snow.

The snow bunting breeds on Arctic islands and farther north than any other bird. The female makes a nest of grasses, moss and lichens on the ground. She lays four to eight eggs and, when they hatch, both parents help to care for the young. Seeds, buds and insects are the snow bunting's main foods.

Sheathbills scavenge any food they can find. These large white birds live in the far south on islands close to the Antarctic. They do catch fish but they also search the beaches for any dead animals they can eat. They also snatch weak or dying young from seals and penguins.

Snowy sheathbill

Snowy owl

Snow bunting

The ptarmigan has white feathers in the winter to help it hide from enemies among the winter snows in the Arctic. But in summer its white plumage would make it very obvious, so the ptarmigan moults and grows brown and grey feathers.

Ptarmigan

Penguins have a thick layer of fat just under their skin to help protect them from the cold. Their feathers are waterproof and very tightly packed for warmth. Penguins live mainly in Antarctica, but some live in South Africa, South America and Australia.

QUIZ

All of these birds live in snow and ice, but some of them live in the north and some live in the south. Can you tell which live in the north, the Arctic, and which live in the south, the Antarctic?

Answers:
All belong in the north, the Arctic, except for the penguins and the snowy sheathbill which belong in the south, the Antarctic.

Emperor penguin

The tundra swan lays its eggs and rears its young in the tundra of the Arctic. The female bird makes a nest on the ground and lays up to five eggs. Both male and female care for the young. In autumn the whole family migrates, travels south to spend the winter in warmer lands.

Tundra swan

Special beaks

The snail kite feeds only on water snails and its long upper beak is specially shaped for this strange diet. When the kite catches a snail, it holds it in one foot while standing on a branch or other perch. It strikes the snail's body with its sharp beak and shakes it from the shell.

▼ The snail kite lives in the southern USA, and Central and South America, but it is now very rare.

Toco toucan

The wrybill is the only bird with a beak that curves to the right. The wrybill is a type of plover which lives in New Zealand. It sweeps its beak over the ground in circles to pick up insects.

Wrybill

The toco toucan's colourful beak is about 19 centimetres long. It allows the toucan to pick fruit and berries at the end of branches that it would not otherwise be able to reach. There are more than 40 different kinds of toucan, and all have large beaks of different colours. The colours and patterns may help the birds attract mates.

Black skimmer

The lower half of the skimmer's beak is longer than the upper half. This allows it to catch fish in a special way. The skimmer flies just above the water with the lower part of its beak below the surface. When it comes across a fish, the skimmer snaps the upper part of its beak down to trap the prey.

I DON'T BELIEVE IT!

The flamingo's legs may look as if they are back to front. In fact, what appear to be the bird's knees are really its ankles!

Flamingo

The crossbill has a very unusual beak which crosses at the tip. The shape of this beak allows the bird to open out the scales of pine cones and remove the seeds it feeds on.

Crossbill

The flamingo uses its beak to filter food from shallow water. It stands in the water with its head down and its beak beneath the surface. Water flows into the beak and is pushed out again by the flamingo's large tongue. Any tiny creatures such as insects and shellfish are trapped on bristles in the beak.

Birds and people

People buying and selling caged birds has led to some species becoming extremely rare. Some pet birds such as budgerigars are bred in captivity, but others such as parrots are taken from the wild, even though this is now illegal. The beautiful hyacinth macaw, which used to be common in South American jungles, is now rare because of people stealing them from the wild to sell.

Red-fan parrot

Hyacinth macaw

King parrot

In some parts of the world, people still keep falcons for hunting. The birds are kept in captivity and trained to kill rabbits and other animals, and bring them back to their master. When the birds are taken out hunting, they wear special hoods over their heads. These are removed when the bird is released to chase its prey.

Falcon

Many kinds of birds are reared for their eggs and meat. Chickens and their eggs are a major food in many countries, and ducks, geese and turkeys are also eaten. These are all specially domesticated species but some wild birds, such as pheasants, partridge and grouse, are also used as food.

Starlings

Starlings are very common city birds. Huge flocks are often seen gathering to roost, or sleep on buildings. Starlings originally lived in Europe and Asia but have been taken to other countries and been just as successful. For example, 100 years ago 120 starlings were released in New York. Now starlings are among the most common birds in North America. The starling is very adaptable. It will eat a wide range of foods including, insects, seeds and fruits, and will nest almost anywhere.

I DON'T BELIEVE IT!

In one city crows wait by traffic lights. When the lights are red they place walnuts in front of the cars. When the lights turn green the cars move over the nuts, breaking the shells. The birds then fly down and pick up the kernels!

MAMMALS

From mighty whales to tiny mice,
discover the fascinating world of mammals.

Skunks • Rhinos • Jaguars • Sloths • Rats • Koalas
Seals • Bears • Pandas • Hyenas • Mice • Porcupines
Lions • Meerkats • Camels • Tigers • Wolves
Elephants • Gorillas • Bats • Cheetahs • Hares
Chimpanzees • Otters • Raccoons • Anteaters
Zebras • Rabbits • Moles • Badgers

What are mammals?

Mammals are warm-blooded animals with a bony skeleton and fur or hair. Being warm-blooded means that a mammal can keep its body at a constant temperature, even if the weather is very cold. The skeleton supports the body and protects the delicate parts inside, such as the heart, lungs and brain. There is one sort of mammal you know very well, it's you!

African savanna elephant

Eurasian beaver

Meerkats

Eurasian otter

European water vole

Ch

Red panda

Greater
fruit bat

Lions

Greater
horseshoe
bat

Western tarsier

Racoon-dog

The mammal world

There are nearly 4500 different types of mammal. Most have babies which grow inside the mother's body. While a baby mammal grows, a special organ called a placenta supplies it with food and oxygen from the mother's body. These mammals are called placental mammals.

▼ This echidna is part of a group of mammals called monotremes. They do not give birth to live young – they lay eggs instead.

Not all mammals' young develop inside the mother's body. Two smaller groups of mammals do things differently. Monotremes, like platypuses and echidnas or spiny anteaters, lay eggs. The platypus lays her eggs in a burrow, but the echidna keeps her single egg in a special dip in her belly until it is ready to hatch.

Mammal mothers feed their babies on milk from their own bodies. The baby sucks this milk from teats on special mammary glands, also called udders or breasts, on the mother's body. The milk contains all the food the young animal needs to help it grow.

Duck-billed platypus

▲ Olive baboons live in Africa in groups called troops of between 20 and 150 animals.

QUIZ

1. How many types of mammal are there?
2. Which types of mammal lay eggs?
3. How big is a baby kangaroo when it is born?
4. What supplies food and oxygen to a baby mammal in the womb?

Answers:
1. nearly 4500 2. Platypus and echidnas
3. 2 centimetres 4. The placenta

Marsupials give birth to tiny young that finish developing in a pouch. A baby kangaroo is only 2 centimetres long when it is born. Tiny, blind and hairless, it makes its own way to the safety of its mother's pouch. Once there, it latches onto a teat in the pouch and begins to feed.

▲ The baby kangaroo stays in the pouch for about six months while it grows.

▲ Fallow deer have a good sense of smell, and excellent sight.

Most mammals have good senses of sight, smell and hearing. Their senses help them watch out for enemies, find food and keep in touch with each other. For many mammals, smell is their most important sense. Plant-eaters such as rabbits and deer sniff the air for signs of danger such as the scent of a predator.

Big and small

The blue whale is the biggest mammal and the largest animal ever known to have lived. It can measure more than 33.5 metres long – that's as long as seven family cars parked end to end – and weigh up to 190,000 kilograms. It spends all its life in the sea.

▼ Mammal species range from the giant blue whale to tiny shrews and bats. Here you can see the blue whale to scale with the largest land mammals, and a tiny human!

Blue whale:
33.5 metres long

Giraffe:
5.5 metres tall

Human:
1.7 metres tall

The elephant is the biggest land mammal. There are three kinds of elephant – the African savanna elephant, the African forest elephant, and the Asian. The African savanna is the biggest, a full-grown male may weigh as much as 7500 kilograms – more than a hundred adult people. It stands about 4 metres high at the shoulder. Elephants may eat more than 300 kilograms of leaves, twigs and fruit each day.

African savanna elephant

Gorilla

Gorillas are the biggest primates. Primates are the group of mammals to which chimpanzees and humans belong. A full-grown male gorilla is about 1.75 metres tall and weighs as much as 275 kilograms.

The giraffe is the tallest of all the mammals. A male giraffe is about 5.5 metres tall – that's more than three or four people standing on each other's shoulders. The giraffe lives in Africa, south of the Sahara desert. Its height helps it reach fresh juicy leaves at the tops of trees.

I DON'T BELIEVE IT!

The African elephant has the biggest nose in the mammmal world. A male's nose, or trunk, measures up to 2.5 metres long. Elephants use their trunks for gathering food, fighting and drinking, as well as for smelling.

Brown bear: 2.4 metres tall

African elephant: 4 metres tall

Hog–nosed bat

The capybara is the largest living rodent. Rodents are the group of mammals that include rats and mice. At about 1.3 metres long the capybara is a giant compared to most rodents. It lives around ponds, lakes and rivers in South America.

The smallest mammal in the world is the tiny hog–nosed bat. A full-grown adult's body is only 3 centimetres long. It weighs about 2 grams – less than a teaspoon of rice!

Capybara

The tiny mouse deer is only the size of a hare. Also known as the chevrotain, this little creature is only about 85 centimetres long and stands about 30 centimetres high at the shoulder. It lives in African forests.

329

Fast movers

The cheetah can run faster than any other animal. It can move at about 100 kilometres an hour, but it cannot run this fast for long. The cheetah uses its speed to catch other animals to eat. It creeps towards its prey until it is only about 100 metres away. Then it races towards it at top speed, ready for the final attack.

▲ The cheetah's long slender legs and muscular body help it to run fast. The long tail balances the body while it is running.

The red kangaroo is a champion jumper.
It can leap along at 40 kilometres an hour
or more. The kangaroo needs to be able to
travel fast. It lives in the dry desert lands of
Australia and often has to journey long
distances to find grass to eat and
water to drink.

▼ The pronghorn is one
of the fastest mammals in
North America. It has to
run to escape its enemies,
such as wolves.

▲ The red kangaroo can leap
9 or 10 metres in a single bound.

The pronghorn is slower than the
cheetah, but it can run for longer.
It can keep up a speed of 70 kilometres
an hour for about ten minutes.

Brown hare

Even the little
brown hare can
run at more than
70 kilometres an
hour. Its powerful
back legs help it
move fast enough
to escape enemies
such as foxes.

SPEED DEMONS!

How do you compare to the fastest
mammal on earth? Ask an adult to
measure how far you can run in 10
seconds. Times this by 6, and then times
the answer by 60 to find out how
many metres you can run in an hour.
If you divide this by 1000 you will get
your speed in kilometres per hour. You
will find it will be far less than the
cheetah's 100 kilometres per hour!

Swimmers and divers

Most swimming mammals have flippers and fins instead of legs. Their bodies have become sleek and streamlined to help them move through the water easily. Seals and sea lions have large, paddle-like flippers which they can use to drag themselves along on land, as well as for swimming power in water. Whales never come to land. They swim by moving their tails up and down and using their front flippers to steer.

◀ The narwhal is one of the strangest looking whales. One of its teeth grows out through a hole in its upper lip to form a tusk that grows up to 2.7 metres long. The narwhal lives in the Arctic Ocean, and can grow up to 6.1 metres long.

The killer whale can swim at 55 kilometres an hour. A fierce hunter, it uses its speed to chase fast-swimming prey such as squid, fish and seals. It sometimes hunts in groups and will even attack other whales. Killer whales live in all the world's oceans. Despite their name, they are the largest of the dolphin family. They grow up to 10 metres long and weigh as much as 9000 kilograms.

This fin is called the dorsal fin. On an adult male whale this fin alone is taller than a man, growing up to 2 metres high.

Killer whale

◄ The bowhead whale, also called the Greenland Right whale, lives in the Arctic Ocean. It grows up to 20 metres long, feeding on tiny creatures that it gets from the water using filters in its mouth called baleen.

QUIZ

1. How deep can a Weddell seal dive?
2. What is the layer of fat on a seal's body called?
3. How fast can a killer whale swim?
4. How do whales move their tails when they swim?

4. Up and down
3. 55 kilometres an hour
1. 600 metres or more 2. Blubber
Answers:

◄ The northern fur seal grows up to 1.8 metres long. It is unusual because its rear flippers are much larger for its size than other species of fur seal.

Weddell seal

▲ The harp seal lives in the Arctic Ocean. It grows to about the same size as a man, up to 1.9 metres. It feeds mainly on fish and shellfish, which it catches on long, deep dives.

The Weddell seal can dive deeper than any other seal. It goes down to depths of 600 metres or more in its search for cod and other fish. The Weddell seal can stay underwater for a long while, and dives of more than an hour have been timed. This seal lives in the icy waters of Antarctica. Its body is covered with a thick layer of fatty blubber which helps to keep it warm.

333

Fliers and gliders

Bats are the only true flying mammals. They zoom through the air on wings made of skin. These are attached to the sides of their body and supported by specially adapted, extra-long bones of the arms and hands. Bats generally hunt at night. During the day they hang upside down by their feet from a branch or cave ledge. Their wings are neatly folded at their sides or around their body.

▲ Fruit-eating bats, such as flying foxes, live in the tropics. They feed mostly on fruit and leaves.

There are more than 950 different types of bat. They live in most parts of the world, but not in colder areas. Bats feed on many different sorts of food. Most common are the insect-eating bats which snatch their prey from the air while in flight. Others feast on pollen and nectar from flowers. Flesh-eating bats catch fish, birds, lizards and frogs.

▲ True vampire bats feed only on the blood of other mammals!

Flying lemurs don't really fly – they just glide from tree to tree. They can glide distances of up to 130 metres with the help of flaps of skin at the sides of the body. When the flying lemur takes off from a branch it holds its limbs out, stretching the skin flaps so that they act like a parachute.

Other gliding mammals are the flying squirrels and gliders. All can glide from tree to tree, like the flying lemur, with the help of flaps of skin at the sides of the body. Flying squirrels live in North America and parts of Asia. Gliders are a type of possum and live in Australia and New Guinea.

I DON'T BELIEVE IT!

A vampire bat consumes about 26 litres of blood a year. That's about as much as the total blood supply of five human beings!

335

Life in snow and ice

The polar bear is the biggest land-based predator in the Arctic. It can run fast, swim well and even dives under the ice to hunt its main prey – ringed seals. It also catches seabirds and land animals such as the Arctic hare and reindeer. The polar bear's thick white fur helps to keep it warm – even the soles of its feet are furry.

▶ The polar bear has a diet that consists almost entirely of meat, feasting on seals, fish and the odd whale. This is unlike other species of bear, which eat mostly plant foods.

Musk ox

Caribou, also known as reindeer, feed in arctic lands. The land around the Arctic Ocean is called the tundra. In the short summer plenty of plants grow, the caribou eat their fill and give birth to their young. When summer is over the caribou trek up to 1000 kilometres south to spend the winter in forests.

The musk ox has a long shaggy outer coat to help it survive the arctic cold. A thick undercoat keeps out the damp. The musk ox eats grass, moss and lichen. In winter it digs through the snow with its hooves to reach its food.

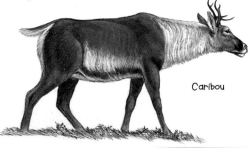

Caribou

The lemming builds its nest under the snow in winter. The nest is made on the ground from dry plants and twigs. The lemming makes tunnels under the snow from its nest to find grass, berries and lichen to eat. During the summer the lemming nests underground.

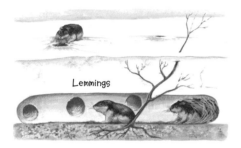

Lemmings

The walrus uses its long tusks for many tasks. They are used to drag itself out of water and onto the ice as well as for defending itself against enemies and rival walruses. The tusks can grow as much as 1 metre long.

Walrus

The leopard seal is the fiercest hunter in the Antarctic. It lives in the waters around Antarctica and preys on penguins, fish and even other seals. There are no land mammals in the Antarctic.

Leopard seal

Some arctic animals such as the Arctic hare and the ermine, or stoat, change colour. In winter these animals have white fur which helps them hide among the snow. In summer, when white fur would make them very easy to spot, their coats turn brown.

337

Creatures of the night

Not all mammals are active during the day. Some sleep during the daylight hours and wake up at night. They are called nocturnal mammals, and there are many reasons for their habits. Bats, for example, hunt at night to avoid competition with daytime hunters, such as eagles and hawks. At night, bats and owls have the skies to themselves.

The tarsier's big eyes help it to see in the dark. This little primate lives in Southeast Asian forests where it hunts insects at night. Its big eyes help it make the most of whatever glimmer of light there is from the moon. Like the bats, it probably finds there is less competition for its insect prey at night.

◀ The western tarsier is only 16 centimetres long, but its huge tail can be up to 27 centimetres long.

▼ Red pandas live in Asia, from the country of Nepal to Myanmar (Burma), and in Southwest China.

The red panda is a night feeder. It curls up in a tree and sleeps during the day, but at night it searches for food such as bamboo shoots, roots, fruit and acorns. It also eats insects, birds' eggs and small animals. In summer, though, red pandas sometimes wake up in the day and climb trees to find fresh leaves to eat.

Hyenas come out at night to find food. During the day they shelter underground. Hyenas are scavengers – this means that they feed mainly on the remains of creatures killed by larger hunters. When a lion has eaten its fill, the hyenas rush in to grab the remains.

Bats hunt at night. Insect feeders, such as the horseshoe bat, manage to find their prey by means of a special kind of animal sonar. The bat makes high-pitched squeaks as it flies. If the waves from these sounds hit an animal, such as a moth, echoes bounce back to the bat. These echoes tell the bat where its prey is.

Large ears hear the echoes

QUIZ

1. What do we call animals that come out only at night?
2. Where does the tarsier live?
3. What is a scavenger?
4. How does the horseshoe bat find its prey?
5. What does the red panda eat?

Answers:
1. Nocturnal 2. Southeast Asia 3. An animal that eats the remains of creatures killed by larger hunters. 4. By animal sonar. 5. Bamboo shoots, fruit, acorns, insects, birds' eggs

Busy builders

Beavers start their home building by damming a stream with branches, stones and mud. They do this to make a deep, quiet lake where they can make a winter food store and a shelter called a lodge. Once the dam is made they begin to build the lodge, usually a dome-shaped structure made of sticks and mud. In summer, beavers feed on twigs, leaves and roots. They also collect extra branches and logs to store for the winter.

The beaver gnaws the tree to fell it and eat the soft bark.

The entrance to the lodge is usually underwater but the single chamber inside is above water level.

READING MAMMALS!

You can make your own mammal bookmark! Ask an adult to help you cut a piece of white card about 4 centimetres wide by 15 centimetres long. Draw a picture of a mammal onto your piece of card and colour it in. Now you have a mammal to help you read!

The harvest mouse makes a nest on grass stems. It winds some strong stems round one another to make a kind of platform. She then weaves some softer grass stems into the structure to form a ball-like shape about 10 centimetres across.

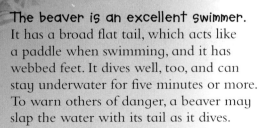

Harvest mouse

The beaver is an excellent swimmer. It has a broad flat tail, which acts like a paddle when swimming, and it has webbed feet. It dives well, too, and can stay underwater for five minutes or more. To warn others of danger, a beaver may slap the water with its tail as it dives.

Family life

Many mammals live alone, except when they have young, but others live in groups. Wolves live in family groups called packs. The pack is led by an adult female and her mate and may include up to 20 other animals.

◀ Grooming is an important part of pack life The more superior members are groomed by the lower ranking wolves.

Lions live in groups called prides. The pride may include one or more adult males, females related to each other, and their young. The average number in a pride is 15. Female young generally stay with the pride of their birth but males must leave before they are full-grown. Lions are unusual in their family lifestyle – all other big cats live alone.

▶ The male lion is considerably bigger than the female. He has shaggy neck fur called a mane.

Meerkats

A type of mongoose called a meerkat lives in large groups of up to 30 animals. The group is called a colony and contains several family units of a pair of adults along with their young. The colony lives in a network of underground burrows. The members of the colony guard each other against enemies.

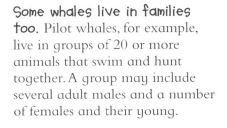

I DON'T BELIEVE IT!

Lions may be fierce but they are also very lazy. They sleep and snooze for more than 20 hours of the day!

Naked mole rats live underground in a colony of animals led by one female. The colony includes about 100 animals and the ruling female, or queen, is the only one that produces young. Other colony members live like worker bees – they dig the burrows to find food for the group, and look after the queen.

Some whales live in families too. Pilot whales, for example, live in groups of 20 or more animals that swim and hunt together. A group may include several adult males and a number of females and their young.

The male elephant seal fights rival males to gather a group of females. This group is called a harem and the male seal defends his females from other males. The group does not stay together for long after mating.

◄ The burrowing mole rat has powerful front legs and claws which it uses to tunnel through the earth.

Desert dwellers

Many desert animals burrow underground to escape the scorching heat. The North African gerbil, for example, stays hidden all day and comes out at night to find seeds and insects to eat. This gerbil is so well adapted to desert life that it never needs to drink. It gets all the liquid it needs from its food.

North African gerbils

▼ Most camels are kept by people in the desert, but some still live wild.

The large ears of the fennec fox help it to lose heat from its body. This fox lives in the North African desert. For its size, it has the largest ears of any dog or fox.

Fennec fox

A camel can last for weeks without drinking water. It can manage on the liquid it gets from feeding on desert plants. But when it does find some water it drinks as much as 80 litres at one time. It does not store water in its hump, but it can store fat.

The bactrian camel has thick fur to keep it warm in winter. It lives in the Gobi Desert in Asia where winter weather can be very cold indeed. In summer, the camel's long shaggy fur drops off, leaving the camel almost hairless.

The kangaroo rat never needs to drink. A mammal's kidneys control how much water there is in the animal's body. The kangaroo rat's kidneys are much more efficient than ours. It can even make some of its food into water inside its body!

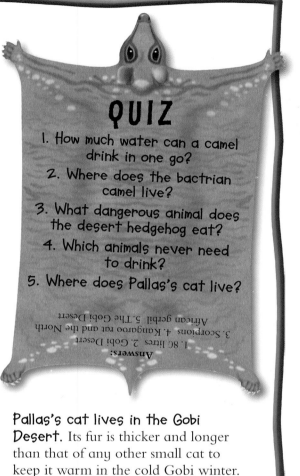

▶ The kangaroo rat is named because it has long, strong back legs and can jump like a kangaroo.

QUIZ

1. How much water can a camel drink in one go?
2. Where does the bactrian camel live?
3. What dangerous animal does the desert hedgehog eat?
4. Which animals never need to drink?
5. Where does Pallas's cat live?

Answers:
1. 80 litres 2. Gobi Desert
3. Scorpions 4. Kangaroo rat and the North African gerbil 5. The Gobi Desert

The desert hedgehog eats scorpions as well as insects and birds' eggs. It carefully nips off the scorpion's deadly sting before eating.

Pallas's cat lives in the Gobi Desert. Its fur is thicker and longer than that of any other small cat to keep it warm in the cold Gobi winter. Pallas's cat lives alone, usually in a cave or a burrow and hunts small creatures such as mice and birds.

Pallas cat

▲ The desert hedgehog digs a short, simple burrow into the sand. It stays there during the day to escape the heat.

On the prowl

Mammals that hunt and kill other creatures are called carnivores. Examples of carnivores are animals such as lions, tigers, wolves and dogs. Meat is a more concentrated food than plants so many carnivores do not have to hunt every day. One kill will last them for several days.

▶ Most carnivores will hunt creatures smaller than themselves. The tiger can more easily catch and kill smaller prey like this water deer.

The tiger is the biggest of the big cats and an expert hunter. It hunts alone, often at night, and buffalo, deer and wild pigs are its usual prey. The tiger cannot run fast for long so it prefers to creep up on its prey without being noticed. Its stripy coat helps to keep it hidden among long grasses. When it is as close as possible to its prey, the tiger makes a swift pounce and kills its victim with a bite to the neck. The tiger clamps its powerful jaws around the victim's throat and suffocates it.

MAKE A FOOD CHAIN

Draw a picture of a large carnivore such as a lion and tie it to a piece of string. Then draw a picture of an animal that the lion catches such as a zebra. Hang that from the picture of the lion. Lastly draw a picture of lots of grass and plants (the food of the zebra). Hang that from the picture of the zebra.

Brown bear

Bears eat many different sorts of food. They are carnivores but most bears, except for the polar bear, eat more plant material than meat. Brown bears eat fruit, nuts and insects and even catch fish. In summer, when salmon swim up rivers to lay their eggs, the bears wade into the shallows and hook fish from the water with their mighty paws.

Hunting dogs hunt in packs. Together, they can bring down a much larger animal. The pack sets off after a herd of plant-eaters such as zebras or gazelles. They try to separate one animal that is perhaps weaker or slower from the rest of the herd.

Hunting dogs

Fighting back

Some animals have special ways of defending themselves from deadly enemies. The nine-banded armadillo protects itself with its body armour. Strong plates made of bone, topped with a layer of horn, cover the armadillo's back, sides and head. Its legs and belly are left unprotected, but if it is attacked the armadillo rolls itself up into tight ball.

Nine-banded armadillo

The skunk defends itself with a bad-smelling fluid. This fluid comes from special glands near the animal's tail. If threatened, the skunk lifts its tail and sprays its enemy. The fluid's strong smell irritates the victim's eyes and makes it hard to breathe, and the skunk runs away.

Porcupine

Skunk

The porcupine's body is covered with as many as 30,000 sharp spines. When an enemy approaches, the porcupine first rattles its spines as a warning. If this fails, the porcupine runs towards the attacker and drives the sharp spines into its flesh.

A rhinoceros may charge its enemies at top speed. Rhinoceroses are generally peaceful animals but a female will defend her calf fiercely. If the calf is threatened, she will gallop towards the enemy with her head down and lunge with her sharp horns. Few predators will stay around to challenge an angry rhino.

I DON'T BELIEVE IT!

Smelly skunks sometimes feed on bees. They roll the bees on the ground to remove their stings before eating them.

Pangolin

▲ The sight of a full-grown rhinoceros charging is enough to make most predators turn and run.

The pangolin's body is protected by tough overlapping scales. These make the animal look rather like a giant pinecone. The pangolin feeds mainly on ants and termites and its thick scales protect it from the stinging bites of its tiny prey.

Deep in the jungle

Jungle mammals live at all levels of the forest from the tallest trees to the forest floor. Bats fly over the tree tops and monkeys and apes swing from branch to branch. Lower down, smaller creatures, such as civets and pottos, hide among the dense greenery.

Moustached bat

Angwantibo

Pygmy chimpanzee

Gorilla

Talapoin

Jaguar

Giant armadillo

Civet

The jaguar is one of the fiercest hunters in the jungle. It lives in the South American rainforest and is the largest cat in South America. The pig-like peccary and the capybara – a large jungle rodent – are among its favourite prey.

The howler monkey has the loudest voice in the jungle. Each troop of howler monkeys has its own special area, called a territory. Males in rival troops shout at each other to defend their territory. Their shouts can be heard from nearly 5 kilometres away.

The sloth hardly ever comes down to the ground. This jungle creature lives hanging from a branch by its special hook-like claws. It is so well adapted to this life that its fur grows downwards – the opposite way to that of most mammals – so that rainwater drips off more easily.

I DON'T BELIEVE IT!

The sloth is the slowest animal in the world. In the trees it moves along at only about 5 metres a minute. On the ground it moves even more slowly – about 2 metres a minute!

Two-toed sloth

Some monkeys, such as the South American woolly monkey, have a long tail that they use as an extra limb when climbing. This is called a prehensile tail. It contains a powerful system of bones and muscles so it can be used for gripping.

Tapirs are plump pig-like animals which live on the jungle floor. There are three different kinds of tapir in the South American rainforests and one kind in the rainforests of Southeast Asia. Tapirs have long bendy snouts and they feed on leaves, buds and grass.

▼ This Brazilian tapir is often found near water and is a good swimmer.

Okapi

The okapi uses its long tongue to pick leaves from forest trees. This tongue is so long that the okapi can lick its own eyes clean! The okapi lives in the African rainforest.

Strange foods

Some mammals only eat one or two kinds of food. The giant panda, for instance, feeds mainly on the shoots and roots of the bamboo plant. It spends up to 12 hours a day eating, and gobbles up about 12 kilograms of bamboo a day. The panda also eats small amounts of other plants such as irises and crocuses, and very occasionally hunts small creatures such as mice and fish. Giant pandas live in the bamboo forests of central China.

▼ People used to think that vampire bats sucked blood up through fangs. Now we know that they lap like a cat.

▲ There are very few giant pandas left in the wild. Their homes are being cut down, which leaves them with little to eat.

The vampire bat feeds only on blood – it is the only bat which has this special diet. The vampire bat hunts at night. It finds a victim such as a horse or cow and crawls up its leg onto its body. The bat shaves away a small area of flesh and, using its long tongue, laps up the blood that flows from the wound. The vampire bat feeds for about 30 minutes, and probably drinks about 26 litres of blood a year.

Tiny ants and termites are the main foods of the giant anteater. The anteater breaks open the insects' nests with its strong hooked claws. It laps up huge quantities of the creatures, their eggs and their young with its long tongue. This tongue is about 60 centimetres long and has a sticky surface that helps the anteater to catch the insects.

Giant anteater

The mighty blue whale eats only tiny shrimp-like creatures called krill. The whale strains these from the water through a special filter system in its mouth called baleen. It may eat up to 4 tonnes of krill a day.

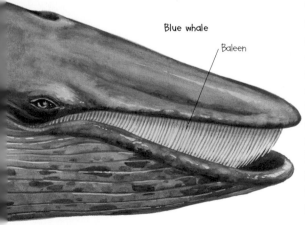

Blue whale

Baleen

QUIZ

1. From how far away can you hear a howler monkey?

2. How fast does a sloth move along the ground?

3. Some monkeys have tails they can grip with. What is the word for them?

4. How much bamboo does a giant panda eat in a day?

5. What does the koala eat?

6. How long is an anteater's tongue?

Answers:
1. Nearly 5 kilometres 2. About 2 metres per minute 3. Prehensile 4. About 12 kilograms 5. Eucalyptus leaves 6. 60 centimetres

The koala eats the leaves of eucalyptus plants. These leaves are very tough and can be poisonous to many other animals. They do not contain much goodness and the koala has to eat for several hours every day to get enough food. It spends the rest of its time sleeping to save energy. The koala's digestive system has adapted to help it cope with this unusual diet.

Koala

Tool users

The chimpanzee is one of the few mammals to use tools to help it find food. It uses a stone like a hammer to crack nuts, and uses sticks to pull down fruit from the trees and for fighting. It also uses sticks to help catch insects.

▶ The chimp pokes a sharp stick into a termite or ant nest. It waits a moment or two and then pulls the stick out, covered with juicy insects which it can eat.

▶ Chimps have also discovered that leaves make a useful sponge for soaking up water to drink or for wiping their bodies. Scientists think that baby chimps are not born knowing how to use tools. They have to learn their skills by watching adults at work.

The sea otter uses a stone to break open its shellfish food. It feeds mainly on sea creatures with hard shells, such as mussels, clams and crabs. The sea otter lies on its back in the water and places a rock on its chest. It then bangs the shellfish against the rock until the shell breaks, allowing the otter to get at the soft meat inside.

▶ The sea otter spends most of its life in the waters of the North Pacific and is an expert swimmer and diver.

The cusimanse is a very clever kind of mongoose. It eats frogs, reptiles, mammals and birds, but it also eats crabs and birds' eggs. When it comes across a meal that is protected by a tough shell, it throws it back between its hind legs against a stone or tree to break it open and get at the tasty insides!

Cusimanse

ANIMAL POSTERS

Take a sheet of paper and trace as many predators from this book as you can find. Colour them in and put a big heading – PREDATORS. Take another sheet and trace all the plant-eaters you can find. Put a big heading – PLANT-EATERS.

PREDATORS   PLANT-EATERS

City creatures

Foxes are among the few large mammals which manage to survive in towns and cities. Once foxes found all their food in the countryside, but now more and more have discovered that city rubbish bins are a good hunting ground. The red fox will eat almost anything. It kills birds, rabbits, eats insects, fruit and berries and takes human leavings.

Fox

Raccoons also live in city areas and raid rubbish bins for food. Like foxes, they eat lots of different kinds of food, including fish, nuts, seeds, berries and insects, as well as what they scavenge from humans. They are usually active at night and spend the day in a den made in a burrow, a hole in rocks or even in the corner of an empty city building.

Rat

Raccoon

Rats and mice are among the most successful of all mammals. They live all over the world and they eat almost any kind of food. The brown rat and the house mouse are among the most common. The brown rat eats seeds, fruit and grain, but it will also attack birds and mice. In cities it lives in cellars and sewers, anywhere there is rotting food and rubbish. The house mouse hides under floors and in cupboards. It will eat any human food it can find, as well as paper, glue and even soap!

I DON'T BELIEVE IT!

Rats will eat almost anything. They have been known to chew through electrical wires, lead piping and even concrete dams. In the United States rats are said to cause up to 1 billion dollars' worth of damage every year!

Fresh water mammals

Most river mammals spend only part of their time in water. Creatures such as the river otter and the water rat live on land and go into the water to find food. The hippopotamus, on the other hand, spends most of its day in water to keep cool. Its skin needs to stay moist, and it cracks if it gets too dry.

▶ The hippo is not a good swimmer but it can walk on the riverbed. It can stay underwater for up to half an hour.

Webbed feet make the water rat a good swimmer. They help the rat push its way through water. Other special features for a life spent partly in water include its streamlined body and small ears.

Water rat

Water opossum

The water opossum is the only marsupial that lives in water. Found around lakes and streams in South America, it hides in a burrow during the day and dives into the river at night to find fish.

▼ When a platypus has found its food, it stores it in its cheeks until it has time to eat it.

The platypus uses its duck-like beak to find food in the riverbed. This strange beak is extremely sensitive to touch and to tiny electric currents given off by prey. The platypus dives down to the bottom of the river and digs in the mud for creatures such as worms and shrimps.

QUIZ

1. When are city foxes most active?
2. Do raccoons eat only seeds and berries?
3. What are the most common types of rats and mice?
4. Which is the only marsupial that lives in water?
5. What does the platypus eat?
6. Where do river dolphins live?
7. How does the water rat swim?

Answers:
1. At night 2. No, they also eat fish, nuts and insects 3. Brown rats and house mice 4. Water opossum 5. Worms, shrimps and snails 6. Asia and South America 7. With the help of its webbed feet

Eurasian otter

Most dolphins are sea creatures but some live in rivers. There are five different kinds of river dolphins living in rivers in Asia and South America. All feed on fish and shellfish. They probably use echolocation, a kind of sonar like that used by bats, to find their prey.

The river otter's ears close off when it is swimming. This stops water getting into them when the otter dives. Other special features are the otter's webbed feet, and its short, thick fur, which keeps its skin dry.

▲ The Ganges dolphin is blind but can find food by skilful use of echolocation.

359

Plant-eaters

Plant-eaters must spend much of their time eating in order to get enough nourishment. A zebra spends at least half its day munching grass. The advantage of being a plant-eater, though, is that the animal does not have to chase and compete for its food like hunters do.

▲ Zebras are fast runners and are capable of outrunning most of their predators, sometimes at speeds of up to 60 kilometres an hour.

Some kinds of bat feed on pollen and nectar. The Queensland blossom bat, for example, has a long brush-like tongue which it plunges deep into flowers to gather its food. As it feeds it pollinates the flowers – it takes the male pollen to the female parts of a flower so that it can bear seeds and fruits.

Queensland blossom bat

Rabbits have strong teeth for eating leaves and bark. The large front teeth are called incisors and they are used for biting leaves and chopping twigs. The incisors keep growing throughout the rabbit's life – if they did not they would soon wear out. Farther back in the rabbit's mouth are broad teeth for chewing.

Rabbit

I DON'T BELIEVE IT!

Manatees are said to have been the origin of sailors' stories about mermaids. Short–sighted sailors may have mistaken these plump sea creatures for beautiful women.

The manatee is a water–living mammal which feeds on plants. There are three different kinds of these large, gentle creatures: two live in fresh water in West Africa and in the South American rainforest, and the third lives in the west Atlantic, from Florida to the Amazon.

Plants are the main foods of most monkeys. Monkeys live in tropical forests where there are plenty of fresh leaves and ripe fruit all year round. Some will also eat insects and other small creatures.

Manatee

Dugong

◀ Manatees, and their relations dugongs, feed on plants such as water weeds, water lilies and seaweeds.

White–cheeked mangabey

361

Digging deep

Champion burrowers of the mammal world are prairie dogs. These little animals are not dogs at all but a kind of plump short-tailed squirrel. There are five different species, all of which live in North America. They live in large burrows, which contain several chambers linked by tunnels.

▲ A family of prairie dogs is called a coterie and contains about 8 animals – a male, several females and young. A large number of coteries live close to each other in huge colonies, called 'towns', which may cover hundreds of kilometres. Prairie dogs feed on grass and other plants.

Moles have specially adapted front feet for digging. The feet are very broad and are turned outwards for pushing through the soil. They have large strong claws. The mole has very poor sight. Its sense of touch is very well developed and it has sensitive bristles on its face.

European mole

Badgers dig a network of chambers and tunnels called a sett. There are special areas in the sett for breeding, sleeping and food stores. Sleeping areas are lined with dry grass and leaves which the badgers sometimes take outside to air for a while.

▼ Badgers usually stay in the burrow during the day and come out at dusk. They are playful creatures and adults are often seen chasing and even leapfrogging with their cubs.

Mothers and babies

Most whales are born tail first. If the baby emerged head first it could drown during the birth process. As soon as the baby has fully emerged, the mother, with the help of other females, gently pushes it up to the surface to take its first breath. The female whale feeds her baby on milk, just like other mammals.

A baby panda weighs only about 100 grams at birth – that's about as big as a white mouse. It is tiny compared to its mother, who may weigh 100 kilograms or more. The newborn cub is blind and helpless, with a thin covering of white fur. By four weeks it has black and white fur like an adult, and its eyes open when it is two to three months old. It starts to walk when it is about four months and begins to eat bamboo at six months.

Giant panda and cub

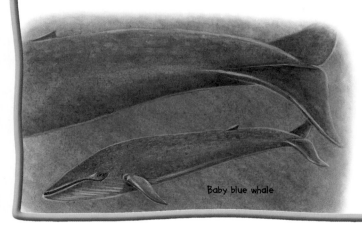

Baby blue whale

The blue whale has a bigger baby than any other mammal. At birth the baby is about 7 metres long and weighs 2000 kilograms – that's more than 30 average people. It drinks as much as 500 litres of milk a day!

Some babies have to be up and running less than an hour after birth. If the young of animals such as antelopes were as helpless as the baby panda they would immediately be snapped up by predators. They must get to their feet and be able to move with the herd as quickly as possible or they will not survive.

QUIZ

1. Where do prairie dogs live?
2. What is the name for the tunnels that badgers dig?
3. How much does a baby blue whale weigh?
4. How long is an elephant's pregnancy?
5. How many babies does the Virginia opossum have?
6. How much does a baby panda weigh?

Answers:
1. North America 2. A sett 3. 2000 kilograms 4. 20-21 months 5. up to 21 babies 6. 100 grams

Virginia opossum

Babies in mother's pouch

The female elephant has the longest pregnancy of any mammal. She carries her baby for 20 to 21 months. The calf weighs about 100 kilograms when it is born. It can stand up soon after the birth and run around after its mother when it is a few days old.

The Virginia opossum has as many as 21 babies at one time – more than any other mammal. The young are only a centimetre long, and all of the babies together weigh only a couple of grams.

SCIENCE

Take a look at how we use science, and why new
machines and inventions affect how we live.

Machines • Fireworks • Heat • Internet • Transport
Sound waves • Light • Lenses • Lasers • Magnets
Electricity • Computers • Electric motors
Materials • Chemicals • Elements • Atoms
Scientists • Medicine • Recycling

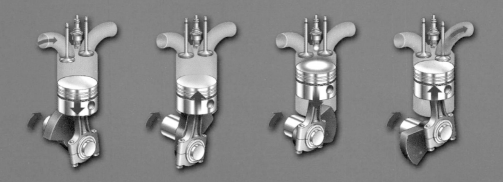

Why do we need science?

Even one hundred books like this could not explain all the reasons why we need science. Toasters, bicycles, mobile phones, computers, cars, light bulbs – all the gadgets and machines we use every day are the results of scientific discoveries. Houses, skyscrapers, bridges and rockets are built using science. Our knowledge of medicines, nature, light and sound comes from science. Then there is the science of predicting the weather, investigating how stars shine, finding out why carrots are orange…

▶ In a big city, almost every vehicle, building, machine and gadget is based on science and technology.

Machines big and small

Machines are everywhere! They help us do things, or make doing them easier. Every time you play on a see-saw, you are using a machine! A lever is a stiff bar that tilts at a point called the pivot or fulcrum. The pivot of the see-saw is in the middle. Using the see-saw as a lever, a small person can lift a big person by sitting further from the pivot.

The screw is another simple but useful scientific machine. It is a ridge, or thread, wrapped around a bar or pole. It changes a small turning motion into a powerful pulling or lifting movement. Wood screws hold together furniture or shelves. A car jack lets you lift up a whole car.

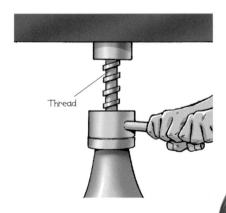

Thread

▲ On a see-saw lever, the pivot is in the middle. Other levers have pivots at the end.

Where would you be without wheels? Not going very far. The wheel is a simple machine, a circular disc that turns around its centre on a bar called an axle. Wheels carry heavy weights easily. There are giant wheels on big trucks and trains and small wheels on rollerblades.

Axle

▶ A car's rear wheels are turned by axles.

▶ Gears change the turning direction of a force. They can slow it down or speed it up – and even convert it into a sliding force (rack and pinion).

Reversing gears   Pinion gear

Sliding rack

Bevel gears

Slow pinion gear

Slow worm gear

▲ Two pulleys together reduce the force needed to lift a heavy girder by one half.

A pulley turns around, like a wheel.

It has a groove around its edge for a cable or rope. Lots of pulleys allow us to lift very heavy weights easily. The pulleys on a tower crane can lift huge steel girders to the top of a skyscraper.

Lever

Pivot

Gears are like wheels, with pointed teeth around the edges.

They change a fast, weak turning force into a slow, powerful one – or the other way around. On a bicycle, you can pedal up the steepest hill in bottom (lowest) gear, then speed down the other side in top (highest) gear.

I DON'T BELIEVE IT!

A ramp is a simple machine called an inclined plane. It is easier to walk up a ramp than to jump straight to the top.

When science is hot!

Fire! Flames! Burning! Heat! The science of heat is important in all kinds of ways. Not only do we cook with heat, but we also warm our homes and heat water. Burning happens in all kinds of engines in cars, trucks, planes and rockets. It is also used in factory processes, from making steel to shaping plastics.

Heat moves by conduction. A hot object will pass on, or transfer, some of its heat to a cooler one. Dip a metal spoon in a hot drink and the spoon handle soon warms up. Heat is conducted from the drink, through the metal.

▲ A firework burns suddenly as an explosive, with heat, light and sound... BANG!

◀ Metal is a good conductor of heat. Put a teaspoon in a hot drink and feel how quickly it heats up.

Heat moves by invisible 'heat rays'. This is called thermal radiation and the rays are infrared waves. The Sun's warmth radiates through space as infrared waves, to reach Earth.

Burning, also called combustion, is a chemical process. Oxygen gas from the air joins to, or combines with, the substance being burned. The chemical change releases lots of heat, and usually light too. If this happens really fast, we call it an explosion.

Temperature is the amount of heat in a substance. It is usually measured in degrees Celsius, °C. Water freezes into ice at 0°C, and boils into steam at 100°C. We take temperatures using a device called a thermometer. Your body temperature is probably about 37°C.

▶ A thermometer may be filled with alcohol and red dye. As the temperature goes up, the liquid rises up its tube to show how hot it is. It sinks back down if the temperature falls.

CARRYING HEAT

You will need:

wooden ruler   metal spoon
plastic spatula   heatproof jug
frozen peas   some butter

Find a wooden ruler, a metal spoon and a plastic spatula, all the same length. Fix a frozen pea to one end of each with butter. Put the other ends in a heatproof jug. Ask an adult to fill the jug with hot water. Heat is conducted from the water, up the object, to melt the butter. Which object is the best conductor?

Heat moves by convection, especially through liquids and gases. Some of the liquid or gas takes in heat, gets lighter and rises into cooler areas. Then other, cooler, liquid or gas moves in to do the same. You can see this as 'wavy' hot air rising from a flame.

▶ See how hot air shimmers over a candle.

Engine power

Imagine having to walk or run everywhere, instead of riding in a car. Engines are machines that use fuel to do work for us and make life easier. Fuel is a substance that has chemical energy stored inside it. The energy is released as heat by burning or exploding the fuel in the engine.

Fan sucks air in

Air is squashed by turbines

Jet fuel is sprayed onto air, and small explosion happens

Most cars have petrol engines. A mixture of air and petrol is pushed into a hollow chamber called the cylinder. A spark from a spark plug makes it explode, which pushes a piston down inside the cylinder (see below). This movement is used by gears to turn the wheels. Most cars have four or six cylinders.

A diesel engine works in a similar way, but without sparks. The mixture of air and diesel is squashed so much in the cylinder that it becomes hot enough to explode. Diesel engines are used where lots of power is needed, in trucks, diggers, tractors and big trains.

▼ This shows the four-stroke cycle of a petrol engine.

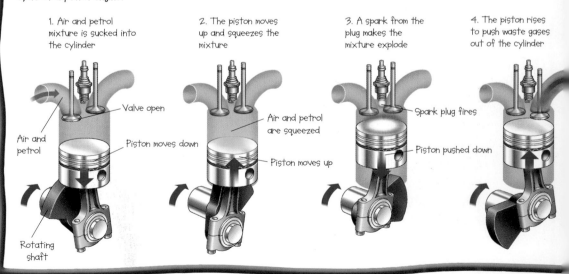

1. Air and petrol mixture is sucked into the cylinder

2. The piston moves up and squeezes the mixture

3. A spark from the plug makes the mixture explode

4. The piston rises to push waste gases out of the cylinder

Valve open

Air and petrol

Piston moves down

Air and petrol are squeezed

Piston moves up

Spark plug fires

Piston pushed down

Rotating shaft

▼ Jet engines are very powerful. They use a mixture of air and fuel to push the plane forward at high speed.

A jet engine mixes air and kerosene and sets fire to it in one long, continuous, roaring explosion. Incredibly hot gases blast out of the back of the engine. These push the engine forward – along with the plane.

An electric motor passes electricity through coils of wire. This makes the coils magnetic, and they push or pull against magnets around them. The push-pull makes the coils spin on their shaft (axle).

Gases roar past exhaust turbines

Hot gases rush out of the engine

Afterburner adds more roaring gases

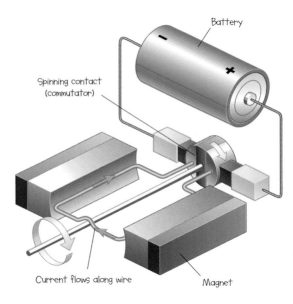

Battery

Spinning contact (commutator)

Current flows along wire

Magnet

QUIZ

What type of engine is found in these vehicles. Is it a jet engine, an electric motor, a petrol engine or a diesel one?

1. Cable–car
2. Formula 1 racing car
3. Fork–lift truck
4. Land–speed record car

Answers:
1. Electric motor
2. Petrol engine
3. Diesel engine 4. Jet engine

Engines which burn fuel give out gases and particles through their exhausts. Some of these gases are harmful to the environment. The less we use engines, the better. Electric motors are quiet, efficient and reliable, but they still need fuel – to make the electricity at the power station.

Science on the move

Without science, we would have to walk everywhere, or ride a horse. Luckily, scientists and engineers have developed many methods of transport, most importantly, the car. Lots of people can travel together in a bus, train, plane or ship. This uses less energy and resources, and makes less pollution.

Passenger terminal

Underground trains to take passengers to and from the terminal

Science is used to stop criminals. Science-based security measures include a 'door frame' that detects metal objects like guns and a scanner which sees inside bags. A sniffer-machine (or dog) can detect the smell of explosives or illegal drugs.

Jetways are extending walkways that stretch out like telescopic fingers, right to the plane's doors. Their supports move along on wheeled trolleys driven by electric motors.

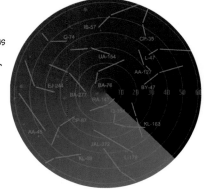

► The radar screen shows each aircraft as a blip, with its flight number or identity code.

◄ Modern airports are enormous. They can stretch for several miles, and they have a constant flow of planes taking off and landing. Hundreds of people are needed to make sure that everything runs smoothly and on time.

Jetway

Every method of transport needs to be safe and on time. In the airport control tower, air traffic controllers track planes on radar screens. They talk to pilots by radio. Beacons send out radio signals, giving the direction and distance to the airport.

On the road, drivers obey traffic lights. On a railway network, train drivers obey similar signal lights of different colours, such as red for stop. Sensors by the track record each train passing and send the information by wires or radio to the control room. Each train's position is shown as a flashing light on a wall map.

▼ Train signals show just two colours – red for stop and green for go.

D-27

Noisy science

Listening to the radio or television, playing music, shouting at each other – they all depend on the science of sound – acoustics. Sounds are like invisible waves in the air. The peak (highest point) of the wave is where a region of air is squashed under high pressure. The trough (lowest point) of the wave is a region where air is expanded under low pressure.

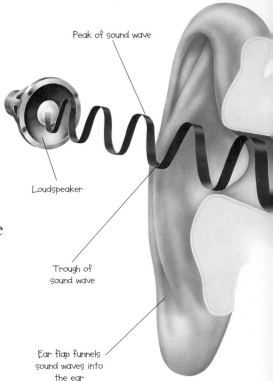

Peak of sound wave

Loudspeaker

Trough of sound wave

Ear flap funnels sound waves into the ear

Scientists measure the loudness or intensity of sound in decibels, dB. A very quiet sound like a ticking watch is 10 dB. Ordinary speech is 50-60 dB. Loud music is 90 dB. A jet plane taking off is 120 dB. Too much noise damages the ears.

▲ We cannot see sound waves but we can certainly hear them. They are ripples of high and low pressure in air.

◄ The decibel scale measures the intensity, or energy, in sound.

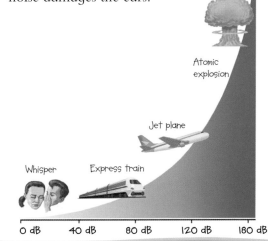

Atomic explosion

Jet plane

Whisper   Express train

| 0 dB | 40 dB | 80 dB | 120 dB | 180 dB |

Whether a sound is high or low is called its pitch, or frequency. It is measured in Hertz, Hz. A singing bird or whining motorcycle has a high pitch. A rumble of thunder or a massive truck has a low pitch. People can hear frequencies from 25 to 20,000 Hz.

Tiny bones
carry vibrations

Cochlea
(fluid filled chamber)

Sound waves vibrate
through fluid

Ear drum
vibrates

Sound waves travel about 330 metres every second. This is fast, but it is one million times slower than light waves. Sound waves also bounce off hard, flat surfaces. This is called reflection. The returning waves are heard as an echo.

Loudspeakers change electrical signals into sounds. The signals in the wire pass through a wire coil inside the speaker. This turns the coil into a magnet, which pushes and pulls against another magnet. The pushing and pulling make the cone vibrate, which sends sound waves into the air.

Sound waves spread out from a vibrating object that is moving rapidly to and fro. Stretch an elastic band between your fingers and twang it. As it vibrates, it makes a sound. When you speak, vocal cords in your neck vibrate. You can feel them through your skin.

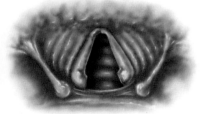

◄ The vocal cords are tough flaps in your voicebox, in your neck.

BOX GUITAR
You will need:
a shoebox   an elastic band
split pins   some card

Cut a hole about 10 centimetres across on one side of an empy shoebox. Push split pins through either side of the hole, and stretch an elastic band between them. Pluck the band. Hear how the air and box vibrate. Cover the hole with card. Is the 'guitar' as loud?

Look out – light's about!

Almost everything you do depends on light and the science of light, which is called optics. Light is a form of energy that you can see. Light waves are made of electricity and magnetism – and they are tiny. About 2000 of them laid end to end would stretch across this full stop.

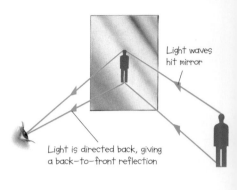

Light waves hit mirror

Light is directed back, giving a back-to-front reflection

▲ Light waves bounce off a mirror.

▼ A prism of clear glass or clear plastic separates the colours in white light.

Like sound, light bounces off surfaces which are very smooth. This is called reflection. A mirror is smooth, hard and flat. When you look at it, you see your reflection.

Ordinary light from the Sun or from a light bulb is called white light. But when white light passes through a prism, a triangular block of clear glass, it splits into seven colours. These colours are known as the spectrum. Each colour has a different length of wave. A rainbow is made by raindrops which work like millions of tiny prisms to split up sunlight.

Light passes through certain materials, like clear glass and plastic. Materials which let light pass through, to give a clear view, are transparent. Those which do not allow light through, like wood and metal, are opaque.

► Glass and water bend, or refract, light waves. This makes a drinking straw look bent where it goes behind the glass and then into the water.

Mirrors and lenses are important parts of many optical (light–using) gadgets. They are found in cameras, binoculars, microscopes, telescopes and lasers. Without them, we would have no close-up photographs of tiny microchips or insects or giant planets – in fact, no photos at all.

Light does not usually go straight through glass. It bends slightly where it goes into the glass, then bends back as it comes out. This is called refraction. A lens is a curved piece of glass or plastic that bends light to make things look bigger, smaller or clearer. Spectacle and contact lenses bend light to help people see more clearly.

▼ A concave lens, which is thin in the middle, makes things look smaller.

▲ A convex lens, which bulges in the middle, makes things look larger.

I DON'T BELIEVE IT!

Light is the fastest thing in the Universe. It travels through space at 300,000 kilometres per second. That's seven times around the world in less than one second!

The power of lasers

Laser light is a special kind of light. Like ordinary light, it is made of waves, but there are three main differences. First, ordinary white light is a mixture of colours. Laser light is just one pure colour. Second, ordinary light waves have peaks (highs) and troughs (lows), which do not line up with each other – laser light waves line up perfectly. Third, an ordinary light beam spreads and fades. A laser beam does not. It can travel for thousands of kilometres as a strong, straight beam.

To make a laser beam, energy is fed in short bursts into a substance called the active medium. The energy might be electricity, heat or ordinary light. In a red ruby laser, the active medium is a rod of ruby crystal. A strong lamp makes the tiny particles in the crystal vibrate. They give off energy, which bounces to and fro inside the crystal, off the mirrors at each end. Eventually, the rays vibrate with each other and they are all the same length. The energy becomes so strong that it bursts through a mirror at the end of the crystal.

Part–silver mirror

Silver mirror

Laser beam emerges

Particles in ruby crystal

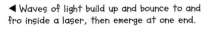

◀ Waves of light build up and bounce to and fro inside a laser, then emerge at one end.

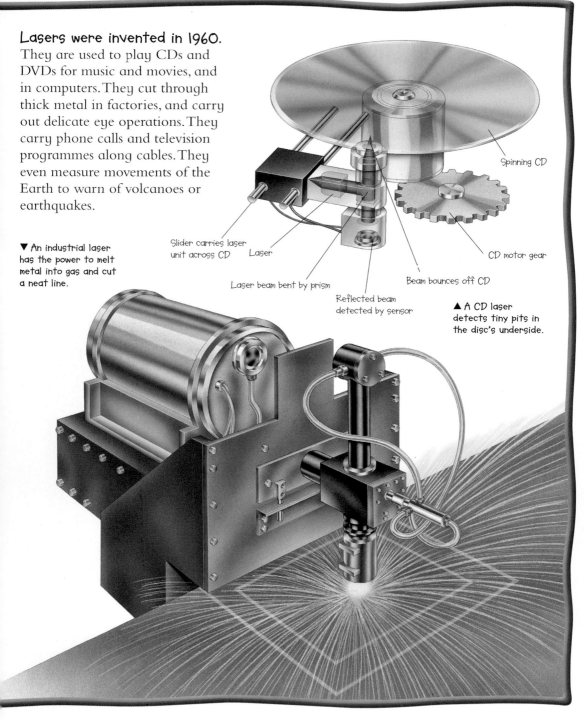

Lasers were invented in 1960.
They are used to play CDs and DVDs for music and movies, and in computers. They cut through thick metal in factories, and carry out delicate eye operations. They carry phone calls and television programmes along cables. They even measure movements of the Earth to warn of volcanoes or earthquakes.

▼ An industrial laser has the power to melt metal into gas and cut a neat line.

Spinning CD

Slider carries laser unit across CD

Laser

CD motor gear

Laser beam bent by prism

Beam bounces off CD

Reflected beam detected by sensor

▲ A CD laser detects tiny pits in the disc's underside.

383

Mystery magnets

Without magnets there would be
no electric motors, computers or
loudspeakers. Magnetism is an invisible
force to do with atoms – tiny particles
that make up everything. Atoms are
made of even smaller particles, including
electrons. Magnetism is linked to the
way that these line up and move. Most
magnetic substances contain iron. As
iron makes up a big part of the metallic
substance steel, steel is also magnetic.

▼ An electromagnet
attracts the body of
a car, which is made
of iron-based steel.

A magnet is a lump of iron or steel which has all
its electrons and atoms lined up. This means that
their magnetic forces all add up. The force surrounds
the magnet, in a region called the magnetic field.
This is strongest at the two parts of the magnet called
the poles. In a bar or horseshoe magnet, the poles are
at the ends.

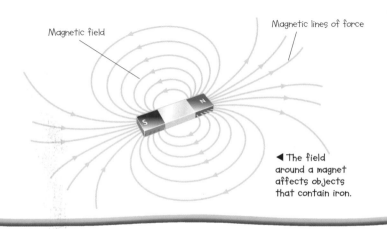

Magnetic field

Magnetic lines of force

◀ The field
around a magnet
affects objects
that contain iron.

When electricity flows through a wire, it makes a weak magnetic field around it. If the wire is wrapped into a coil, the magnetism becomes stronger. This is called an electromagnet. Its magnetic force is the same as an ordinary magnet, but when the electricity goes off, the magnetism does too. Some electromagnets are so strong, they can lift whole cars.

A magnet has two different poles – north and south. A north pole repels (pushes away) the north pole of another magnet. Two south poles also repel each other. But a north pole and a south pole attract (pull together). Both magnetic poles attract any substance containing iron, like a nail or a screw.

QUIZ

Which of these substances or objects is magnetic?

1. Metal spoon 2. Plastic spoon
3. Pencil 4. Drinks can
5. Food can 6. Screwdriver
7. Cooking foil

Answers:
1.Yes 2.No 3.No
4.No 5.Yes 6.Yes 7.No

Electric sparks!

Flick the switch and things happen. The television goes off, the computer comes on, lights shine and music plays. Electricity is our favourite form of energy. We send it along wires and plug hundreds of machines into it. Imagine no washing machine, no electric light and no vacuum cleaner!

▶ Electricity is bits of atoms moving along a wire.

Atom

Electron

Electricity depends on electrons, tiny parts of atoms. In certain substances, when electrons are 'pushed', they hop from one atom to the next. When billions do this every second, electricity flows. The 'push' is from a battery or the generator at a power station. Electricity only flows if it can go in a complete loop or circuit. Break the circuit and the flow stops.

Electricity flows easily through some substances, including water and metals. These are electrical conductors. Other substances do not allow electricity to flow. They are insulators. Insulators include wood, plastic, glass, card and ceramics. Metal wires and cables have coverings of plastic, to stop the electricity leaking away.

Positive contact

◀ A battery has a chemical paste inside a metal casing.

Negative contact on base

A battery makes electricity from chemicals. Two different chemicals next to each other, such as an acid and a metal, swap electrons and get the flow going. Electricity's pushing strength is measured in volts. Most batteries are about 1.5, 3, 6 or 9 volts, with 12 volts in cars.

Electricity from power stations is carried along cables on high pylons, or buried underground. This is known as the distribution grid. At thousands of volts, this electricity is extremely dangerous. For use in the home, it is changed to 220 volts (in Britain). But it can still easily kill a person.

▼ A power station makes enough electricity for thousands of homes.

◄ High pylons hold electric cables safely above ground.

Mains electricity is made at a power station. A fuel such as coal or oil is burned to heat water into high-pressure steam. The steam pushes past the blades of a turbine and makes them spin. The spinning motion turns coils of wire near powerful magnets, and this makes electricity flow in the coils.

MAKE A CIRCUIT

You will need:

a lightbulb · a battery
some wire · a plastic ruler
a metal spoon · some dry card

Join a bulb to a battery with pieces of wire, as shown. Electricity flows round the circuit and lights the bulb. Make a gap in the circuit and put various objects into it, to see if they allow electricity to flow again. Try a plastic ruler, a metal spoon and some dry card.

Making sounds and pictures

The air is full of waves we cannot see or hear, unless we have the right machine. Radio waves are a form of electrical and magnetic energy, just like heat and light waves, microwaves and X-rays. All of these are called electromagnetic waves and they travel at an equal speed – the speed of light.

Satellite

Radio waves

Radio waves carry their information by being altered, or modulated, in a certain pattern. The height of a wave is called its amplitude. If this is altered, it is known as AM (amplitude modulation). Look for AM on the radio display.

Radio waves are used for both radio and television. They travel vast distances. Long waves curve around the Earth's surface. Short waves bounce between the Earth and the sky.

The number of waves per second is called the frequency. If this is altered, it is known as FM (frequency modulation). FM radio is clearer than AM, and less affected by weather and thunderstorms.

▼ All these waves are the same form of energy. They all differ in length.

▲ A radio set picks up radio waves using its long aerial or antenna.

| Long radio waves | Shorter radio waves (TV) | Microwaves | Light waves | X–rays | Short X–rays | Gamma rays |

Radio and TV programmes may be sent out as radio waves from a tall tower on the ground. The tower is called a transmitter. Sometimes waves may be broadcast (sent) by a satellite in space. Or the programmes may not even arrive as radio waves. They can come as flashes of laser light, as cable TV and radio.

I DON'T BELIEVE IT!

You can listen to a radio on the Moon, but not in a submarine. Radio waves travel easily though space, but they hardly pass at all through water.

▶ A dish-shaped receiver picks up radio waves for TV channels.

Inside a TV set, the pattern of radio waves is changed into electrical signals. Some go to the loudspeaker to make the sounds. Others go to the screen to make the pictures. Inside most televisions, the screen is at the front of a glass container called a tube. At the back of the tube are electron guns. These fire streams of electrons. The inside of the screen is coated with thousands of tiny coloured dots called phosphors. When electrons hit the dots, they glow and make the picture.

Electron stream

Glowing dots (phosphors)

Gun

▶ A TV screen's three colours of patches or dots combine to make up the other colours.

389

Compu-science

Computers are amazing machines. But they have to be told exactly what to do. So we put in instructions and information, by various means. These include typing on a keyboard, inserting a disc, using a joystick or games board, or linking up a camera, scanner or another computer.

CD or DVD drive (reader)

Most computers are controlled by instructions from a keyboard and a mouse. The mouse moves a pointer around on the screen and its click buttons select choices from lists called menus.

Main computer case

Microchips on circuit board

Floppy disc drive

Silicon 'wafer'

Plastic casing

◄ This close up of a slice of silicon 'wafer' shows the tiny parts which receive and send information in a computer.

Wire 'feet' link to other part in the computer

Some computers are controlled by talking to them! They pick up the sounds using a microphone. This is VR, or voice recognition technology.

The 'main brain' of a computer is its Central Processing Unit. It is usually a microchip – millions of electronic parts on a chip of silicon, hardly larger than a fingernail. It receives information and instructions from other microchips, carries out the work, and sends back the results.

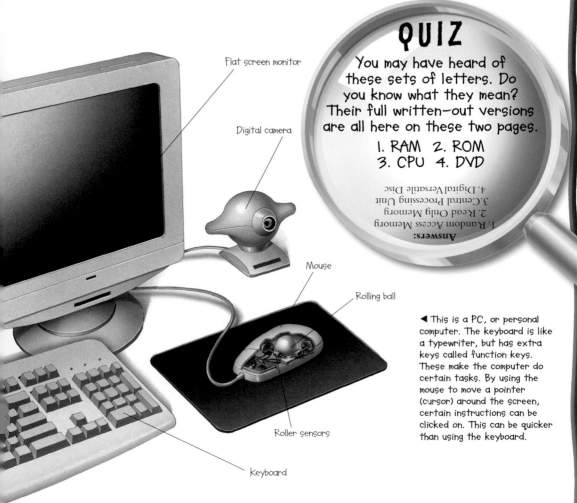

Flat screen monitor

Digital camera

QUIZ

You may have heard of these sets of letters. Do you know what they mean? Their full written—out versions are all here on these two pages.

1. RAM 2. ROM
3. CPU 4. DVD

Answers:
1. Random Access Memory
2. Read Only Memory
3. Central Processing Unit
4. Digital Versatile Disc

Mouse

Rolling ball

◀ This is a PC, or personal computer. The keyboard is like a typewriter, but has extra keys called function keys. These make the computer do certain tasks. By using the mouse to move a pointer (cursor) around the screen, certain instructions can be clicked on. This can be quicker than using the keyboard.

Roller sensors

Keyboard

Information and instructions are contained in the computer in memory microchips. There are two kinds. Random Access Memory is like a jotting pad. It keeps changing as the computer carries out its tasks. Read Only Memory is like an instruction book. It usually contains the instructions for how the computer starts up and how all the microchips work together.

Once the computer has done its task, it feeds out the results. These usually go to a screen called a monitor, where we see them. But they can also go to a printer, a loudspeaker or even a robot arm. Or they can be stored on a disc such as a magnetic disc, compact disc or Digital Versatile Disc (DVD).

Web around the world

The world is at your fingertips – if you are on the Internet. The 'Net' is one of the most amazing results of modern-day science. It is a worldwide network of computers, linked like one huge electrical spider's web.

A modem changes telephone signals to computer signals

▶ The web spans the world as signals of electricity, radio, light and microwaves.

Email stands for electronic mail – it is a quick way of sending messages to other Internet users

▲ As mobile phones get smaller, they can also connect to the Net using their radio link.

Signals travel from computer to computer in many ways. These include electricity along telephone wires, flashes of laser light along fibre-optic cables or radio waves between tall towers. Information is changed from one form to another in a split second. It can also travel between computers on different sides of the world in less than a second using satellite links.

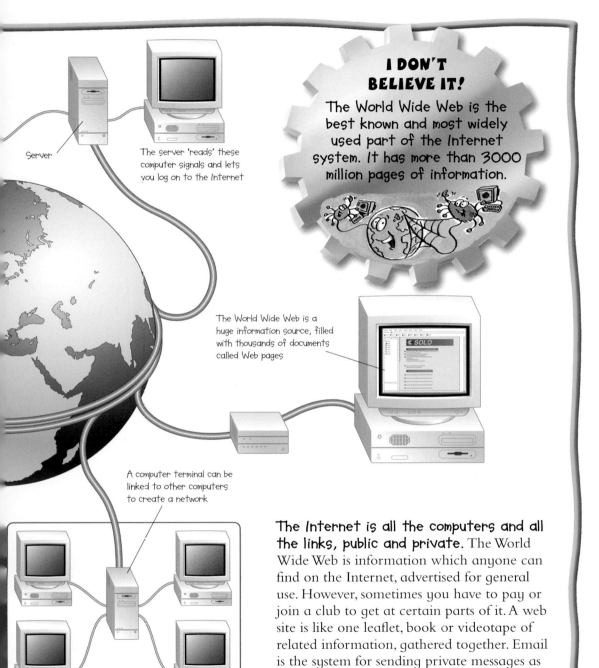

Server

The server 'reads' these computer signals and lets you log on to the Internet

I DON'T BELIEVE IT!

The World Wide Web is the best known and most widely used part of the Internet system. It has more than 3000 million pages of information.

The World Wide Web is a huge information source, filled with thousands of documents called Web pages

A computer terminal can be linked to other computers to create a network

The Internet is all the computers and all the links, public and private. The World Wide Web is information which anyone can find on the Internet, advertised for general use. However, sometimes you have to pay or join a club to get at certain parts of it. A web site is like one leaflet, book or videotape of related information, gathered together. Email is the system for sending private messages as words, pictures and sounds, from one person to another.

What's it made of?

You would not make a bridge out of straw, or a cup out of thin paper! Choosing the right substance or material for the job is part of materials science. All the substances in the world can be divided into several groups. The biggest group is metals such as iron, copper, silver, and gold. Most metals are strong, hard and shiny, and carry heat and electricity well. They are used where materials must be tough and long-lasting.

Plastics are made mainly from the substances in petroleum (crude oil). There are so many kinds – some are hard and brittle while others are soft and bendy. They are usually long-lasting, not affected by weather or damp, and they resist heat and electricity.

▼ A racing car has thousands of parts made from hundreds of materials. Each is suited to certain conditions such as stress, temperature and vibrations.

Each tyre is made of thick, tough rubber to withstand high speeds

The main body of the car is made from carbon fibre, a light but very strong material

The front wing is a special shape – this produces a force that presses the car down onto the track

The car's axles are made from titanium – a very strong, light metal

Ceramics are materials based on clay or other substances dug from the Earth. They can be shaped and dried, like a clay bowl. Or they can be fired – baked in a hot oven called a kiln. This makes them hard and long-lasting, but brittle and prone to cracks. Ceramics resist heat and electricity very well.

Glass is produced from the raw substances limestone and sand. When heated at a high temperature, these substances become a clear, gooey liquid, which sets hard as it cools. Its great advantage is that you can see through it.

Metal

Fibre

Ceramic

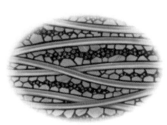

◀ Metal, fibre and ceramic can combine to make a composite material (above). The way all of these ingredients are arranged can affect the composite's strength.

Composites are mixtures or combinations of different materials. For example, glass strands are coated with plastic to make GRP – glass-reinforced plastic. This composite has the advantages of both materials.

Rear wing

The engine can produce about 10 times as much power as an ordinary car – but it needs to be as light as possible

MAKE YOUR OWN COMPOSITE

You will need:
flour   newspaper strips
water   balloon   pin

You can make a composite called pâpier maché from flour, newspaper and water. Tear newspaper into strips. Mix flour and water into a paste. Dip each strip in the paste and place it around a blown-up balloon. Cover the balloon and allow it to dry. Pop the balloon with a pin, and the composite should stay in shape.

The world of chemicals

The world is made of chemical substances. Some are completely pure. Others are mixtures of substances – such as petroleum (crude oil). Petroleum provides us with thousands of different chemicals and materials, such as plastics, paints, soaps and fuel. It is one of the most useful, and valuable, substances in the world.

▶ The huge tower (fractionating column) of an oil refinery may be 50 metres high.

In an oil refinery, crude oil is heated in a huge tower. Some of its different substances turn into fumes (vapours) and rise up the tower. The fumes turn back into liquids at different heights inside the tower, due to the different temperatures at each level. We get petrol in this way. Remaining at the bottom of the tower are thick, gooey tars, asphalts and bitumens – which are used to make road surfaces.

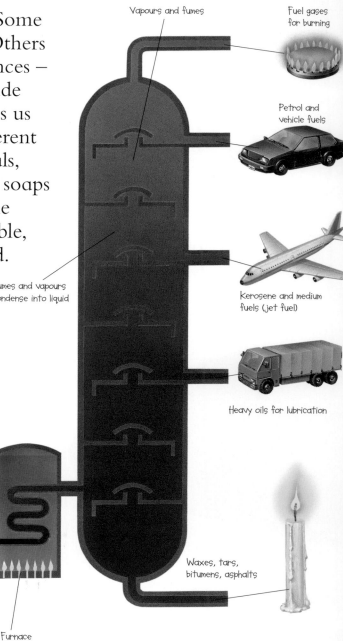

Vapours and fumes

Fuel gases for burning

Petrol and vehicle fuels

Fumes and vapours condense into liquid

Kerosene and medium fuels (jet fuel)

Heavy oils for lubrication

Waxes, tars, bitumens, asphalts

Furnace

One group of chemicals is called acids. They vary in strength from very weak citric acid which gives the sharp taste to fruits such as lemons, to extremely strong and dangerous sulphuric acid in a car battery. Powerful acids burn and corrode, or eat away, substances. Some even corrode glass or steel.

Another group of chemicals is bases. They vary in strength from weak alkaloids, which give the bitter taste to coffee beans, to strong and dangerous bases in drain cleaners and industrial polishes. Bases feel soapy or slimy and, like acids, they can burn or corrode.

▼ Indicator paper changes colour when it touches different substances. Acids turn it red, alkalis make it bluish-purple. The deeper the colour, the stronger the acid or base.

Acidic substance

Neutral substance

Alkaline substance

Acids and bases are 'opposite' types of chemicals. When they meet, they undergo changes called a chemical reaction. The result is usually a third type of chemical, called a salt. The common salt we use for cooking is one example. Its chemical name is sodium chloride.

FROTHY FUN

You will need:

some vinegar   washing soda

Create a chemical reaction by adding a few drops of vinegar to a spoonful of washing soda in a saucer. The vinegar is an acid, the soda is a base. The two react by frothing and giving off bubbles of carbon dioxide gas. What is left is a salt (but not to be eaten).

Pure science

The world seems to be made of millions of different substances – such as soil, wood, concrete, plastics and air. These are combinations of simpler substances. If you could take them apart, you would see that they are made of pure substances called elements.

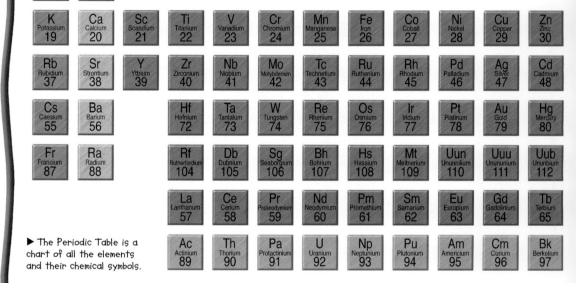

▶ The Periodic Table is a chart of all the elements and their chemical symbols.

Hydrogen is the simplest element.
This means it has the smallest atoms. It is a very light gas, which floats upwards in air. Hydrogen was once used to fill giant airships. But there was a problem – hydrogen catches fire easily and explodes. In fact, stars are made mainly of burning hydrogen, which is why they are so hot and bright.

About 90 elements are found naturally on and in the Earth. In an element, all of its particles, called atoms, are exactly the same as each other. Just as important, they are all different from the atoms of any other element.

▼ The elements can be arranged in a table. Each has a letter, like C for carbon. It also has a number showing how big or heavy its atoms are compared to those of other elements.

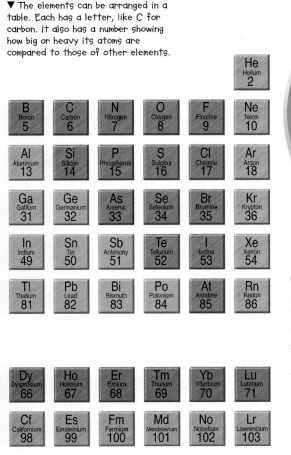

| He Helium 2 |
B Boron 5	C Carbon 6	N Nitrogen 7	O Oxygen 8	F Flourine 9	Ne Neon 10
Al Alumnium 13	Si Silicon 14	P Phosphorus 15	S Sulphur 16	Cl Chlorine 17	Ar Argon 18
Ga Gallium 31	Ge Germeinium 32	As Arsenic 33	Se Selenium 34	Br Bromine 35	Kr Krypton 36
In Indium 49	Sn Tin 50	Sb Antimony 51	Te Tellurium 52	I Iodine 53	Xe Xenon 54
Tl Thalium 81	Pb Lead 82	Bi Bismuth 83	Po Polonium 84	At Astatine 85	Rn Radon 86

| Dy Dysprosium 66 | Ho Holmium 67 | Er Erbium 68 | Tm Thulium 69 | Yb Ytterbium 70 | Lu Lutetium 71 |
| Cf Californium 98 | Es Einsteinium 99 | Fm Fermium 100 | Md Mendelevium 101 | No Nobelium 102 | Lr Lawrencium 103 |

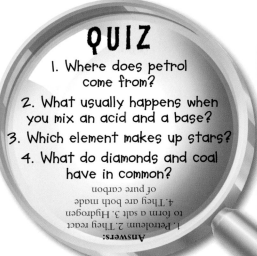

QUIZ

1. Where does petrol come from?

2. What usually happens when you mix an acid and a base?

3. Which element makes up stars?

4. What do diamonds and coal have in common?

Answers:
1. Petroleum 2. They react to form a salt 3. Hydrogen 4. They are both made of pure carbon

Uranium is a heavy and dangerous element. It gives off harmful rays and tiny particles, called radioactivity. These can cause sickness, burns and diseases such as cancer. Radioactivity is a type of energy and, under careful control, it may be used as fuel in nuclear power stations.

Aluminium is an element which is a metal, and it is one of the most useful in modern life. It is light and strong, it does not rust, and it is resistant to corrosion. Saucepans, drinks cans, cooking foil and jet planes are made mainly of aluminium.

Carbon is a very important element in living things – including our own bodies. It joins easily with atoms of other elements to make large groups of atoms called molecules. When it is pure, carbon can be two different forms. These are soft, powdery soot, and hard, glittering diamond. The form depends on how the carbon atoms join to each other.

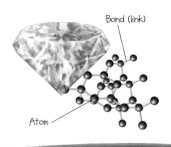

▶ Carbon can be hard diamond or soft soot, which is made of sheets of joined atoms.

Bond (link)

Atom

Small science

Many pages in this book mention atoms. They are the smallest bits of a substance. They are so tiny, even a billion atoms would be too small to see. But scientists have carried out experiments to find out what's inside an atom. The answer is – even smaller bits. These are sub-atomic particles, and there are three main kinds.

At the centre of each atom is a blob called the nucleus. It contains an equal number of two kinds of sub-atomic particles. These are protons and neutrons. The proton is like the north pole of a magnet. It is positive, or plus. The neutron is not. It is neither positive or negative.

Electron

Nucleus

I DON'T BELIEVE IT!

One hundred years ago, people thought the electrons were spread out in an atom, like the raisins in a raisin pudding.

Atoms of the various elements have different numbers of protons and neutrons. An atom of hydrogen has just one proton. An atom of helium, the gas put in party balloons to make them float, has one proton and one neutron. An atom of the heavy metal called lead has 82 protons and neutrons.

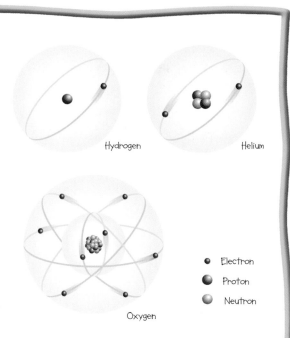

Hydrogen

Helium

● Electron

● Proton

○ Neutron

Oxygen

► The bits inside an atom give each substance its features, from exploding hydrogen to life-giving oxygen.

Movement of electrons

◄ Uranium is a tough, heavy, dangerous metal. Each atom of uranium has 92 electrons whizzing around its nucleus.

Around the centre of each atom are sub–atomic particles called electrons. They whizz round and round the nucleus. In the same way that a proton in the nucleus is positive or plus, an electron is negative or minus. The number of protons and neutrons is usually the same, so the plus and minus numbers are the same. (Electrons are the bits which jump from atom to atom when electricity flows).

It is hard to imagine that atoms are so small. A grain of sand, smaller than this o, contains at least 100 billion billion atoms. If you could make the atoms bigger, so that each one becomes as big as a pin head, the grain of sand would be two kilometres high!

Scientists at work

There are thousands of different jobs and careers in science. Scientists work in laboratories, factories, offices, mines, steelworks, nature parks and almost everywhere else. They find new knowledge and make discoveries using a process called the scientific method.

First comes an idea, called a theory or hypothesis. This asks or predicts what will happen in a certain situation. Scientists continually come up with new ideas and theories to test. One very simple theory is – if I throw a ball up in the air, will it come back down?

The scientist carries out an experiment or test, to check what happens. The experiment is carefully designed and controlled, so that it will reveal useful results. Any changes are carried out one at a time, so that the effect of each change can be studied. The experiment for our simple theory is – throw the ball up in the air.

Measuring and recording are very important as part of the experiment. All the changes are measured, written down, and perhaps photographed or filmed as well.

▼ Scientists carrying out research in a laboratory gather information and record all of their findings.

The results are what happens during and at the end of the experiment. They are studied, perhaps by drawing graphs and making tables. You can probably guess the result of our experiment – the ball falls back down.

At the end of this scientific process, the scientist thinks of reasons or conclusions about why certain things happened. The conclusion for our experiment is – something pulls the ball back down. But science never stands still. There are always new theories, experiments and results. This is how science progresses, with more discoveries and inventions every year.

QUIZ

Put these activities in the correct order, so that a scientist can carry out the scientific method.

1. Results 2. Experiment
3. Conclusions 4. Theory
5. Measurements

Answer:
4, 2, 5, 1, 3

Science in nature

Science and its effects are found all over the natural world. Scientists study animals, plants, rocks and soil. They want to understand nature, and find out how science and its technology affect wildlife.

One of the most complicated types of science is ecology. Ecologists try to understand how the natural world links together. They study how animals and plants live, what animals eat, and why plants grow better in some soils than others. They count the numbers of animals and plants and may trap animals briefly to study them, or follow the growth of trees in a wood. When the balance of nature is damaged, ecologists can help to find out why.

Banded demoiselle damselfly

Water scorpion

Rainbow trout

Water beetle

▼ One of the most important jobs in science is to study damage and pollution in the natural world. Almost everything we make or do affects wild places with their animals and plants. Factories, power stations and roadways crammed with vehicles are especially harmful, as chemicals spread in the air and seep into soil and water.

Reedmace

Power station

Heron

Otter

Warbler

Ecologists use many forms of high-tech science in their studies. They may fit an animal with a radio-collar so that its movements can be tracked. Special cameras see in the dark and show how night hunters catch their prey. Radar used to detect planes can also follow flocks of birds. The sonar (echo-sounding) equipment of boats can track shoals of fish or whales.

I DON'T BELIEVE IT!

Science explains how animals such as birds or whales find their way across the world. Some detect the Earth's magnetism, and which way is north or south. Others follow changes in gravity, the force which pulls everything to the Earth's surface.

Body science

One of the biggest areas of science is medicine.
Medical scientists work to produce better drugs,
more spare parts for the body and more machines
for use by doctors. They also carry out
scientific research to find out how
people can stay healthy and
prevent disease.

▶ As a runner gets tired, his heart pumps
harder. Its beats can be detected and
shown on an ECG machine.

ECG machine
showing display

Sensor pad

As parts of the body work, such as the
muscles and nerves, they produce tiny
pulses of electricity. Pads on the skin pick
up these pulses, which are displayed as a wavy
line on a screen or paper strip. The ECG
(electro-cardiograph) machine shows the heart
beating. The EEG (electro-encephalograph)
shows nerve signals flashing around the brain.

Laser beam hits retina inside eye

▶ Laser beams can be used to treat people who are short-sighted, or people with failing eyesight.

Laser beams are ideal for delicate operations, or surgery, on body parts such as the eye. The beam makes very small, precise cuts. It can be shone into the eye and made most focused, or strongest, inside. So it can make a cut deep within the eye, without any harm to the outer parts.

MAKE A PULSE MACHINE

You will need:
modelling clay   a drinking straw

Find your pulse by feeling your wrist, just below the base of your thumb, with a finger of the other hand. Place some modelling clay on this area, and stick a drinking straw into it. Watch the straw twitch with each heartbeat. Now you can see and feel your pulse. Check your pulse rate by counting the number of heartbeats in one minute.

▼ An endoscope is inserted into the body to give a doctor a picture on screen. The treatment can be given immediately.

The endoscope is like a flexible telescope made of fibre-optic strands. This is pushed into a body opening such as the mouth, or through a small cut, to see inside. The surgeon looks into the other end of the endoscope, or at a picture on a screen.

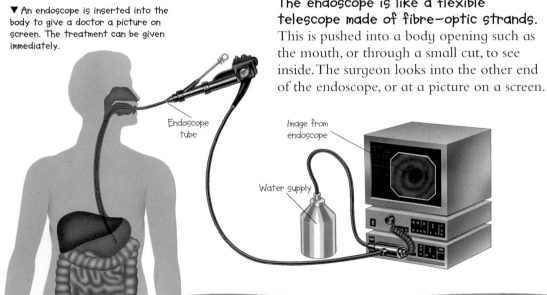

Endoscope tube

Image from endoscope

Water supply

Science in the future

Many modern machines and processes can cause damage to our environment and our health. The damage includes acid rain, destruction of the ozone layer and the greenhouse effect, leading to climate change and global warming. Science can help to find solutions. New filters and chemicals called catalysts can reduce dangerous fumes from vehicle exhausts and power stations, and in the chemicals in factory waste pipes.

◀ Fumes, waste and chemicals cause terrible pollution in many cities.

One very important area of science is recycling. Many materials and substances can be recycled – glass, paper, plastics, cans, scrap metals and rags. Scientists are working to improve the process. Products should be designed so that when they no longer work, they are easy to recycle. The recycling process itself is also being made more effective.

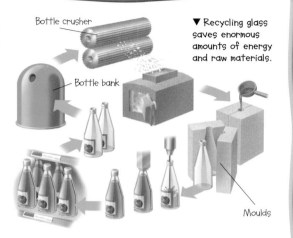

Bottle crusher

Bottle bank

▼ Recycling glass saves enormous amounts of energy and raw materials.

Moulds

QUIZ

If you become a scientist, which science would you like to study? See if you can guess what these sciences are:

1. Meteorology 2. Biology
3. Astronomy 4. Ecology

Answers:
1. Weather and climate
2. Animals, plants and other living things
3. Stars, planets and objects in space
4. The way nature works

▼ The energy in flowing water can be turned into electricity at a hydroelectric power station.

We use vast amounts of energy, especially to make electricity and as fuel in our cars. Much of this energy comes from crude oil (petroleum), natural gas and coal. But these energy sources will not last for ever. They also cause huge amounts of pollution. Scientists are working to develop cleaner forms of energy, which will produce less pollution and not run out. These include wind power from turbines, solar power from photocells, and hydroelectric and tidal power from dams.

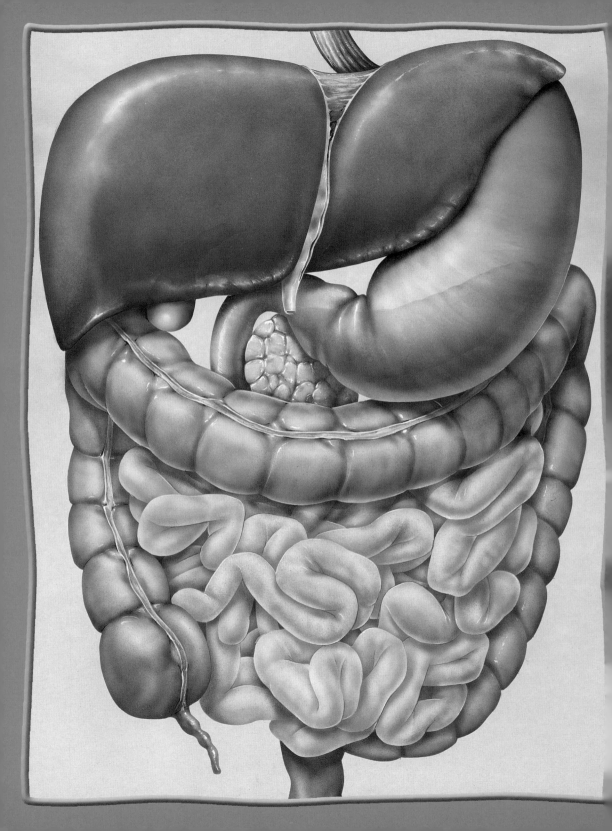

HUMAN BODY

Our bodies are like amazing machines. Take a closer look at body systems and how they work.

Babies • Growing up • Skin • Hair • Nails • Health
Joints • Muscles • Breathing • Lungs • Food • Teeth
Digestion • Blood • Heart • Ears • Eyes • Nose
Tongue • Nerves • Hormones • Brain • Skeleton

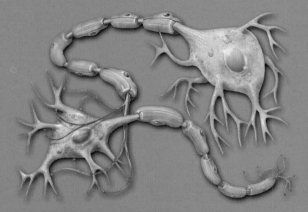

Outside, inside

There are more than six billion human bodies in the world. If you could say hello to all of them, even quickly, it would take you more than 300 years. In some ways, all of these human bodies are very similar, especially on the inside. Each one has a heart and brain, bones and guts, arms and legs and skin. But each human body is also individual, especially on the outside. You have your own appearance, size and shape, facial features, hairstyle and clothes. You also have your own personality, with likes and dislikes, and special things that make you happy or sad. So human bodies may be very similar in how they look, but not in what they do. You are unique, your own self.

▶ We tend to notice small differences on the outside of human bodies, such as height, width, hair colour and clothes. This allows us to recognize our family and friends.

Baby body

A full-grown human body is made of billions of microscopic parts, called cells. But in the beginning, the body is a single cell, smaller than this full stop. Yet it contains all the instructions, known as genes, for the whole body to grow and develop.

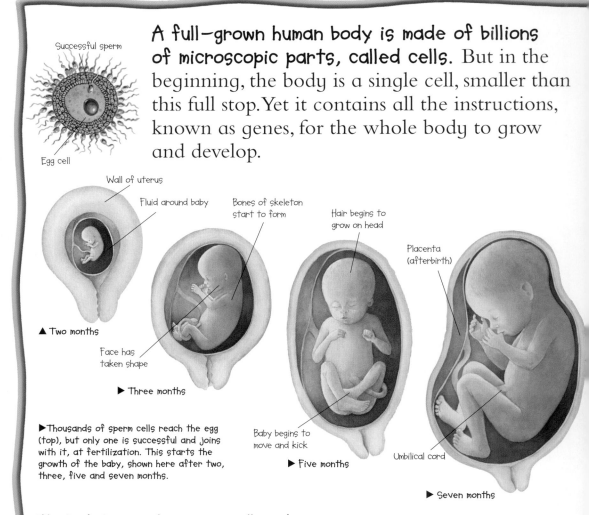

Successful sperm

Egg cell

Wall of uterus

Fluid around baby

Bones of skeleton start to form

Hair begins to grow on head

Placenta (afterbirth)

▲ Two months

Face has taken shape

▶ Three months

Baby begins to move and kick

Umbilical cord

▶ Five months

▶ Seven months

▶ Thousands of sperm cells reach the egg (top), but only one is successful and joins with it, at fertilization. This starts the growth of the baby, shown here after two, three, five and seven months.

The body begins when an egg cell inside the mother joins up with sperm from the father. The egg cell splits into two cells, then into four cells, then eight, and so on. The bundle of cells embeds itself in the mother's womb (uterus), which protects and nourishes it. Soon there are thousands of cells, then millions, forming a tiny embryo. After two months the embryo has grown into a tiny baby, as big as your thumb, with arms, legs, eyes, ears and mouth.

After nine months in the womb, the baby is ready to be born. Strong muscles in the walls of the womb tighten, or contract. They push the baby through the opening, or neck of the womb, called the cervix, and along the birth canal. The baby enters the outside world.

A newborn baby may be frightened and usually starts to cry. Inside the womb it was warm, wet, dark, quiet and cramped. Outside there are lights, noises, voices, fresh air and room to stretch. The crying is also helpful to start the baby breathing, using its own lungs.

I DON'T BELIEVE IT!

The human body never grows as fast again as it does during the first weeks in the womb. If the body kept growing at that rate, every day for 50 years, it would be bigger than the biggest mountain in the world!

▼ Nine months

Wall of womb is stretched

Placenta

◄ Inside the womb, the baby cannot breathe air or eat food. Nutrients and oxygen pass from mother to baby through the blood vessels in the ropelike umbilical cord.

Umbilical cord

Baby is born head–first

Cervix (neck of womb)

Being born can take an hour or two – or a whole day or two. It is very tiring for both the baby and its mother. After birth, the baby starts to feel hungry and it feeds on its mother's milk. Finally, mother and baby settle down for a rest and some sleep.

415

The growing body

A new baby just seems to eat, sleep and cry. It feeds on milk when hungry and sleeps when tired. Also, it cries when it is too hot, too cold, or when its nappy needs changing.

A new baby is not totally helpless. It can do simple actions called reflexes, to help it survive. If something touches the baby's cheek, it turns its head to that side and tries to suck. If the baby hears a loud noise, it opens its eyes wide, throws out its arms and cries for help. If something touches the baby's hand and fingers, it grasps tightly.

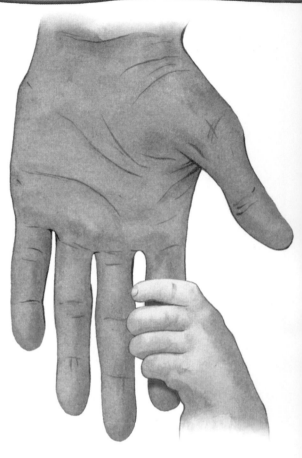

▲ In the grasping reflex, the baby tightly holds anything that touches its hand or fingers. Its grip is surprisingly strong!

WHAT HAPPENS WHEN?

Most babies learn to do certain actions in the same order. The order is mixed up here. Can you put it right?

walk, crawl, roll over, sit up, smile, stand

Answers:
smile, roll over, sit up,
crawl, stand, walk

A new baby looks, listens, touches and quickly learns. Gradually it starts to recognize voices, faces and places. After about six weeks, it begins to smile. Inside the body, the baby's brain is learning very quickly. The baby soon knows that if it laughs, people will laugh back. If it cries, someone will come to look after it.

▼ Most babies crawl before they walk, but some go straight from sitting or 'bottom–shuffling' to walking.

As a baby grows into a child, at around 18 months, it learns ten new words every day, from 'cat' and 'dog' to 'sun' and 'moon'. There are new games such as piling up bricks, new actions such as throwing and kicking, and new skills such as using a spoon at mealtimes and scribbling on paper.

At about three months old, most babies can reach out to hold something, and roll over when lying down. By the age of six months, most babies can sit up and hold food in their fingers. At nine months, many babies are crawling well and perhaps standing up. By their first birthday, many babies are learning to walk and starting to talk.

At the age of five, when most children start school, they continue to learn an amazing amount. This includes thinking or mental skills such as counting and reading, and precise movements such as writing and drawing. They learn out of the classroom too – how to play with friends and share.

▶ Playing is lots of fun, but it's learning too, as children develop control over the muscles in their fast-growing bodies.

On the body's outside

Skin's surface is made of tiny cells which have filled up with a hard, tough substance called keratin, and then died. So when you look at a human body, most of what you see is 'dead'! The cells get rubbed off as you move, have a wash and get dry.

Skin rubs off all the time, and grows all the time too. Just under the surface, living cells make more new cells that gradually fill with keratin, die and move up to the surface. It takes about four weeks from a new skin cell being made to when it reaches the surface and is rubbed off. This upper layer of skin is called the epidermis.

▲ Skin may feel smooth, but its surface is made of millions of tiny flakes, far too small to see.

▼ This view shows skin magnified (enlarged) about 50 times.

Skin's lower layer, the dermis, is thicker than the epidermis. It is made of tiny, bendy, threadlike fibres of the substance collagen. The dermis also contains small blood vessels, tiny sweat glands, and micro-sensors that detect touch.

Hair

Oil gland

Pain sensors

Epidermis

Dermis

Light touch sensor

Hair follicle

Heavy pressure sensor

▼ Skin is tough, but it sometimes needs help to protect the body. Otherwise it, and the body parts beneath, may get damaged.

Safety helmet protects head and brain

Elbow-pads cushion fall

Knee-pads prevent hard bumps

Gloves save fingers from scrapes and breaks

One of skin's important jobs is to protect the body. It stops the delicate inner parts from being rubbed, knocked or scraped. Skin also prevents body fluids from leaking away and it keeps out dirt and germs.

Skin helps to keep the body at the same temperature. If you become too hot, sweat oozes onto your skin and, as it dries, draws heat from the body. Also, the blood vessels in the lower layer of skin widen, to lose more heat through the skin. This is why a hot person looks sweaty and red in the face.

Skin gives us our sense of touch. Millions of microscopic sensors in the lower layer of skin, the dermis, are joined by nerves to the brain. Different sensors detect different kinds of touch, from a light stroke to heavy pressure, heat or cold, and movement. Pain sensors detect when skin is damaged. Ouch!

SENSITIVE SKIN

You will need:

a friend   sticky-tack
two used matchsticks   ruler

1. Press some sticky-tack on the end of the ruler. Press two matchsticks into the sticky-tack, standing upright, about 1 centimetre apart.
2. Make your friend look away. Touch the back of their hand with both matchstick ends. Ask your friend: 'Is that one matchstick or two?' Sensitive skin can detect both ends.
3. Try this at several places such as the finger, wrist, forearm, neck and cheek.

Hair and nails

There are about 120,000 hairs on the head, called scalp hairs. There are also eyebrow hairs and eyelash hairs. Grown-ups have hairs in the armpits and between the legs, and men have hairs on the face. And everyone, even a baby, has tiny hairs all over the body – 20 million of them!

▼ Black curly hair is the result of black melanin from a flat hair follicle

▲ Blonde wavy hair is the result of carotene from an oval hair follicle

◄ Hair contains pigments (coloured substances) – mainly melanin (dark brown) and some carotene (yellowish). Different amounts of pigments, and the way their tiny particles are spread out, cause different hair colours.

▲ Straight red hair is the result of red melanin from a round hair follicle

▶ Straight black hair is the result of black melanin from a round follicle

Each hair grows from a deep pit in the skin, called a follicle. The hair is only alive where it gets longer, at its base or root, in the bottom of the follicle. The rest of the hair, called the shaft, is like the surface of the skin – hard, tough, dead and made of keratin. Hair helps to protect the body, especially where it is thicker and longer on the head. It also helps to keep the body warm in cold conditions.

Scalp hairs get longer by about 3 millimetres each week, on average. Eyebrow hairs grow more slowly. No hairs live for ever. Each one grows for a time, then it falls out, and its follicle has a 'rest' before a new hair sprouts. This is happening all the time, so the body always has some hairs on each part.

Nails, like hairs, grow at their base (the nail root) and are made of keratin. Also like hairs, nails grow faster in summer than in winter, and faster at night than by day. Nails lengthen by about half a millimetre, on average, each week.

▼ The growing nail root is hidden under skin. The nail slides slowly along the nail bed.

Nail root

Nail root

Cuticle (skin edge)

Nail bed

Bone inside finger

Nails have many uses, from peeling off sticky labels to plucking guitar strings or scratching an itch. They protect and stiffen the ends of the fingers, where there are nerves that give us our sense of touch.

▶ Nails make the fingertips stronger and more rigid for pressing hard on guitar strings. Slightly longer nails pluck the strings.

I DON'T BELIEVE IT!

A scalp hair grows for up to five years before it falls out and gets replaced. Left uncut during this time, it would be about one metre long. But some people have unusual hair that grows faster and for longer. Each hair can reach more than 5 metres in length before dropping out.

The bony body

The human body is strengthened, supported and held up by parts that we cannot see – bones. Without bones, the body would be as floppy as a jellyfish! Bones do many jobs. The long bones in the arms work like levers to reach out the hands. The finger bones grasp and grip. The leg bones are also levers when we walk and run. Bones protect softer body parts. The domelike skull protects the brain. The ribs in the chest are like the bars of a cage to protect the heart and lungs inside. Bones also produce blood cells, as explained on the opposite page.

▶ The skeleton forms a strong framework inside the body. The only artificial (man-made) substances that can match bone for strength and lightness are some of the materials used to make racing cars and jet planes.

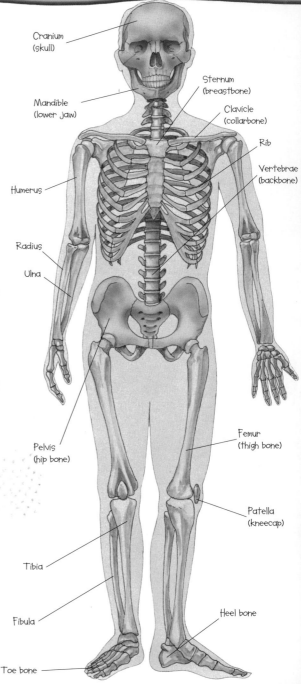

Cranium (skull)

Sternum (breastbone)

Mandible (lower jaw)

Clavicle (collarbone)

Rib

Vertebrae (backbone)

Humerus

Radius

Ulna

Pelvis (hip bone)

Femur (thigh bone)

Patella (kneecap)

Tibia

Fibula

Heel bone

Toe bone

All the bones together make up the skeleton. Most people have 206 bones, from head to toe as follows:
- 8 in the upper part of the skull, the cranium or braincase
- 14 in the face
- 6 tiny ear bones, 3 deep in each ear
- 1 in the neck, which is floating and not directly connected to any other bone
- 26 in the spinal column or backbone
- 25 in the chest, being 24 ribs and the breastbone
- 32 in each arm, from shoulder to fingertips (8 in each wrist)
- 31 in each leg, from hip to toetips (7 in each ankle)

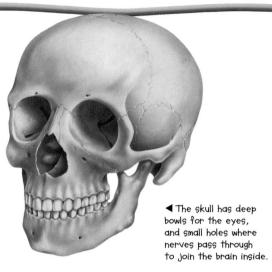

◄ The skull has deep bowls for the eyes, and small holes where nerves pass through to join the brain inside.

NAME THE BONE!

Every bone has a scientific or medical name, and many have ordinary names too. Can you match up these ordinary and scientific names for various bones?

1. Mandible 2. Femur 3. Clavicle
4. Pelvis 5. Patella 6. Sternum

a. Thigh bone b. Breastbone
c. Kneecap d. Hip bone
e. Collarbone f. Lower jaw bone

Answers:
1f 2a 3e 4d 5c 6b

▶ Bone has a hard layer outside, a spongy layer next, and soft marrow in the middle.

Bone contains threads of the tough, slightly bendy substance called collagen. It also has hard minerals such as calcium and phosphate. Together, the collagen and minerals make a bone strong and rigid, yet able to bend slightly under stress. Bones have blood vessels for nourishment and nerves to feel pressure and pain. Also, some bones are not solid. They contain a jellylike substance called marrow. This makes tiny parts for the blood, called red and white blood cells.

Marrow

Spongy bone

Compact (hard) bone

End or head of bone

Nerves and blood vessels

'Skin' of bone (periosteum)

The flexible body

Without joints, almost the only parts of your body that could move would be your tongue and eyebrows! Joints between bones allow the skeleton to bend. You have more than 150 joints. The largest are in the hips and knees. The smallest are in the fingers, toes, and between the tiny bones inside each ear which help you hear.

There are several kinds of joints, depending on the shapes of the bone ends, and how much the bones can move. Bend your knee and your lower leg moves forwards and backwards, but not sideways. This is a hinge-type joint. Bend your hip and your leg can move forwards, backwards, and also from side to side. This is a ball–and–socket joint.

▶ In the shoulder, the upper arm bone's rounded head fits into a socket in the shoulder blade.

Collarbone

Head of upper arm bone

Shoulder blade

TEST YOUR JOINTS

Try using these different joints carefully, and see how much movement they allow. Can you guess the type of joint used in each one – hinge or ball–and–socket?

1. Fingertip joint (smallest knuckle)
2. Elbow
3. Hip
4. Shoulder

Answers:
1. hinge 2. hinge
3. ball-and-socket 4. ball-and-socket

Inside a joint where the bones come together, each bone end is covered with a smooth, shiny, slippery, slightly springy substance, known as cartilage. This is smeared with a thick liquid called synovial fluid. The fluid works like the oil in a car, to smooth the movements and reduce rubbing and wear between the cartilage surfaces.

The bones in a joint are linked together by a baglike part, the capsule, and strong, stretchy, straplike ligaments. The ligaments let the bones move but stop them coming apart or moving too far. The shoulder has seven strong ligaments.

◀ The arm joints are very flexible, but they can also work as strongly as the leg joints to hold up the whole body.

In some joints, there are cartilage coverings over the bone ends and also pads of cartilage between the cartilage! These extra pads are called articular discs. There is one in each joint in the backbone, between the spinal bones, which are called vertebrae. There are also two of these extra cartilages, known as menisci, in each knee joint. They help the knee to 'lock' straight so that we can stand up without too much effort.

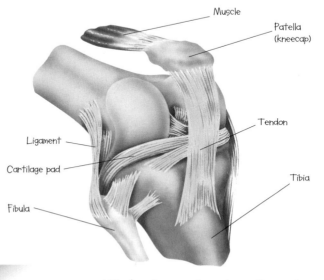

Muscle

Patella (kneecap)

Tendon

Ligament

Cartilage pad

Tibia

Fibula

▲ The knee has many ligaments, cartilage pads (menisci) and strong tendons that anchor muscles.

When muscles pull

Almost half the body's weight is muscles, and there are more than 640 of them! Muscles have one simple but important job, which is to get shorter, or contract. A muscle cannot get longer.

A muscle is joined to a bone by its tendon. This is where the end of the muscle becomes slimmer or tapers, and is strengthened by strong, thick fibres of collagen. The fibres are fixed firmly into the surface of the bone.

▼ A tendon is stuck firmly into the bone it pulls, with a joint stronger than superglue!

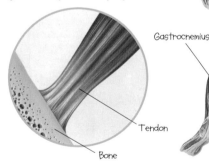

Tendon

Bone

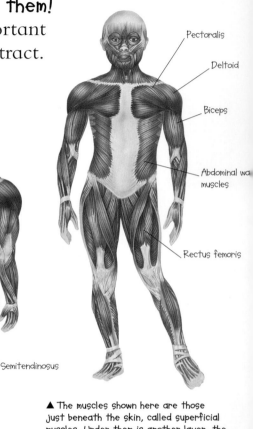

Trapezius

Gluteus

Gastrocnemius

Semitendinosus

Pectoralis

Deltoid

Biceps

Abdominal wall muscles

Rectus femoris

▲ The muscles shown here are those just beneath the skin, called superficial muscles. Under them is another layer, the deep muscle layer. In some areas there is an additional layer, the medial muscles.

Some muscles are wide or broad, and shaped more like flat sheets or triangles. These include the three layers of muscles in the lower front and sides of the body, called the abdominal wall muscles. If you tense or contract them, they pull your tummy in to make you look thinner.

Most muscles are long and slim, and joined to bones at each end. As they contract they pull on the bones and move them. As this happens, the muscle becomes wider, or more bulging in the middle. To move the bone back again, a muscle on the other side of it contracts, while the first muscle relaxes and is pulled longer.

I DON'T BELIEVE IT!

It's easier to smile than to frown. There are about 40 muscles under the skin of the face. You use almost all of these to make a deep frown, but only about half of them to show a broad grin.

◀ A weightlifter's muscles can raise more than three times the body weight above the head.

Every muscle in the body has a scientific or medical name, which is often quite long and complicated. Some of these names are familiar to people who do exercise and sports. The 'pecs' are the pectoralis major muscles across the chest. The 'biceps' are the biceps brachii muscles in the upper arms, which bulge when you bend your elbow.

If you take plenty of exercise or play sport, you do not gain new muscles. But the muscles you have become larger and stronger. This keeps them fit and healthy. Muscles which are not used much may become weak and floppy.

▶ Muscles work in two-way pairs, like the biceps and triceps, which bend and straighten the elbow.

Biceps

Triceps

Biceps gets shorter and the elbow moves

To move the arm back down, the triceps shortens and the biceps gets longer

Muscle power

Muscles have many shapes and sizes, but inside they are all similar. They have bundles of long, hairlike threads called muscle fibres, or myofibres. Each muscle fibre is slightly thinner than a hair. A big muscle has many thousands of them. Most are about 3 or 4 centimetres long. In a big muscle, many fibres of different lengths lie alongside each other and end-to-end.

Muscle fibre

Nerve branches

Muscle fibre

Muscle fibril

▶ While arm muscles prepare to make the racket hit the ball, hundreds of other muscles keep the body poised and balanced.

Each muscle fibre is made of dozens or hundreds of even thinner parts, called muscle fibrils or myofibrils. There are millions of these in a large muscle. And, as you may guess, each fibril contains hundreds of yet thinner threads! There are two kinds, actin and myosin. As the actins slide past and between the myosins, the threads get shorter – and the muscle contracts.

Muscles are controlled by the brain, which sends messages to them along stringlike nerves. When a muscle contracts for a long time, its fibres 'take turns'. Some of them shorten powerfully while others relax, then the contracted ones relax while others shorten, and so on.

Body of muscle

Actin

Myosin

◀ The main part of a muscle is the body or belly, with hundreds of muscle fibres inside.

▼ Dozens of arm and hand muscles move a pen precisely, a tiny amount each time.

WHICH MUSCLES?

Can you match the names of these muscles, with different parts of the body?

a. Gluteus maximus b. Masseter
c. Sartorius d. Cardiac muscle
e. Pectoralis major

1. Heart 2. Chest 3. Front of thigh
4. Buttock 5. Mouth

Answers:
a4 b5 c3 d1 e2

The body's biggest muscles are the ones you sit on – the gluteus maximus muscles in the buttocks. The longest muscle is the sartorius, across the front of the thigh. Some of its fibres are more than 30 centimetres in length. The most powerful muscle, for its size, is the masseter in the lower cheek, which closes the jaws when you chew.

The breathing body

The body cannot survive more than a minute or two without breathing. This action is so important, we do it all the time without thinking. We breathe to take air into the body. Air contains the gas oxygen, which is needed to get energy from food to power all of the body's vital life processes.

▲ A space suit protects an astronaut, and contains air to breathe in the emptiness of space.

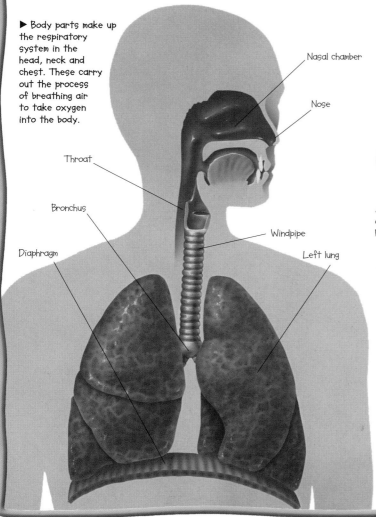

▶ Body parts make up the respiratory system in the head, neck and chest. These carry out the process of breathing air to take oxygen into the body.

Nasal chamber

Nose

Throat

Bronchus

Windpipe

Diaphragm

Left lung

Parts of the body that work together to carry out a main task are called a system – so the parts that carry out breathing are the respiratory system. These parts are the nose, throat, windpipe, the air tubes or bronchi in the chest, and the lungs.

The nose is the entrance for fresh air to the lungs – and the exit for stale air from the lungs. The soft, moist lining inside the nose makes air warmer and damper, which is better for the lungs. Tiny bits of floating dust and germs stick to the lining or the hairs in the nose, making the air cleaner.

◄ The human voice can make a wide range of sounds, from loud to soft, and low to high.

The windpipe, or trachea, is a tube leading from the back of the nose and mouth, down to the lungs. It has about 20 C-shaped hoops of cartilage in its wall to keep it open, like a vacuum cleaner hose. Otherwise the pressure of body parts in the neck and chest would squash it shut.

HUMMMMMM!

You will need:
A stopwatch

Do you think making sounds with your voice-box uses more air than breathing? Find out by following this experiment.

1. Take a deep breath in, then breathe out at your normal rate, for as long as you can. Time the out-breath.

2. Take a similar deep breath in, then hum as you breathe out, again for as long as you can. Time the hum.

3. Try the same while whispering your favourite song, then again when singing.

At the top of the windpipe, making a bulge at the front of the neck, is the voice–box or larynx. It has two stiff flaps, vocal cords, which stick out from its sides. Normally these flaps are apart for easy breathing. But muscles in the voice-box can pull the flaps almost together. As air passes through the narrow slit between them it makes the flaps shake or vibrate – and this is the sound of your voice.

▼ The vocal cords are held apart for breathing (left) and pulled together for speech (right).

431

Breathing parts

The main parts of the respiratory (breathing) system are the two lungs in the chest. Each one is shaped like a tall cone, with the pointed end at shoulder level.

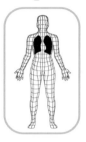

Right lung

Left bronchus

Muscles in wall of bronchus

Air space inside bronchus

View along inside of bronchus

Air comes in and out of the lungs along the windpipe, which branches at its base to form two main air tubes, the bronchi. One goes to each lung. Inside the lung, each bronchus divides again and again, becoming narrower each time. Finally the air tubes, thinner than hairs, end at groups of tiny 'bubbles' called alveoli.

I DON'T BELIEVE IT!

On average, the air breathed in and out through the night by a sleeping person, would fill an average-sized bedroom. This is why some people like to sleep with the door or window open!

There are more than 100 million tiny air bubbles, or alveoli, in each lung. Inside, oxygen from breathed-in air passes through the very thin linings of the alveoli to equally tiny blood vessels on the other side. The blood carries the oxygen away, around the body. At the same time a waste substance, carbon dioxide, seeps through the blood vessel, into the alveoli. As you breathe out, the lungs blow out the carbon dioxide.

Breathing needs muscle power!

The main breathing muscle is the dome-shaped diaphragm at the base of the chest. To breathe in, it becomes flatter, making the lungs bigger, so they suck in air down the windpipe. At the same time, rib muscles lift the ribs, also making the lungs bigger. To breathe out, the diaphragm and rib muscles relax. The stretched lungs spring back to their smaller size and blow out stale air.

Air in

Air out

Diaphragm pulls down

Diaphragm relaxes

▲ Breathing uses two main sets of muscles, the diaphragm and those between the ribs.

▶ After great activity, the body breathes faster and deeper, to replace the oxygen used by the muscles for energy.

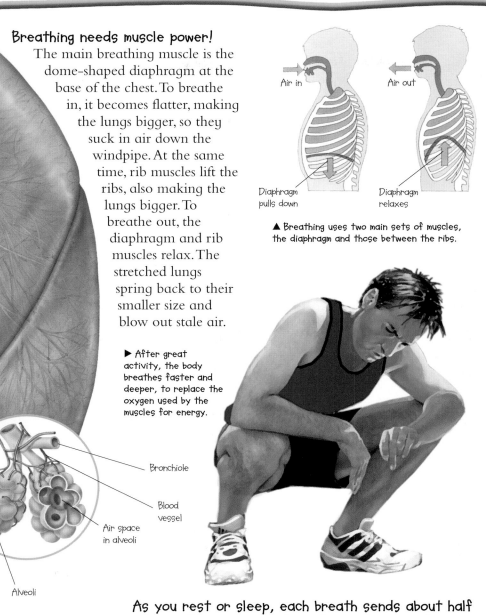

Bronchiole

Blood vessel

Air space in alveoli

Alveoli

▲ Inside each lung, the main bronchus divides again and again, into thousands of narrower airways called bronchioles.

As you rest or sleep, each breath sends about half a litre of air in and out, 15 to 20 times each minute. After great activity, such as running a race, you need more oxygen. So you take deeper breaths faster – 3 litres or more of air, 50 times or more each minute.

The hungry body

All machines need fuel to make them go, and the body is like a living machine whose fuel is food. Food gives us energy for our body processes inside, and for breathing, moving, talking and every other action we make. Food also provides raw materials that the body uses to grow, maintain itself and repair daily wear-and-tear.

▶ Fish, low-fat meats like chicken, and dairy produce such as eggs all contain plenty of valuable proteins.

▶ Foods such as bread, pasta and rice contain lots of starch, which is a useful energy source.

We would not put the wrong fuel into a car engine, so we should not put unsuitable foods into the body. A healthy diet needs a wide variety of different foods, especially fresh vegetables and fruits, which have lots of vital nutrients. Too much of one single food may be unhealthy, especially if that food is very fatty or greasy. Too much of all foods is also unhealthy. It makes the body overweight, which increases the risk of various illnesses.

▶ Cheeses, and fatty and oily foods, are needed in moderate amounts. Plant oils are healthier than fats and oils from animal sources.

There are six main kinds of nutrients in foods, and the body needs balanced amounts of all of them.

• Proteins are needed for growth and repair, and for strong muscles and other parts.

• Carbohydrates, such as sugars and starches, give plenty of energy.

• Some fats are important for general health and energy.

• Vitamins help the body to fight germs and disease.

• Minerals are needed for strong bones and teeth and also healthy blood.

• Fibre is important for good digestion and to prevent certain bowel disorders.

▲ Fresh fruits such as bananas, and vegetables such as carrots, have lots of vitamins, minerals and fibre, and are good for the body in lots of ways.

FOOD FOR THOUGHT

Which of these meals do you think is healthier?

Meal A
Burger, sausage and lots of chips, followed by ice-cream with cream and chocolate.

Meal B
Chicken, tomato and a few chips, followed by fresh fruit salad with apple, banana, pear and melon.

Answer:
Meal B

435

Bite, chew, gulp

The hardest parts of your whole body are the ones that make holes in your food – teeth. They have a covering of whitish or yellowish enamel, which is stronger than most kinds of rocks! Teeth need to last a lifetime of biting, nibbling, gnashing, munching and chewing. They are your own food processors.

There are four main shapes of teeth. The front ones are incisors, and each has a straight, sharp edge, like a spade or chisel, to cut through food. Next are canines, which are taller and more pointed, used mainly for tearing and pulling. Behind them are premolars and molars, which are lower and flatter with small bumps, for crushing and grinding.

Incisor

Canine

Premolar

Molar

Jaw bone

Root

◀ In an adult, each side (left and right) of each jaw (upper and lower) usually has eight different-shaped teeth, of four main types.

A tooth may look almost dead, but it is very much alive. Under the enamel is slightly softer dentine. In the middle of the tooth is the dental pulp. This has blood vessels to nourish the whole tooth, and nerves that feel pressure, heat, cold and pain. The lower part of the tooth, strongly fixed in the jaw bone, is the root. The enamel-covered part above the gum is the crown.

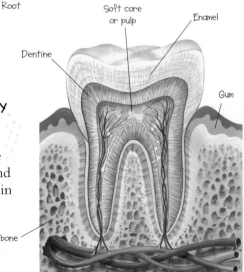

Dentine

Soft core or pulp

Enamel

Gum

Jaw bone

▶ At the centre of a tooth is living pulp, with many blood vessels and nerve endings that pass into the jaw bone.

Teeth are very strong and tough, but they do need to be cleaned properly and regularly. Germs called bacteria live on old bits of food in the mouth. They make waste products which are acid and eat into the enamel and dentine, causing holes called cavities. Which do you prefer – cleaning your teeth after main meals and before bedtime, or the agony of toothache?

▶ Clean your teeth by brushing in different directions and then flossing between them. They will look better and stay healthier for longer.

▼ The first set of teeth lasts about ten years, while the second set can last ten times longer.

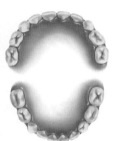

First set
(milk or deciduous teeth)

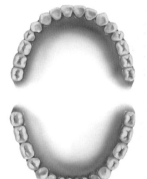

Second set
(adult or permanent set)

Teeth are designed to last a lifetime. Well, not quite, because the body has two sets. There are 20 small teeth in the first or baby set. The first ones usually appear above the gum by about six months of age, the last ones at three years old. As you and your mouth grow, the baby teeth fall out from about seven years old. They are replaced by 32 larger teeth in the adult set.

After chewing, food is swallowed into the gullet (oesophagus). This pushes the food powerfully down through the chest, past the heart and lungs, into the stomach.

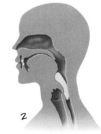

1
tongue pushes food to the back of the throat

2
throat muscles squeeze the food downwards

3
the oesophagus pushes food to the stomach

437

Food's long journey

The digestive system is like a tunnel about 9 metres long, through the body. It includes parts of the body that bite food, chew it, swallow it, churn it up and break it down with natural juices and acids, take in its goodness, and then get rid of the leftovers.

The stomach is a bag with strong, muscular walls. It stretches as it fills with food and drink, and its lining makes powerful digestive acids and juices called enzymes, to attack the food. The muscles in its walls squirm and squeeze to mix the food and juices.

The stomach digests food for a few hours into a thick mush, which oozes into the small intestine. This is only 4 centimetres wide, but more than 5 metres long. It takes nutrients and useful substances through its lining, into the body.

Liver

Pancreas

Small intestine (ileum)

Caecum (start of large intestine)

Appendix

Rectum

The large intestine follows the small one, and it is certainly wider, at about 6 centimetres, but much shorter, only 1.5 metres. It takes in fluids and a few more nutrients from the food, and then squashes what's left into brown lumps, ready to leave the body.

Stomach

Large intestine

▶ The lining of the small intestine has thousands of tiny finger-like parts called the villi, which take nutrients from food, into the blood and lymph system.

◀ The digestive parts almost fill the lower part of the main body, called the abdomen.

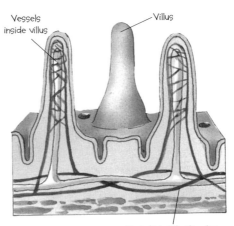

Vessels inside villus

Villus

Vessels in intestine lining

The liver and pancreas are also parts of the digestive system. The liver sorts out and changes the many nutrients from digestion, and stores some of them. The pancreas makes powerful digestive juices that pass to the small intestine to work on the food there.

I DON'T BELIEVE IT!

What's in the leftovers? The brown lumps called bowel motions or faeces are only about one-half undigested or leftover food. Some of the rest is rubbed-off parts of the stomach and intestine lining. The rest is millions of 'friendly' but dead microbes (bacteria) from the intestine. They help to digest our food for us, and in return we give them a warm, food-filled place to live.

Blood in the body

The heart beats to pump the blood all around the body and pass its vital oxygen and nutrients to every part. The same blood goes round and round, or circulates, in its network of blood vessels. So the heart, blood vessels and blood are known as the circulatory system.

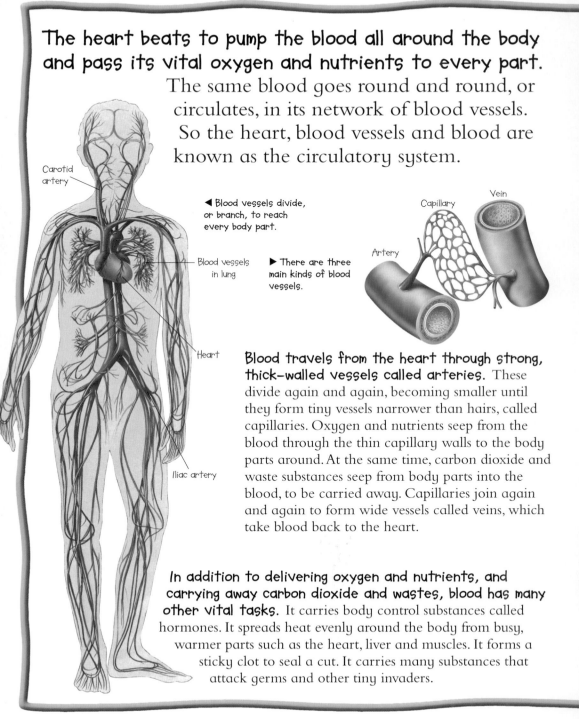

Carotid artery

◄ Blood vessels divide, or branch, to reach every body part.

Blood vessels in lung

► There are three main kinds of blood vessels.

Capillary

Vein

Artery

Heart

Iliac artery

Blood travels from the heart through strong, thick-walled vessels called arteries. These divide again and again, becoming smaller until they form tiny vessels narrower than hairs, called capillaries. Oxygen and nutrients seep from the blood through the thin capillary walls to the body parts around. At the same time, carbon dioxide and waste substances seep from body parts into the blood, to be carried away. Capillaries join again and again to form wide vessels called veins, which take blood back to the heart.

In addition to delivering oxygen and nutrients, and carrying away carbon dioxide and wastes, blood has many other vital tasks. It carries body control substances called hormones. It spreads heat evenly around the body from busy, warmer parts such as the heart, liver and muscles. It forms a sticky clot to seal a cut. It carries many substances that attack germs and other tiny invaders.

Blood has four main parts. The largest is billions of tiny, saucer-shaped red cells, which make up almost half of the total volume of blood and carry oxygen. Second is the white cells, which clean the blood, prevent disease and fight germs. The third part is billions of tiny platelets, which help blood to clot. Fourth is watery plasma, in which the other parts float.

QUIZ

Can you match these blood parts and vessels with their descriptions?
a. Artery b. Vein c. White blood cell
d. Red blood cell e. Platelet f. Capillary

1. Large vessel that takes blood back to the heart
2. Tiny vessel allowing oxygen and nutrients to leave blood
3. Large vessel carrying blood away from the heart
4. Oxygen-carrying part of the blood
5. Disease-fighting part of the blood
6. Part that helps blood to clot

Answers:
a3 b1 c5 d4 e6 f2

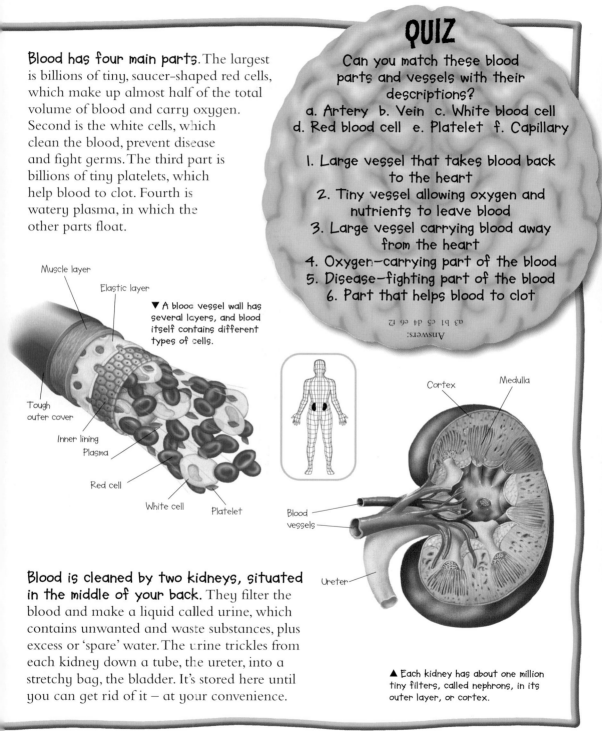

▼ A blood vessel wall has several layers, and blood itself contains different types of cells.

Muscle layer

Elastic layer

Tough outer cover

Inner lining

Plasma

Red cell

White cell

Platelet

Cortex

Medulla

Blood vessels

Ureter

Blood is cleaned by two kidneys, situated in the middle of your back. They filter the blood and make a liquid called urine, which contains unwanted and waste substances, plus excess or 'spare' water. The urine trickles from each kidney down a tube, the ureter, into a stretchy bag, the bladder. It's stored here until you can get rid of it – at your convenience.

▲ Each kidney has about one million tiny filters, called nephrons, in its outer layer, or cortex.

441

The beating body

The heart is about as big as its owner's clenched fist. It is a hollow bag of very strong muscle, called cardiac muscle or myocardium. This muscle never tires. It contracts once every second or more often, all through life. The contraction, or heartbeat, squeezes blood inside the heart out into the arteries. As the heart relaxes it fills again with blood from the veins.

Inside, the heart is not one baglike pump, but two pumps side by side. The left pump sends blood all around the body, from head to toe, to deliver its oxygen (systemic circulation). The blood comes back to the right pump and is sent to the lungs, to collect more oxygen (pulmonary circulation). The blood returns to the left pump and starts the whole journey again.

▶ The heart is two pumps side by side, and each pump has two chambers, the upper atrium and the lower ventricle.

To upper body

Aorta (main artery)

Pulmonary artery to lung

From upper body

To lung

From lung

Right atrium

Valve

Right ventricle

From lower body

To lower body

Inside the heart are four sets of bendy flaps called valves. These open to let blood flow the right way. If the blood tries to move the wrong way, it pushes the flaps together and the valve closes. Valves make sure the blood flows the correct way, rather than sloshing to and fro, in and out of the heart, with each beat.

▶ The heartbeat is the regular squeezing of the heart muscle to pump blood around the body.

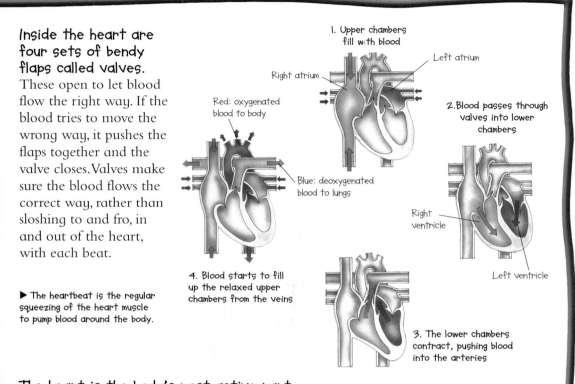

1. Upper chambers fill with blood

Left atrium

Right atrium

Red: oxygenated blood to body

2. Blood passes through valves into lower chambers

Blue: deoxygenated blood to lungs

Right ventricle

Left ventricle

4. Blood starts to fill up the relaxed upper chambers from the veins

3. The lower chambers contract, pushing blood into the arteries

The heart is the body's most active part, and it needs plenty of energy brought by the blood. The blood flows through small vessels, which branch across its surface and down into its thick walls. These are called the coronary vessels.

The heart beats at different rates, depending on what the body is doing. When the muscles are active they need more energy and oxygen, brought by the blood. So the heart beats faster, 120 times each minute or more. At rest, the heart slows to 60 to 80 beats per minute.

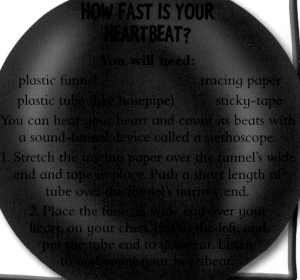

HOW FAST IS YOUR HEARTBEAT?

You will need:

plastic funnel   tracing paper
plastic tube (like hosepipe)   sticky-tape

You can hear your heart and count its beats with a sound-funnel device called a stethoscope.

1. Stretch the tracing paper over the funnel's wide end and tape in place. Push a short length of tube over the funnel's narrow end.

2. Place the funnel's wide end over your heart, on your chest, just to the left, and put the tube end to your ear. Listen to and count your heartbeat.

Looking and listening

The body finds out about the world around it by its senses – and the main sense is eyesight. The eyes detect the brightness, colours and patterns of light rays, and change these into patterns of nerve signals that they send to the brain. More than half of the knowledge, information and memories stored in the brain come into the body through the eyes.

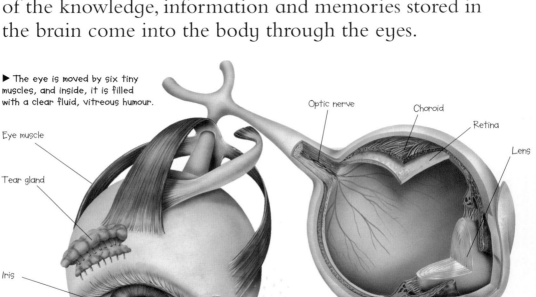

▶ The eye is moved by six tiny muscles, and inside, it is filled with a clear fluid, vitreous humour.

Optic nerve

Choroid

Retina

Lens

Eye muscle

Tear gland

Iris

Pupil

Lens muscle

Tear duct to nose

Each eye is a ball about 2.5 centimetres across. At the front is a clear dome, the cornea, which lets light through a small, dark-looking hole just behind it, the pupil. The light then passes through a pea-shaped lens which bends the rays so they shine a clear picture onto the inside back of the eye, the retina. This has 125 million tiny cells, rods and cones, which detect the light and make nerve signals to send along the optic nerve to the brain.

▼ In the retina are wider cone cells, narrower rod cells, and many nerve cells with long fibres connecting them.

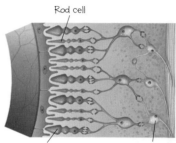

Rod cell

Cone cell

Nerve cells

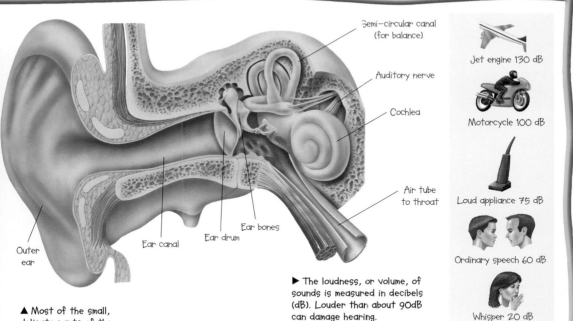

Semi-circular canal (for balance)

Auditory nerve

Cochlea

Air tube to throat

Ear bones

Ear drum

Ear canal

Outer ear

Jet engine 130 dB

Motorcycle 100 dB

Loud appliance 75 dB

Ordinary speech 60 dB

Whisper 20 dB

▶ The loudness, or volume, of sounds is measured in decibels (dB). Louder than about 90dB can damage hearing.

▲ Most of the small, delicate parts of the ear are inside the head, well protected by skull bones around them.

BRIGHT AND DIM

Look at your eyes in a mirror. See how the dark hole which lets in light, the pupil, is quite small. The coloured part around the pupil, the iris, is a ring of muscle.

Close your eyes for a minute, then open them and look carefully. Does the pupil quickly get smaller?

While the eyes were closed, the iris made the pupil bigger, to try and let in more light, so you could try to see in the darkness. As you open your eyes, the iris makes the pupil smaller again, to prevent too much light from dazzling you.

The ear is far more than the bendy, curly flap on the side of the head. The ear flap funnels sound waves along a short tunnel, the ear canal, to a fingernail-sized patch of tight skin, the eardrum. As sound waves hit the eardrum it shakes or vibrates, and passes the vibrations to a row of three tiny bones. These are the ear ossicles, the smallest bones in the body. They also vibrate and pass on the vibrations to another part, the cochlea, which has a curly, snail-like shape.

Inside the cochlea, the vibrations pass through fluid and shake rows of thousands of tiny hairs which grow from specialized hair cells. As the hairs vibrate, the hair cells make nerve signals, which flash along the auditory nerve to the brain.

445

Smelling and tasting

▼ The parts that carry out smelling are in the roof of the large chamber inside the nose.

Olfactory cells

Mucus lining

Nasal cavity

You cannot see smells, which are tiny particles floating in the air – but your nose can smell them. Your nose is more sensitive than you realize. It can detect more than 10,000 different scents, odours, perfumes, fragrances, pongs and niffs. Smell is useful because it warns us if food is bad or rotten, and perhaps dangerous to eat. That's why we sniff a new or strange food item, almost without thinking, before trying it.

▼ Olfactory (smell) cells have micro-hairs facing down into the nasal chamber, which detect smell particles landing on them.

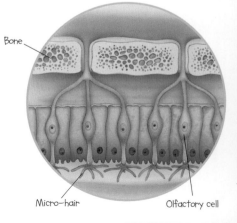

Bone

Micro-hair

Olfactory cell

Smell particles drift with breathed-in air into the nose and through the nasal chamber behind it. At the top of the chamber are two patches of lining, each about the area of a thumbnail and with 250 million microscopic hairs. The particles land on the sticky hairs, and if they fit into landing sites called receptors there, like a key into a lock, then nerve signals flash along the olfactory nerve to the brain.

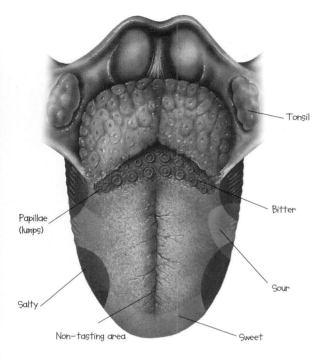

Tonsil

Papillae
(lumps)

Bitter

Sour

Salty

Non-tasting area

Sweet

The body's most flexible muscle is also the one which is coated with 10,000 micro-sensors for taste – the tongue. Each micro-sensor is a taste bud shaped like a tiny onion. Most taste buds are along the tip, sides and rear upper surface of the tongue. They are scattered around the much larger flaps and lumps on the tongue, which are called papillae.

◀ The taste buds are mainly around the edges of the tongue, not on the main middle area.

Taste works in a similar way to smell, but it detects flavour particles in foods and drinks. The particles touch tiny hairs sticking up from hair cells in the taste buds. If the particles fit into receptors there, then the hair cell makes nerve signals, which go along the facial and other nerves to the brain.

SWEET AND SOUR

The tongue detects only four basic flavours – sweet at the tip, salty along the front sides, sour along the rear sides, and bitter across the back.

Which of these foods is sweet, salty, bitter or sour?

1. Coffee 2. Lemon 3. Bacon
4. Ice cream

Answers:
1. bitter 2. sour 3. salty 4. sweet

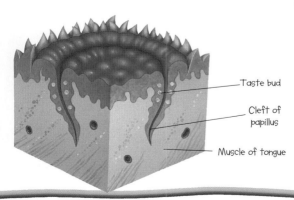

Taste bud

Cleft of
papillus

Muscle of tongue

◀ The large pimple-like lumps at the back of the tongue, called papillae, have tiny taste buds in their deep clefts.

The nervous body

The body is not quite a 'bag of nerves', but it does contain thousands of kilometres of these pale, shiny threads. Nerves carry tiny electrical pulses known as nerve signals or neural messages. They form a vast information-sending network that reaches every part, almost like the body's own Internet.

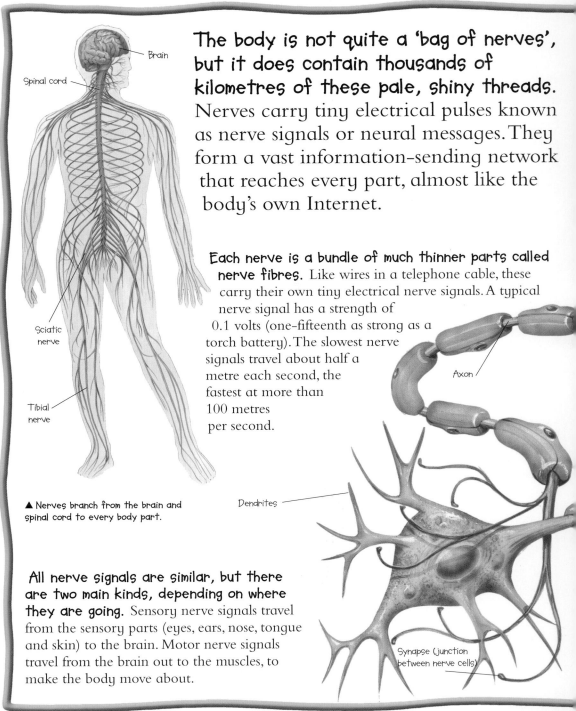

Brain

Spinal cord

Sciatic nerve

Tibial nerve

▲ Nerves branch from the brain and spinal cord to every body part.

Each nerve is a bundle of much thinner parts called nerve fibres. Like wires in a telephone cable, these carry their own tiny electrical nerve signals. A typical nerve signal has a strength of 0.1 volts (one-fifteenth as strong as a torch battery). The slowest nerve signals travel about half a metre each second, the fastest at more than 100 metres per second.

Axon

Dendrites

Synapse (junction between nerve cells)

All nerve signals are similar, but there are two main kinds, depending on where they are going. Sensory nerve signals travel from the sensory parts (eyes, ears, nose, tongue and skin) to the brain. Motor nerve signals travel from the brain out to the muscles, to make the body move about.

TIME TO REACT!

You will need:
a friend   ruler

1. Ask your friend holds the ruler by the end with the highest measurement, letting it hang down. Put your thumb and fingers level with the other end, ready to grab.

2. Get your friend to let the ruler go, for you to grasp it as it falls. Measure where your thumb is on the ruler. Swap places so your friend has a go.

3. The person who grabs the ruler nearest its lower end has the fastest reactions. To grab the ruler, nerve signals travel from the eye, to the brain, and back out to the muscles in the arm and hand.

Hormones are part of the body's inner control system. A hormone is a chemical made by a gland. It travels in the blood and affects other body parts, for example, making them work faster or release more of their product.

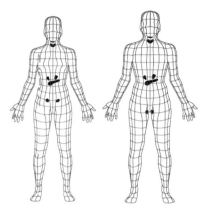

▼ Female and male bodies have much the same hormone-making glands, except for the reproductive parts – ovaries in the female (left) and testes in the male (right).

The main hormonal gland, the pituitary, is also the smallest. Just under the brain, it has close links with the nervous system. It mainly controls other hormonal glands. One is the thyroid in the neck, which affects the body's growth and how fast its chemical processes work. The pancreas controls how the body uses energy, by its hormone, insulin. The adrenal glands are involved in the body's balance of water, minerals and salts, and how we react to stress and fear.

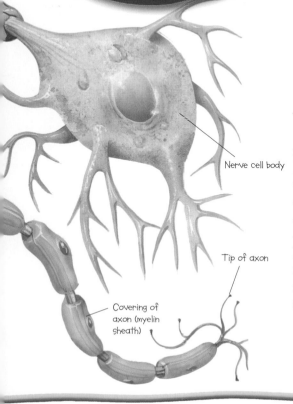

Nerve cell body

Tip of axon

Covering of axon (myelin sheath)

◀ The brain and nerves are made of billions of specialized cells, nerve cells or neurons. Each has many tiny branches, dendrites, to collect nerve messages, and a longer, thicker branch, the axon or fibre, to pass on the messages.

The brainy body

Your brain is as big as your two fists side by side. It's the place where you think, learn, work out problems, remember, feel happy and sad, wonder, worry, have ideas, sleep and dream.

▼ The two wrinkled hemispheres (halves) of the cerebrum, where thinking happens, are the largest brain parts.

Cerebral hemisphere

Thalamus

Hippocampus

Cerebellum

Brain stem

The main part of the brain is its bulging, wrinkled upper part, the **cerebrum.** Different areas of its surface (cerebral cortex) deal with nerve signals to and from different parts of the body. For example, messages from the eyes pass to the lower rear part of the cerebrum, called the visual centre. They are sorted here as the brain cells work out what the eyes are seeing. There are also areas for touch, hearing, taste and other body processes.

Yet the brain looks like a wrinkly lump of grey–pink jelly! On average, it weighs about 1.4 kilograms. It doesn't move, but its amazing nerve activity uses up one-fifth of all the energy needed by the body.

The cerebellum is the rounded, wrinkled part at the back of the brain. It processes messages from the motor centre, sorting and coordinating them in great detail, to send to the body's hundreds of muscles. This is how we learn skilled, precise movements such as writing, skateboarding or playing music (or all three), almost without thinking.

The brain stem is the lower part of the brain, where it joins the body's main nerve, the spinal cord. The brain stem controls basic processes vital for life, like breathing, heartbeat, digesting food and removing wastes.

The brain really does have 'brain waves'. Every second it receives, sorts and sends millions of nerve signals. Special pads attached to the head can detect these tiny electrical pulses. They are shown on a screen or paper strip as wavy lines called an EEG, electro-encephalogram.

▼ Different areas or centres of the brain's outer layer, the cerebral cortex, deal with messages from and to certain parts of the body.

Touch area
Movement area
Thought area
Vision area
Speech area
Hearing area

▼ The brain's 'waves' or EEG recordings change, depending on whether the person is alert and thinking hard, resting, falling asleep or deeply asleep.

I DON'T BELIEVE IT!

The brain never sleeps! EEG waves show that it is almost as busy at night as when we are awake. It still controls heartbeat, breathing and digestion. It also sifts through the day's events and stores memories.

The healthy body

No one wants to be ill – and it is very easy to cut down the risk of becoming sick or developing disease. For a start, the body needs the right amounts of different foods, especially fresh foods like vegetables and fruits. And not too much food either, or it becomes unhealthily fat.

Another excellent way to stay well is regular sport or exercise. Activity keeps the muscles powerful, the bones strong and the joints flexible. If it speeds up your breathing and heartbeat, it keeps your lungs and heart healthy too.

◀ Germs on hands can get onto our food and then into our bodies. So it is important to wash hands before mealtimes.

Germs are everywhere – in the air, on our bodies and on almost everything we touch. If we keep clean by showering or bathing, and especially if we wash our hands after using the toilet and before eating, then germs have less chance to attack us.

Health is not only in the body, it's in the mind. Too much worry and stress can cause many illnesses, such as headaches and digestive upsets. This is why it's so important to talk about troubles and share them with someone who can help.

◀ Exercise keeps the body fit and healthy, and it should be fun too. It is always best to reduce risks of having an accident by wearing a cycle helmet for example.

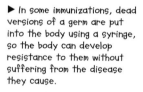

▶ In some immunizations, dead versions of a germ are put into the body using a syringe, so the body can develop resistance to them without suffering from the disease they cause.

Doctors and nurses help us to recover from sickness, and they also help prevent illness. Regular check-ups at the dentist, optician and health centre are vital. For most people immunizations (vaccinations) also help to protect against diseases. It is good to report any health problem early, before they become too serious to treat.

Old age is getting older! More people live to be 100 years or more and for many of them, their bodies are still working well. How would you like to spend your 100th birthday?

INVENTIONS

Explore fascinating inventions such as the
discovery of fire and amazing laser technology.

Computers • Microscopes • Telescopes
Musical instruments • Telephones • Television
Tools • Fire • Wheels • Bicycles • Weapons • Boats
Maps • Clocks • Windmills • Engines • Printing
Cameras • Hot-air balloons • Jets • CDs
Microwaves • Rockets • Space shuttles

Inventors of the Stone Age

Humans have always been inventors.
Over 400,000 years ago, our ancient
relatives made stone tools such as axes.
Then about 30,000 years ago they
discovered how to sew skins together to
make clothes. Bones were first used as
musical instruments over 20,000 years
ago. Early people also learned how
to use fire and invented cooking and
ways of lighting the darkness. Because
they lived by hunting animals, early
humans invented bows and arrows
to which they added sharp stone tips.
They learned how to keep warm
and dry by building shelters and
homes made from tree branches,
rocks and huge woolly
mammoth tusks.

▶ Stone Age clothes were
made out of animal skins sewn
together using a bone needle.

The first tools

The first inventors lived about 2.5 million years ago. They were small, human-like creatures who walked upright on two legs. Their first inventions were stone tools. They hammered stones with other stones to shape them. These rough tools have been found in Tanzania in Africa. Scientists call this early relative of ours 'handy man'.

Stone Age people made really sharp weapons and tools by chipping a stone called flint. They dug pits and tunnels in chalky ground to find the valuable flint lumps. Their digging tools were made from reindeer antlers.

▶ Stone Age hunters trapped woolly mammoths in pits and killed them with spears.

Early hunters were able to kill the largest animals. With flint tips on their weapons, they overcame wild oxen and horses and even killed huge, woolly mammoths. They used their sharp flint tools to carve up the bodies. The flint easily sliced through tough animal hides.

◀ Flint tools were shaped to fit comfortably into the hand, with finely chipped cutting edges that could cut through large bones.

The axe was a powerful weapon.
A new invention, the axe handle, made it possible to strike very hard blows. Fitted with a sharp stone head, the axe was useful for chopping down trees for firewood and building shelters.

▶ Axe heads were valuable, and were traded with people who had no flint.

I DON'T BELIEVE IT!

Some Stone Age hunters used boomerangs! They made them out of mammoth tusks thousands of years before Australian boomerangs, and used them for hunting.

Saws could cut through the hardest wood. Flint workers discovered how to make very small flint flakes. They fixed the flakes like teeth in a straight handle of wood or bone. If the teeth broke, they could fix new ones. Saws were used to cut through tough bones as well as wood.

▼ Saws were made from about 12,000 BC, and had flint 'teeth' held in place by resin.

459

The fire makers

People once used fire created by lightning.
Discovering how to use fire made life a lot
easier. The first fire users lived in Africa more
than 250,000 years ago. Over thousands of
years, these people spread into Europe and
Asia. Winters were very cold further north.
Fire helped people stay warm. They went on
to discover how to twirl a fire stick very fast.
This was done by placing the loop of a
bowstring around the stick and moving the
bow back and forth. After thousands of
years, people invented a way to make
sparks from steel by hitting it with
a flint. Now they could carry
their fire-making tinderboxes
around with them.

▶ Fire provided early people with warmth,
light and heat to cook food. The temperature
deep within a cave stays the same whatever
the weather outside.

MAKING HEAT

When your hands are cold you
rub them together. Do this slowly.
They feel the same. Now rub them
together really fast. Feel how your
hands get warmer. Rubbing things
together is called friction.
Friction causes heat.

Fire makes food taste good.
The invention of cooking made
food safer, because cooking kills
germs. Cooking roots and meat
on a fire makes them more tender
as well as tastier. Humans are the
only animals that cook food.

**Humans invented lamps to light
deep, dark caves.** The lamps
were saucers of clay or stone that
burned animal fat, with moss for
a wick. Campfire flames kept
wild animals away at night. They
also cooked food and kept people
warm. People could see to make
wall paintings in the caves.

New ways of moving

With wheels you can move enormous weights. Once, heavy weights were dragged along the ground, sometimes on sledges. In Scandinavia, parts of 7000-year-old sledges have been found. Over 5500 years ago, the Sumerians of Mesopotamia began to use wheels made from carved planks fastened together.

Metal rim

Plank fastening

▲ Plank wheels were very heavy, and metal rims helped hold them together.

▼ Spoked wheels made chariots light, fast and easy to steer.

Warriors had light, strong wheels on their fighting chariots. Wheels with spokes are lighter than solid plank wheels. From about 1800BC, the ancient Egyptians were using light chariots with spoked wheels. Horses pulled them fast in battle. The ancient Greeks and Romans used them for chariot races as well as for fighting.

Spoke   Light rim   Lightweight frame

Hobby (1818)

Velocipede (1861)
(Boneshaker)

Penny Farthing (early 1870s)

Mountain bike (1976)

◀ From the earliest boneshaker to today's mountain bike, the bicycle has always been popular.

Railway lines were once made of wood! Wheels move easily along rails. Horses pulled heavy wagons on these wagonways over 400 years ago. William Jessop invented specially shaped metal wheels to run along metal rails in 1789. Modern trains haul enormous loads at great speed along metal rails.

In 1861, bikes with solid tyres were called boneshakers! However, an even earlier version of the bicycle was invented by the Frenchman, Count of Sivrac, in 1790. It had no pedals and was moved by the feet pushing against the ground. The invention of air-filled rubber tyres made cycling more comfortable.

Cars with gigantic wheels can drive over other cars! Big wheels give a smooth ride. At some motor shows, trucks with enormous wheels compete to drive over rows of cars. Tractors with huge wheels were invented to drive over very rough ground.

QUIZ
WHICH CAME FIRST?

1. (a) the chariot, or (b) the sledge?
2. (a) solid wheels, or (b) spoked wheels?
3. (a) rails, or (b) steam engines?
4. (a) tyres with inner-tubes, or (b) solid tyres?
5. (a) the boneshaker, or (b) the mountain bike?

Answers:
1.b 2.a 3.a 4.b 5.a

▶ Wheels this size are usually only found on giant dump trucks. These carry heavy loads such as rocks or soil that can be tipped out.

Harvesting the earth

The first farmers used digging sticks. In the area now called Iraq, about 9000 BC, farmers broke the ground and planted seeds of wheat and barley. They used knives made of flint flakes fixed in a bone or wooden handle to cut the ripe grain stalks. The quern was an invention for grinding grain into flour between two stones.

▲ Curved knives made of bone or wood were used for harvesting grain.

Humans pulled the first ploughs. They were invented in Egypt and surrounding countries as early as 4000 BC. Ploughs broke the ground and turned over the soil faster and better than digging sticks. Later on, oxen and other animals pulled ploughs. The invention of metal ploughs made ploughing much easier.

◄ Ploughed furrows made it easier to sow, water and harvest crops.

New inventions changed farming forever.

For thousands of years farming hardly changed. Then, about 300 years ago, there were many new inventions. One of these was a seed-drill, invented by Englishman Jethro Tull. Pulled by a horse, it sowed seeds at regular spaces in neat rows. It was less wasteful than the old method of throwing grain onto the ground.

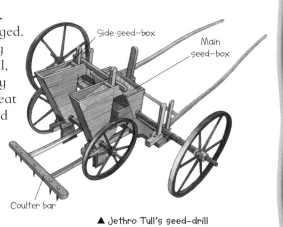

Side seed-box

Main seed-box

Coulter bar

▲ Jethro Tull's seed-drill sowed three rows of seed at a time.

Modern machines harvest huge fields of wheat in record time.

The combine harvester was invented to cut the crop and separate grain at the same time. Teams of combine harvesters roll across America's wide plains harvesting the wheat. What were once huge areas of land covered with grass now provide the grain for America's bread.

Scientists are changing the way plants grow.

They have invented ways of creating crop plants with built-in protection from pests and diseases. Other bumper crop plants grow well in places where once they could not grow at all because of the soil or weather.

▼ The latest combine harvesters have air-conditioned, soundproofed cabs and some even have sound systems.

Under attack!

Using a spear thrower is like having an arm twice the normal length. Spear throwers were invented about 15,000 BC. Hunters and warriors used them to hurl spears harder and farther than ever before. People all over the world invented this useful tool, and Australian Aborigines still use it.

◀ One end of the spear thrower is cupped to hold the spear butt.

▼ Bowmen often stood behind lines of sharpened stakes that protected them from enemies on horseback.

Arrows from a longbow could pass through iron armour. Bows and arrows were invented at least 20,000 years ago. More than 900 years ago, the English longbow was made from a yew branch. Archers used it to fire many arrows a long distance in a short time. By law, all Englishmen had to practise regularly with the longbow. It helped them win many famous battles.

I DON'T BELIEVE IT!

Longbow archers could aim and fire six arrows per minute. The arrow sometimes went straight through an enemy's armour and out the other side.

Crossbows had to be wound up for each shot. They were invented over 2000 years ago in the Mediterranean area, and fired a metal bolt or short arrow. They were powerful and accurate, but much slower than longbows. Soldiers used them in sieges throughout Europe from about AD 1000 onwards. But in battles, where speed was important, crossbows were often beaten by longbows.

▶ Crossbows were the first mechanical hand weapons, and at one time the Church tried to ban them.

In the Bible, David killed the giant, Goliath, with a pebble from a sling. The sling is an ancient weapon probably invented by shepherds. They used it when guarding their flocks, and still do in some countries. The slinger holds the two loose ends, and puts a pebble in the pouch. Then he whirls it round his head and lets go of one end. The pebble flies out at the target.

A schoolboy's catapult can do a lot of damage. The rubber strips are like bowstrings, which can fire a pebble from a pouch, like a sling. Some anglers use a catapult to fire food to attract fish to the water's surface.

From stone to metal

Sometimes pieces of pure natural gold or copper can be found in the ground. The earliest metal workers from about 8000 BC, in the eastern Mediterranean, beat these metals with stone tools. They made the first copper weapons and gold ornaments.

▶ Gold is quite soft, and early goldsmiths beat it into a variety of shapes, and made patterns of hammered indentations on its surface.

Blowing air onto flames makes them hotter. About 8500 years ago people discovered how to melt metals out of the rocks, or ores, containing them. They invented bellows – animal-skin bags, to blow air onto the flames. The hot flames melted the metal out of the ore. We call this 'smelting' the metal.

Bronze weapons stay sharper for longer than copper ones. About 5500 years ago, metal workers invented bronze by smelting copper ores and tin ores together. They used the bronze to make hard, sharp swords, spearheads and axe heads.

◀ Molten bronze was poured into moulds of stone or clay to make tools.

▶ Bronze axes were sharper, and less easily damaged than stone ones.

Armies with iron weapons can beat armies with bronze weapons. Iron is harder than bronze, but needs a very hot fire to smelt it. About 1500 BC, metal workers began to use charcoal in their fires. This burns much hotter than ordinary wood and is good for smelting iron.

▲ After smelting, iron was beaten into shape to make strong, sharp weapons.

◀ Iron chains are made by hammering closed the red-hot links.

The Romans were excellent plumbers. They made water pipes out of lead instead of wood or pottery. Lead is soft, easily shaped and is not damaged by water.

Some modern steelworks are the size of towns. Steel is made from iron, and was first invented when small amounts of carbon were mixed into molten iron. Steel is very hard, and used to build many things, including ships and skyscrapers.

▶ Molten steel is poured from huge vats and rolled out into long sheets.

Boats and sail

Viking explorers reached America 1000 years ago. The world's first boats were log rafts, useful for carrying heavy loads, but very slow. Viking boats were fast, and could travel far across the open sea. Sails were invented at least 5000 years ago, and the Vikings used both sails and oars.

▶ Viking boats were made of long planks fitted onto wooden frames, and steered by means of a long oar fastened near the stern (back of the ship). They could be sailed across deep oceans, or rowed up shallow rivers, and made river journeys from the Baltic as far as the Black Sea.

I DON'T BELIEVE IT!

In 450 BC a merchant called Himilco sailed from North Africa to Britain. He ended up in Cornwall and bought Cornish tin!

About 300 years ago sailing ships sailed all the world's oceans. Some, like the British man-of-war fighting ships, were enormous, with many sails and large crews of sailors. Countries such as Britain, France, Spain and Holland had large navies made up of these ships.

Some sailing boats race around the world non-stop. Modern sailing boats use many inventions, such as machines to roll up the sails and gears that allow the boat to steer itself. These boats are tough, light and very fast.

Wonderful clay

Stone Age hunters used baked clay to do magic. At least 30,000 years ago in Central Europe they discovered that some clay went hard in the sun, and even harder in a fire. They made little clay figures of animals and humans. These were probably used in magic spells to help the hunters catch food. Hardening clay in a fire was the start of the invention of pottery.

◀ Some early clay figures may have been made to represent ancestors or gods and goddesses.

▶ Kilns produced much higher temperatures than open fires, and the heat could be controlled.

Hard clay bowls changed the way people ate. The first known pots were made around 10,000 BC in Japan. They were shaped by hand and hardened in fires. They could hold liquid, and were used to boil meat and plants. This made the food tastier and more tender. Around 7000 BC, potters in Southeast Asia used a new invention – a special oven to harden and waterproof clay, called a kiln.

Potters' wheels were probably invented before cart wheels. About 3500 BC in Mesopotamia (modern Iraq), potters invented a wheel on which to turn lumps of clay and shape round pots. By spinning the clay, the potter could make smooth, perfectly round shapes quickly.

Clay pot

Heat duct

Fuel

Brick–making was invented in hot countries without many trees. The first brick buildings were built in 9000 BC in the Jordan Valley. House builders made bricks from clay and straw, and dried them in the hot sun. By 3500 BC, bricks hardened in kilns were used in important buildings in Mesopotamia.

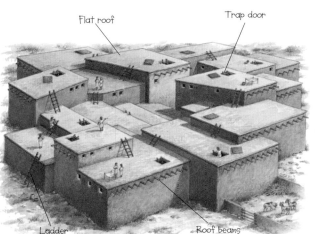

Flat roof

Trap door

Ladder

Roof beams

▶ With the invention of bricks, it was possible to construct large buildings. In 6000 BC, the Turkish town of Catal Hüyük had houses with rooftop openings connected by ladders instead of doors.

Modern factories make thousands of pots at a time. They are 'fired' in huge kilns. Wheels with electric motors are used, though much factory pottery is shaped in moulds. Teams of workers paint patterns.

MAKE A COILED POT

Roll modelling clay into a long, 'snake' shape. Coil some of it into a flat circle. Continue to coil, building the coils upward. Try and make a bowl shape, and finally smooth out the ridges.

▼ Decorating pottery by hand and reproducing the pattern accurately requires much skill.

Sailing into the unknown

Early sailors looked at the stars to find their way about. Around 1000 BC, Phoenician merchants from Syria were able to sail out of sight of land without getting lost. They knew in which direction certain stars lay. The North Star, in the Plough constellation (star group), always appears in the north.

▲ The Plough moves across the night sky but always points to the North Star.

Magnetic compasses always point north and south. They allow sailors to navigate (find their way) even when the stars are invisible. The Chinese invented the magnetic compass about 3000 years ago. It was first used in Europe about 1000 years ago.

▶ Using stick and shell maps, Pacific islanders successfully crossed thousands of kilometres of ocean.

◀ Compasses have a magnetized needle placed on a pivot so it can turn easily. Beneath this is a card with marked points to show direction.

Early maps showed where sea monsters lived. The first world map was drawn by the Greek Ptolemy in AD 160. Greek maps of around 550 BC showed the known world surrounded by water in which monsters lived. Over 500 years ago, Pacific islanders had maps of sticks and shells, showing islands and currents. The first globe was invented in 1492 by a German, Martin Behain.

Shell = island   Reed binding   Stick = current

▼ The chronometer was invented by Englishman John Harrison in 1735. It was a reliable timepiece, specially mounted to remove the effect of a ship's motion at sea.

Mirrors

Telescope

Moving arm

▶ The sextant was developed in the mid-1700s and was an important navigation aid until the 1900s.

Scale

18th-century sailors could work out exactly where they were on the oceans. They used an instrument called a sextant, invented in 1731. The sextant measured the height of the Sun from the horizon. The chronometer was an extremely reliable clock that wasn't affected by the motion of the sea.

USING A COMPASS

Take a compass outside and find out which direction is north. Put a cardboard arrow with 'N' on it on the ground pointing in the right direction. Then try to work out the directions of south, west and east.

New direction-finding inventions can tell anyone exactly where they are. A hand-held instrument, called a GPS receiver, receives signals from satellites in space. It shows your position within a few metres. These receivers can be built into cars, ships, planes – even laptop computers!

Satellite orbit

Global Positioning Satellite (GPS)

◀ Modern navigation instruments use signals from several satellites to pinpoint their position.

475

Weapons of war

I DON'T BELIEVE IT!

In 1453 the biggest cannon in the world could fire a half-tonne cannon ball for a mile. It was used by the Turkish Sultan Mehmet to win the siege of Constantinople.

The Romans invented massive rock-hurling weapons. In medieval times, armies in Europe and the Middle East still used the same weapons in city and castle sieges. The trebuchet slung great rocks or burning material over city walls. The ballista fired missiles such as stones or spears with huge force at the enemy.

The first gunpowder was used in fireworks. The Chinese invented gunpowder over 1000 years ago. In 1221 they used it to make exploding bombs and in 1288 they invented the first gun, a cannon. Cannons and mortars, which fired bombs or large stone balls very high through the air, were used in European sieges from the 14th century onwards. The first small firearms carried by soldiers appeared in the 15th century.

Siege tower

The battering ram could smash through massive city walls and gates. The Egyptians may have invented it in 2000 BC to destroy brick walls. It was a huge tree-trunk, often with an iron head, swung back and forth in a frame. Sometimes it had a roof to protect the soldiers from rocks and arrows from above.

Ballista

▶ Medieval sieges of well-protected forts or cities sometimes lasted for months.

476

Greek fire was a secret weapon that burned in water. The Greeks invented it in the 7th century AD to destroy ships attacking Constantinople. A chemical mixture was squirted at enemies through copper pipes. It was still being used many centuries later in medieval sieges, pumped down onto the heads of attackers.

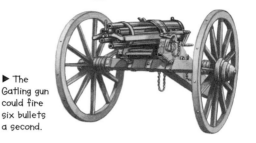

▶ The Gatling gun could fire six bullets a second.

Gunpowder was used in tunnels to blow up castle walls. Attackers in a siege dug tunnels under the walls and supported them with wooden props. Then, they blew up or burned away the props so that the walls collapsed.

Modern machine guns can fire thousands of bullets per minute. Richard Gatling, an American, invented the first machine gun in 1862. As in all modern guns, each machine-gun bullet has its own metal case packed with deadly explosives.

Trebuchet

Battering ram

Measuring time

The huge stone slabs of Stonehenge can be used as a calendar. Some of its stones are lined up with sunrise on the longest day of the year. It was built and rebuilt in Wiltshire in southern England between 3000 BC and 1550 BC.

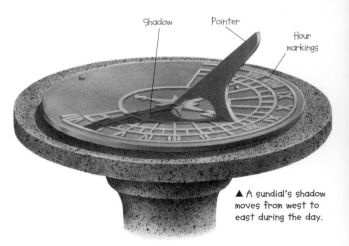

Shadow   Pointer   Hour markings

▲ A sundial's shadow moves from west to east during the day.

One of the earliest clocks was a stick stuck in the ground. Invented in Egypt up to 4000 years ago, the length of the shadow showed the time of day. Later sundials had a face marked with hours, and a pointer that cast a shadow.

▼ Raising the huge main stones of Stonehenge required the muscles of many workers and the know–how of skilled Bronze Age engineers.

Candles, water and sand can all be used to tell the time. The Egyptians invented a clock that dripped water at a fixed rate about 1400 BC. Candle clocks were marked with rings, and in the hourglass, invented about AD 1300, sand ran between two glass globes.

▶ A candle clock (below) and an hourglass (right) show a time period has passed, not the time of day.

▼ Until the invention of quartz movements, wristwatches contained springs and cogs.

Winder

Main spring   Gear wheel   Ratchet wheel

You can't see any moving parts in a modern quartz clock. Early clocks depended on movement. A Dutchman, Christiaan Huygens, invented a clock in 1656 which depended on a swinging pendulum. About the same time, clocks driven by coiled springs were invented. Modern quartz crystal clocks work on invisible vibrations and are very accurate. They were first produced in 1929.

MAKE A SHADOW CLOCK

Fix about 60 centimetres of garden cane upright in a flat piece of ground. Use lollipop sticks or twigs to mark the length of the shadow every hour, from 9 a.m. to 4 p.m. if possible. Which hour casts the shortest shadow?

Answer:
12 o'clock midday

▶ Wrist watches were not made until 1790. Many modern watches have a liquid crystal display (LCD) and show changing numerals instead of hour and minute hands.

Some clocks are like toys. Swiss cuckoo clocks contain a bird on a spring that flies out of a little door and 'cuckoos' the time. Some 18th-century clocks looked like ships, and their guns fired to mark the hours.

Harvesting nature's energy

The first inventions to use wind-power were sailing boats. Invented around 3500 BC by the Egyptians, and also by the Sumerians of Mesopotamia, the first sailing boats had a single square sail. By AD 600, windmills for grinding grain had been invented in Arab countries. Some European windmills, in use from about AD 1100 onwards, could be turned to face the wind.

The first waterwheels invented were flat, not upright. Used around 100 BC in Yugoslavia and Albania, they needed very fast streams to drive them. One century later, Roman upright waterwheels worked better and had gears to slow them down. As well as grinding corn, some were used to drive pumps or saws.

Direction vane

Sail

Main drive

Rotation point

Gears

Millstones

Flour chute

▶ Many windmills were made entirely of wood apart from the millstones.

◀ In overshot watermills, the water strikes the top of the millwheel.

▶ Trevithick's locomotive used high-pressure steam, and he demonstrated it in 1808 on a circular track in London, at speeds of up to 16 kilometres an hour.

Early steam engines often threatened to explode. Thomas Savery's 1698 steam pump, invented in Devon, England, wasted fuel and was dangerous. Englishman Richard Trevithick developed a steam engine to move on tracks in 1804.

Spinning magnets can create an electric current. Michael Faraday and other scientists invented the first magnetic electricity generators (producers) in the 1830s. Today, huge dams use the power of millions of tonnes of flowing water to turn electricity generating machinery. They still use moving magnets to make electricity.

The strength of the wind usually increases the higher up you are. Some of the largest wind turbines in use today stand as high as a 20-storey building, with propellers spanning more than the length of a football pitch. They produce enough electricity to power 1400 homes or more.

I DON'T BELIEVE IT!

The earliest steam engine was totally useless. A 3rd century BC Greek engineer invented a steam machine with a spinning metal ball. Unfortunately no one could think of any use for it.

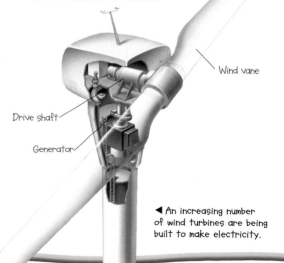

Wind vane

Drive shaft

Generator

◀ An increasing number of wind turbines are being built to make electricity.

Marks on a page

The first writing was made up of pictures. Writing was invented by the Sumerians 5500 years ago. They scratched their writing onto clay tablets. The most famous word pictures are the 'hieroglyphs' of ancient Egyptians from about 5000 years ago. Cuneiform writing was made up of wedge shapes pressed into clay with a reed. It followed the Sumerian picture writing.

▼ Phoenician

▼ Classical Greek

Α Β Γ Δ Ε Ϝ

▼ Roman

A B C D E F

▼ Cyrillic

А Б В Г Д Е

▼ Modern Hebrew

▼ Modern Arabic

▼ Ancient Egyptian

▼ Chinese

人 月 子 水 雨 木

▼ Japanese

星 面 海 水 下

▲ Ancient picture writing used hundreds of different signs, but most modern alphabets have far fewer letters.

▲ Some of the religious books handwritten by monks were decorated with beautiful illustrations.

The world's first book was a roll of paper made from reeds. It was produced in Egypt between 1500 BC and 1350 BC and was called 'The Book of the Dead'. Christian monks used to write their religious books on sheets of parchment made from animal skins.

◀ The first printing presses were made of wood, and used movable wooden letters.

Reading suddenly became much more popular after the invention of printing. A German, John Gutenberg, was an early inventor of a printing press with movable letters in the 15th century. By the end of the century there were printing presses all over Europe.

Once, people were expert at doing sums on their fingers. The first written numbers were invented about 3100 BC by Middle Eastern traders. Around AD 300, the Chinese invented a counting machine called an abacus. It was a frame with beads strung on wires. Some people still use them.

I DON'T BELIEVE IT!

Some early Greek writing was called, 'the way an ox ploughs the ground'. It was written from right to left, then the next line went left to right, and so on, back and forth.

◀ Experts can do complicated sums very fast on an abacus.

Computers do sums at lightning speed. Early modern computers were invented in the United States and Europe in the 1930s and 1940s. Today, computers are small, cheap and extremely powerful. They can store whole libraries of information. The Internet allows everyone to share information and send email messages immediately almost anywhere in the world.

Making things bigger

Small pieces of glass can make everything look bigger. Spectacle-makers in Italy in the 14th century made their own glass lenses to look through. These helped people to read small writing. Scientists later used these lenses to invent microscopes, to see very small things, and telescopes, to see things far away.

▲ Spectacles became important as more people began to read books.

Scientists saw the tiny bacteria that cause illness for the first time with microscopes. The Dutch invented the first microscopes, which had one lens. In the 1590s Zacharias Janssen of Holland invented the first microscope with two lenses, which was much more powerful.

The Dutch tried to keep the first telescope a secret. Hans Lippershey invented it in 1608, but news soon got out. Galileo, an Italian scientist, built one in 1609. He used it to get a close look at the Moon and the planets.

QUIZ

1. Are lenses made from (a) glass, or (b) steel?
2. Which came first, (a) the telescope, or (b) spectacles?
3. Do you study stars with (a) a microscope, or (b) a telescope?
4. Which are smaller, (a) bacteria, or (b) ants
5. Is the Moon (a) closer than the planets, or (b) further away than the planets?

Answers:
1.a 2.b 3.b 4.a 5.a

▲ Early microscopes with two or more lenses, like those of English inventor Robert Hooke (1635–1703), were powerful, but the image was unclear.

You cannot look through a radio telescope.
An American, Grote Reber, invented the first one and built it in his backyard in 1937. Radio telescopes pick up radio signals from space with a dish-shaped receiver. The signals come from distant stars, and, more recently, from human space probes.

▲ Telescopes changed the mistaken idea that the Universe revolved around the Earth.

▼ An electron microscope can magnify a mosquito to monster size, and reveal tiny creatures that are normally invisible.

▲ Most radio telescope dishes can be moved to face in any direction.

Modern microscopes make things look thousands of times bigger. A German, Ernst Ruska, invented the first electron microscope in 1933. It made things look 12,000 times their actual size. The latest microscopes can magnify things millions of times.

Making music

Humans are the only animals that play tunes on musical instruments. Stone Age people invented rattles and other noise-makers, and made them from mammoth bones and tusks. Instruments you hit or rattle are called percussion instruments. They are still used in modern orchestras.

Over 20,000 years ago Stone Age Europeans invented whistles and flutes. They made them out of bones or antlers. Modern flutes still work in a similar way, by covering and uncovering holes in a tube while blowing down it.

Some of the earliest harps invented were made from the shells of tortoises. The first harps were played in Sumeria and Egypt about 5000 years ago. Modern harps, like most ancient harps, have strings of different lengths.

Percussion

Bassoon (woodwind section)

▼ The instruments of the modern orchestra are grouped in several sections and include the violin in the string section, the bassoon in the woodwind section and the trombone in the brass section.

Trombone (brass section)

Pianos have padded hammers inside, which strike the strings. The first piano-like instrument was invented in about 1480 and its strings were plucked when the keys were pressed, not struck. It made a softer sound than a modern piano.

▶ The grand piano's strings are laid out horizontally in a harp-shaped frame.

The trumpet is one of the loudest instruments in the orchestra. A trumpet was found in Tutankhamen's tomb in Egypt dating back to 1320 BC. Over 2000 years ago, Celtic warriors in northern Europe blew great bronze trumpets shaped like mammoth tusks to frighten their enemies.

Bagpipes sound as strange as they look. They were invented in India over 2000 years ago. The Roman army had bagpipe players. In the Middle Ages, European and Middle Eastern herdsmen sometimes played bagpipes while they looked after their animals.

Violin
(string section)

Conductor

Keeping in touch

Some African tribes used to use 'talking drums' to send messages. Native Americans used smoke signals, visible several miles away. Before electrical inventions such as the telephone, sending long-distance messages had to be a simple process.

◀ Smoke from burning vegetation could be broken up into signals by lowering and raising a blanket over the smoke.

▼ Each position of the semaphore signaller's arms forms a different letter. What does this message say?

1 = S

2 = I

Wooden arms on tall poles across the country sent signals hundreds of miles in 18th-century France. Claude Chappe invented this system, now called semaphore, in 1797. Until recently, navies used semaphore flags to signal from ship to ship. In 1838 American Samuel Morse invented a code of short and long bursts of electric current or light, called dots and dashes. It could send messages along a wire, or could be flashed with a light.

3 = G

4 = N

The telephone can send your voice around the world. A Scotsman, Alexander Graham Bell, invented it in the 1870s. When you speak, your voice is changed into electric signals that are sent along to a receiver held by the other user. Within 15 years there were 140,000 telephone owners in the United States.

5 = A

6 = L

Radio signals fly through the air without wires. An Italian, Guglielmo Marconi, invented the radio or 'wireless' in 1899. Radio stations send signals, carried on invisible radio waves, which are received by an antenna. A Scot, John Logie Baird, invented an early TV system in 1926. TV pictures can travel through the air or along wires.

Satellite

TV studio

NTBC

TV camera

I DON'T BELIEVE IT!

Early TV performers had to wear thick, clownlike makeup. The pictures were so fuzzy that viewers could not make out their faces otherwise.

▲ Live Tv images can be beamed to a satellite in space, then redirected to the other side of the world.

With a mobile phone you can talk to practically anyone wherever you are. Your voice is carried on radio waves called microwaves and passed from antenna to antenna until it reaches the phone you are calling. Some of the antennas are on space satellites.

Taking to the skies

The first hot–air balloon passengers were a sheep, a duck and a cockerel. The French Montgolfier brothers invented the hot-air balloon in 1782. The first human passengers often had to put out fires, as the balloon was inflated by hot air created by burning straw and wool!

▲ The Montgolfier hot–air balloon made the first untethered, manned flight from Paris in 1783.

Many inventors have tried to fly by flapping birdlike wings. All have failed. One of the first bird-men crashed to his death at a Roman festival in the 1st century AD.

The first aircraft flight lasted just 12 seconds. The Wright brothers invented their airplane and flew it in 1903 in the United States. In 1909 a Frenchman, Louis Blériot, flew across the Channel. In World War I, airplanes were used in combat. In World War II, aircraft such as the British Spitfire beat off German air attacks.

▲ Formed in 1965, the Royal Air Force Aerobatic Team, known as the Red Arrows, uses Hawk jets. They need perfect timing to perform their close formation flying and aerobatics at high speed.

The first model helicopter was made by Leonardo da Vinci as long ago as 1480. In 1877, an Italian, Enrico Forlanini, invented a steam helicopter which flew for 60 seconds and reached a height of 15 metres. Modern helicopters can hover and land almost anywhere and are often used for rescue missions at land and sea.

In 1948 a jet plane flew faster than the speed of sound. Englishman Frank Whittle invented the first jet engine in 1930. Most modern aircraft are jets without propellers. Teams of jets, like the Red Arrows, often perform stunts at air shows.

I DON'T BELIEVE IT!

In 1783 the first hydrogen balloon was attacked and destroyed by terrified farm workers when it landed. It had flown 24 kilometres.

Keeping a record

The first sound recording was the nursery rhyme, 'Mary had a little lamb'. In 1877 an American, Thomas Edison, invented a way of recording sounds by causing a needle to scratch marks on a cylinder or tube. Moving the needle over the marks again repeated the sounds. Performers spoke or sang into a horn, and the sounds were also played back through it.

To play the first disc records, you had to keep turning a handle. Emile Berlin, a German, invented disc recording in 1887. The discs were played with steel needles, and soon wore out. They also broke easily if you dropped them. Long-playing discs appeared in 1948. They had 20 minutes of sound on each side and were made of bendy plastic, which didn't break so easily.

▲ Thomas Edison produced many important inventions, including sound recording, electric light bulbs and an early film-viewing machine.

▼ Early record players had to be wound up between records, and the loudspeaker was a large horn.

QUIZ

1. Were the first recordings on (a) discs, or (b) cylinders?

2. Which came first, (a) movies, or (b) long-playing records?

3. Do modern cameras take pictures on (a) glass plates, or (b) rolls of film?

4. CDs are played with diamond needles – true or false?

5. Were the first movies shown in (a) the 19th century, or (b) the 20th century?

Answers:
1.b 2.a 3.b 4.false 5.a

492

▶ Popular automatic cameras are controlled by an electronic chip. They are simple to use and take excellent photographs.

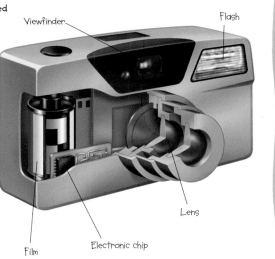

Viewfinder

Flash

Lens

Film

Electronic chip

It took eight hours to take the world's first photograph in 1826.

Frenchman Joseph Nicéphore Niépce was the inventor, and the first photograph was of rooftops. Early cameras were huge, and the photos were on glass plates. In 1889 American George Eastman invented rolls of film, making photography much easier.

▲ The Lumière brothers, who invented the movie projector, also made films and opened the first public cinema.

You can cram a lot of music into one CD.

CDs – compact discs – are small and light. The invention was first introduced by record companies in 1983. Inside the player a beam of light called a laser 'reads' the coded sound off the disc.

▶ With a portable CD player you can enjoy your music anywhere.

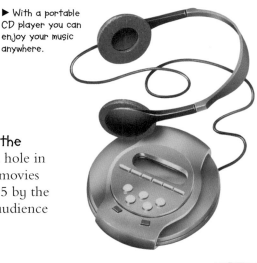

Only one person at a time could watch the first movies.

The viewer peered through a hole in a box. Thomas Edison's company invented movies in 1888. The invention of a projector in 1895 by the French Lumière brothers allowed a whole audience to watch the film on a screen.

Round the house

A horse and cart were needed to move the first successful vacuum cleaner around. An English engineer, Hubert Cecil Booth, invented it in 1902. The first 'Hoover' electric vacuum cleaner was built from a wooden box, an electric fan and an old sack in 1907 in America.

▼ Refrigerators were once large, noisy and had little food space.

▲ The first vacuum cleaners worked by opening and closing a bellows with a handle.

Early refrigerators, invented in the 19th century, killed many people. They leaked the poisonous gas that was used to cool them. In 1929 the gas was changed to a non-poisonous one called freon. We now know that freon causes damage to the planet's atmosphere, so that is being changed too.

QUIZ
1. Did the first 'Hoover' need (a) a horse, or (b) an electric fan?
2. Were early refrigerators dangerous because (a) they blew up or (b) they leaked poison gas?
3. The Cretans had china toilets 4000 years ago – true or false?
4. Do light bulbs contain (a) water, (b) air, or (c) neither?
5. Who opened the first electric light company, (a) Thomas Twyford, or (b) Thomas Edison?

Answers:
1.b 2.b 3.false 4.c 5.b

A melted chocolate bar led to the invention of the microwave oven. An American, Percy L. Spencer, invented it in 1953 after noticing that a microwave machine where he worked had melted the chocolate in his pocket. In a microwave oven the microwaves make the food heat itself up from the inside. Eggs may explode because of this.

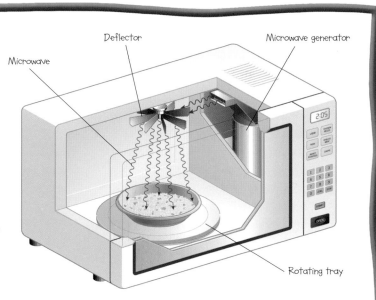

Deflector

Microwave generator

Microwave

Rotating tray

▲ In a microwave oven the microwaves are deflected by metal vanes down onto the food below.

There is no air inside a light bulb. If there was, it would burn out in no time. The first light bulbs failed because air could get in. American Thomas Edison invented an air-tight light bulb in 1879 that could burn for a long time. He opened the first electric light company in 1882.

Vacuum bulb

◀ In a light bulb, electricity causes a wire filament to glow brightly in the airless bulb.

Filament

Screw thread

Power contact

4000 years ago in Crete in Greece the king's palaces had flushing toilets. They used rainwater. In England, toilets that flushed when you pulled a handle were invented in the 18th century. In 1885 Thomas Twyford invented the first all-china flushing toilet.

From Earth into space

Concorde flew at twice the speed of sound, nearly 2150 kilometres an hour. This is at least twice as fast as the earliest jets. The huge jet airliner crossed the Atlantic at a height of over 18,000 metres.

◀ Concorde carried hundreds of passengers in luxury across the Atlantic in a fraction of the usual air crossing time – under 3 hours.

Rockets helped the Chinese drive away a Mongol army in the 13th century. The rockets used gunpowder, which the Chinese had invented 300 years earlier, but had only used in fireworks.

I DON'T BELIEVE IT!

A 15th-century Chinaman, Wan Hu, tried to make a flying machine out of 47 rockets and two kites. His servants lit all the rockets at the same time, and Wan Hu disappeared forever in a massive explosion.

◀ The Chinese were the first to use gunpowder in war, as in this hand-held gun for firing missiles.

German war rockets in World War II could travel 321 kilometres to hit England. They were invented by a scientist called Werner von Braun. After the war he helped the United States build space rockets.

The Apollo II spacecraft landed the first men on the Moon in 1969. On Earth people watched on TV as Neil Armstrong and Buzz Aldrin stepped down onto the Moon's surface.

The Space Shuttle travels on a giant fuel tank with side rockets into space. Then the tank and rockets drop away and the shuttle circles the Earth at a height of 241 kilometres. American scientists invented the reusable Space Shuttle, which first flew in 1981.

► The three-stage Saturn V rocket carried the spacecraft of the first men to land on the Moon. It weighed over 2700 tonnes.

► The Space Shuttle uses rockets to enter space, but comes back without them, landing almost like a normal aircraft.

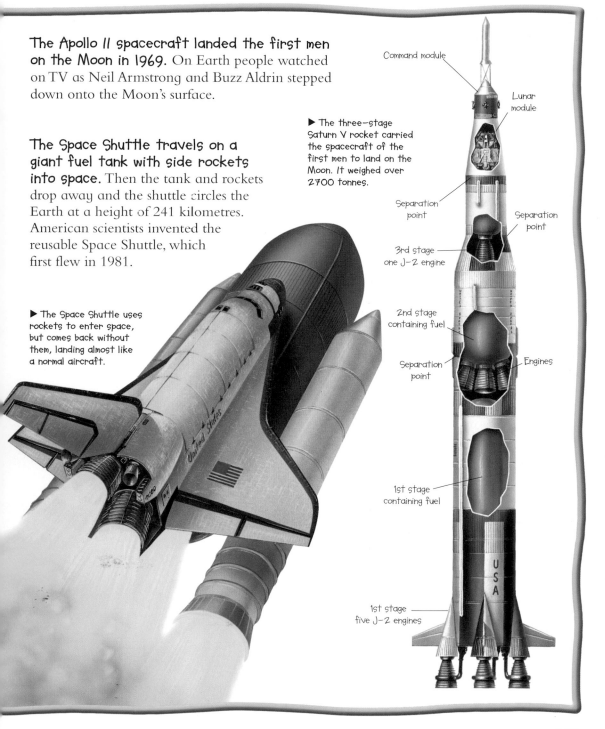

Command module

Lunar module

Separation point

Separation point

3rd stage one J-2 engine

2nd stage containing fuel

Separation point

Engines

1st stage containing fuel

USA

1st stage five J-2 engines

Index

C

Index

Index

H

Index

Index

Index

Index

Index